SOUTHERN MAN
A MEMOIR

SOUTHERN MAN
(A MEMOIR)
MUSIC AND MAYHEM IN
THE AMERICAN SOUTH
ALAN WALDEN
WITH S.E. FEINBERG

A JAWBONE BOOK
Published in the UK
and the USA by
Jawbone Press
Office G1
141–157 Acre Lane
London SW2 5UA
England
www.jawbonepress.com

ISBN 978-1-911036-71-5

Printed in the Czech Republic
by PBTISK

1 2 3 4 5 25 24 23 22 21

CONTENTS

OVERTURE A TOUGH BUSINESS......**5**

PRELUDE MACON AND EGGS......**7**

ACT ONE SOUL
OF THE SOUTH

SCENE 1 OTIS, JOHNNY, AND ME.....**16**

SCENE 2 A SIMPLE MAN FROM
MACON......**19**

SCENE 3 WHERE I CAME FROM......**24**

SCENE 4 DO YOU HEAR THE
MOCKINGBIRDS?......**27**

SCENE 5 SEPARATED BY RACE BUT
NOT FROM SOUL......**31**

SCENE 6 THE POWER TO MELT
PREJUDICE......**38**

SCENE 7 YOU'LL SING WHEN I
TELL YOU TO SING......**47**

SCENE 8 YEAH, MAN, THE SOUTH
WAS JUMPING......**48**

SCENE 9 PHIL AWAITED THOSE
ORDERS AND HE AWAITED
THOSE ORDERS AND HE
AWAITED THOSE ORDERS
SOME MORE......**50**

SCENE 10 GET OUT OF HERE YOU SON
OF A BITCH! YOU TRYING
TO HUSTLE MY SON?......**56**

SCENE 11 YOU AIN'T GOING
TO MISS THAT GIG,
JOHNNIE TAYLOR......**60**

SCENE 12 YOU'VE GOT BALLS. WHAT
CAN I DO FOR YOU?...... **62**

SCENE 13 GIVE ME THAT BOTTLE
AND LET ME CHUG A
LITTLE SOUL...... **65**

SCENE 14 SHOOTOUT AT THE
OK CORRAL...... **67**

SCENE 15 NIGHT RIDERS...... **70**

SCENE 16 DON'T BE WRITING ABOUT
DOM PÉRIGNON WHEN
ALL YOU KNOW ABOUT
IS DRINKING BUD......**73**

SCENE 17 PHIL COMES HOME......**77**

SCENE 18 WHEN THE WOMEN
FAINTED, THEY FELL
BACK, AND THEIR HEADS
WOULD SMACK ON
SOLID WOOD......**81**

SCENE 19 HEY, MAN, YOU EVER
HEAR OF MACON,
GEORGIA?......**85**

SCENE 20 GOT TO GET DOWN IN
THE SOUTH......**86**

SCENE 21 THE RANCH......**97**

SCENE 22 WE GOT THEM WHAT
THEY WANTED AS LONG
AS THEY WERE PLAYING
OUR RECORDS......**104**

SCENE 23 SEEMS LIKE I'VE BEEN
LOOKING FOR TALENT
MY WHOLE LIFE......**109**

SCENE 24 WE JUST WANTED TO FIND
OUT WHAT IT FELT LIKE
TO HANG A WHITE BOY
OUT THE WINDOW......**115**

SCENE 25 YOU'LL NEVER GIVE
ANOTHER ENEMA AS
LONG AS YOU LIVE......**120**

SCENE 26 I JUST HEARD LITTLE
RICHARD WAS AT THE
PEACOCK......**123**

SCENE 27 YOU NEED TO LET A
THIEF STEAL EVERY
ONCE IN A WHILE TO
KEEP HIM HONEST......**128**

SCENE 28 GOT TO GIVE THEM SOME
SATISFACTION......**131**

SCENE 29 THE EUROPEAN SOUL
INVASION......**136**

SCENE 30 MONTEREY POP &
'(SITTIN' ON) THE DOCK
OF THE BAY'......**139**

SCENE 31 IF YOU LET ME HAVE
ANOTHER DAY......**144**

SCENE 32　OTIS WAS SUPERMAN......**146**

SCENE 33　DREAMS OF MY BEST FRIENDS......**151**

SCENE 34　AFRICA SCREAMS......**155**

SCENE 35　MACHINE GUN RONNIE THOMPSON AND STARING DOWN LESTER MADDOX......**158**

SCENE 36　FREE AT LAST, FREE AT LAST, GOD ALMIGHTY, I'M SCARED TO DEATH!......**160**

INTERLUDE　THE PIANO......**164**

ACT TWO A MOST SPLENDID RENAISSANCE

SCENE 1　LONGHAIRS, BEER, AND THE HOTTEST GUITARS IN THE WORLD......**166**

SCENE 2　COVER OF ROLLING STONE?......**171**

SCENE 3　TEMPORARILY INSANE DUE TO TOURING WITH A ROCK 'N' ROLL BAND......**174**

SCENE 4　BROTHERS AGAINST BROTHERS......**179**

SCENE 5　A PRAYER IN A COTTON FIELD......**183**

SCENE 6　THE TOUGHEST KIDS IN THE WORLD......**185**

SCENE 7　LYNYRD SKYNYRD— TURN IT UP!......**191**

SCENE 8　I'D LET HIM HEAR THE WHISTLE OF A TWO-BY-FOUR......**196**

SCENE 9　THESE BOYS ARE NIGHT CRAWLERS......**202**

SCENE 10　A BEAUTIFUL DAY IN THE SWAMP WITH GATORS, TADPOLES, AND 'SWEET HOME ALABAMA'......**206**

SCENE 11　EVERYONE KNEW THEY HAD JUST WRANGLED A MONSTER......**208**

SCENE 12　EVERYONE IN THE ROOM WAS VERY INTERESTING AND I WAS VERY INTERESTING AND EVERYTHING WAS VERY VERY INTERESTING......**213**

SCENE 13　THE TRUTH OF THE MATTER IS......**217**

SCENE 14　TAKING IT OVER THE MOUNTAIN......**221**

SCENE 15　CRY FOR THE BAD MAN......**224**

SCENE 16　A BULL BY THE HORNS......**229**

SCENE 17　THEY GOT THEMSELVES A BIRD SONG!......**232**

SCENE 18　WE GOT YOUR ASS, CLIVE......**238**

SCENE 19　THEY PUSHED IT TOO HARD AND CRASHED IN A SWAMP......**245**

SCENE 20　THE END OF MY FRIEND TWIGGS......**246**

SCENE 21　THE MUSIC OF MOTORCYCLES—THE HELLS ANGELS MEET THE OUTLAWS......**247**

SCENE 22　BEING A GOOD MANAGER, BOOKING AGENT, PROMOTER, FRIEND......**252**

SCENE 23　TRUST......**255**

SCENE 24　THE WHITE GIRLS WERE GETTING TOO EXCITED......**260**

SCENE 25　NASHVILLE CAT......**264**

SCENE 26　NEVER GIVE UP......**265**

POSTLUDE　COME CLOSE TO ME AND GET WARM......**268**

END CREDITS......**270**

A TOUGH BUSINESS
OVERTURE

We had our time, now
Good and bad, now
I can't forget a man
I sho' ain't gonna forget him, now.

— 'Champagne And Wine,' Otis Redding,
Alan Walden, Roy Lee Johnson

Everyone thinks the music business is easy and that all you have to do is perform and play and have fun. The music business is very rough and tough and dirty—it was Frank Sands who told me the story about Joe Glazer sticking a guy in a barrel of acid.

In Miami, Florida, the DJ conventions were exciting during the hot, soulful years. You met DJs from across the country, and some from overseas. Otis was winning the top award, posthumously, so I was excited about this happening.

I went back to my room and there was an urgent message from Phil. I called and he told me to leave the hotel immediately. The 'Black Mafia' from Harlem had shown up and were beating up anyone who was white. One guy was beat up in the lobby. They grabbed a friend of mine from New Orleans while he was in the shower. One held him by his testicles while another smashed them with his hard fist.

5

These guys were not playing. I checked into a cheap hotel down the street and stayed hidden until the awards show.

We all went to the awards escorting Zelma Redding, Otis's widow. Right after the awards, Phil got Zelma and me to go with them to enjoy a few drinks.

'I'm tired of running and hiding,' I told Phil. 'I'm going to stay a while.'

'You're going to get your ass kicked,' Phil warned me, before he and Zelma left.

MACON AND EGGS
PRELUDE
BY S.E. FEINBERG

I woke up early in an exquisitely restored nineteenth-century apartment on Cherry Street—my digs in Macon for a couple of nights—and started out on my walk around the quiet streets, on a crisp early autumn morning. I wanted to introduce myself to this place where a musical and social renaissance dominated the R&B and southern rock 'n' roll scene during the sixties and seventies. Along with L.A., Chicago, New York, Nashville, Memphis, Liverpool, and London, Macon, Georgia, was one of the world's music power spots.

My rendezvous with Alan Walden was scheduled for 10:30, and I wanted to be on time—had to be on time. Rumer, the popular British singer and composer, had set up the meeting, and it took some doing to coordinate all of the pieces. The purpose of the meeting was to see if Alan and I could get along—more importantly, trust each other. I understood that he didn't talk to too many people, so I knew our initial time together would have to count.

Rumer had first mentioned Alan Walden to me while we were on our way to the Glastonbury Music Festival a few years back, during P.F. Sloan's book and music tour. Phil and she had been performing around London. I recall Rumer telling me the story of the Waldens while passing Stonehenge. I was intrigued by Rumer's passionate narrative about these small-town cats who didn't care about what color a person was, only about the music they played. She had me.

I had no idea how the meeting was going to play out, but I did know that writers a lot more successful than me had tried to punch into his circle. Rumer had laid all of the pipe; now I had to see if any water could flow. A northerner being late to a meeting with a very punctual southern man would be a bad start and possibly, I feared, fatal.

I was particularly struck by the old train station with 'colored waiting room' chiseled into the cement building as a reminder of how things were. The old train station is right near the Tubman Museum and, always being interested in connections, this circled around to my wife's relation, Thomas Garrett, who worked with Harriet Tubman and was one of the most successful 'station masters' along the Underground Railroad. Thomas was the inspiration for Simeon Halliday in *Uncle Tom's Cabin*.

I was feeling Macon. I was feeling the warmth of this lovely, historic, southern town. I was tuning into the soul of this place that was all about people and history and music, which served as its soundtrack, and served it very well.

I walked up by the old Capricorn Studios—aware of some of its history, the place having been founded in 1969 by the Walden brothers and Frank Fenter.

On this morning, things were in a state of renovation, which gave the neighborhood a sense of hope. On a future visit with Alan, Rumer, and her husband, composer/producer Rob Shirakbari, we got down into the echo chambers in the basement and were able to crawl into several of them. Each tiled echo chamber was shaped differently to create a unique effect. I could hear the music of The Allman Brothers

Band or Percy Sledge or The Charlie Daniels Band and so many others still permeating through those chambers—a spelunking adventure I will not soon forget.

I took a poke at Grant's Lounge. I knew that almost every musician stopped in there to play a set or just to hang out and dig the vibe. I walked over to the Tic Toc Room, formerly Miss Anne's Tic Toc Lounge, where Little Richard used to wash dishes, and where he truly refined his chops.

I had biscuits, two fried eggs, ham, and coffee at H&H. That is the legendary restaurant where The Allman Brothers Band were often fed by Mama Louise, the woman who once owned the place with her partner, Mama Hill. Mama Louise now serves as a kind of official greeter. I had been told that if you were new in town and had something going on, you were supposed to introduce yourself to her. That's what I was told, and I was game.

Mama Louise sat up in the back. I introduced myself to her and told her I was in town to meet Alan Walden.

'All right,' she said. 'That's good.'

I didn't know too much about the details of the partnership between Phil Walden, Alan Walden, and Otis Redding and those very early years of R&B and the dangerous night rides through the Georgia woods in Cadillacs and Lincolns. I didn't know too much about Alan building a raggedy, tough-ass band called Lynyrd Skynyrd into a worldwide phenomenon. I was in Macon to meet Alan and hopefully learn as much as I could about the man and the place—his life and what he loved and cared about.

I was aware that Macon supposedly had underground tunnels filled with hidden Confederate gold. The poet, Sidney Lanier, was born in

Macon. I knew that Duane Allman and Berry Oakley were killed on their motorcycles in Macon, and that The Allman Brothers Band lived almost everywhere in Macon at one time or another. Everywhere you walk, there are mushrooms engraved into the sidewalk, indicating where The Allman Brothers Band hung out or lived. I had heard that Tennessee Williams was inspired to write *Cat On A Hot Tin Roof* in Macon. There was definitely a sense of mystery and wonder to the place. And music. Macon is all about music. I was happy to be there. I liked Macon.

Not wanting to be late, I started driving out of town and I got as lost as a person can get in this life. I wasn't worried about being lost so much as I was being late. Heck, my GPS was even lost. That poor GPS woman sitting at her kitchen table with a cigarette hanging out of her mouth and maps in front of her just couldn't get me out of this jam like she had gotten me out of so many before. The more lost I got, the more confused I got, and then a sort of fight-or-flight reflex kicked in. I knew I was in the vicinity of Alan's property, but I might as well have been in Saskatchewan.

Finally, in desperation, I saw a US Postal Service truck pulling over to another country house and maneuvered my car in front of it, hemming it in next to a tall azalea bush. The postman stuck his head out of his truck and was more shocked than angry—not frightened, since he was probably carrying.

'What in hell is going on here?'

'I'm so sorry. I'm trying to find an address.'

'Well, there's more ways to do it than scaring me half to death! You can't just pull in front of a US Postal Service vehicle,' the man forcefully explained.

'You're right,' I said, apologetically, rather embarrassed that I had actually pulled such a stupid stunt.

'Well, who are you looking for?'

'Alan Walden,' I said. 'You know how to get to his house?'

'Yes, I do,' he said.

'I came all the way from California.'

'California!' he exclaimed. He looked me over with suspicion but must have seen something that indicated I was no danger to Alan. 'Okay. Well. You see that lake over there?'

'Yes sir, I do.'

'You see that dam over there?'

'Dam? Yeah. I guess so.'

'You cross over that dam there.'

'I cross over the dam to get to Alan Walden's house?'

'Yeah.'

'How?'

'How? You walk over it. You cross right over that spillway. You walk right across to the other side.'

'Well . . . is there a way to maybe . . .'

'You get to the other side there and you make a left. You walk on the bank for about a quarter mile. You'll come to a little dock where there are a couple of chairs. That's where Alan sits sometimes. Up in the field there should be a John Deere tractor. You know what a John Deere tractor looks like?'

'Well, is there any way to drive to his house?'

'Drive right up to his house?' the postman asked. 'Well, sure. If you want to do it that way. You drive down this road and make a right. You cross over a bridge and make a left and drive some along there and make your first right kind of. That puts you on the main road, more or less. You drive down that road about a mile, mile and a half or so. You come to an old horse farm as such. When you get to that old horse farm, you've gone farther than you want to go. You turn around and you drive until you come to a nursing home. When you come to that nursing home, you've gone too far the other way. You turn around and in between that nursing home and that horse farm there is a road that doesn't look like a road.' And then he stopped talking and looked at me as if I didn't understand the directions or there must be something wrong with me or that he enjoyed confusing me, thinking I was maybe from the city and not knowing that I was just as 'country' as he was—possibly more. But I did my best to understand what he was telling me—and, honestly, my misplaced pride got in the way of asking him to repeat any of those directions, which I truly did not understand completely, and we know that pride goes before a fall. So I followed them as best as I could, and I pretty much did what he told me . . . more or less or so.

I came to the old horse farm and I knew I had gone too far. I turned around and got to the nursing home, or a large house with the markings of a nursing home—senior citizens sitting out front on rocking chairs—and reckoned I had gone too far in the other direction. Halfway between the old horse farm and the nursing home was a road that didn't look like a road. I wasn't really sure if that was the road but I drove down it until I saw Alan's house, a large home overlooking the beautiful lake that the postman was wanting me to 'walk across on the dam there.' I pulled around to where I saw a John Deere 4700 tractor. I was greatly relieved that I was five minutes early.

Dogs started to bark, and I went right to the tractor because it was, coincidently, the very same tractor that I have, and it seemed to be suffering from some of the same ills as mine.

A voice came from inside the house.

'Who's out there?'

'It's me. Steve Feinberg. I'm here for our meeting!'

'Hold on a minute.'

In a little bit, Alan Walden came walking out of the house—his several dogs following him, most of them sighted. I reached for his hand and he shook my hand in a friendly manner. He was a fit, older gentleman, and his hair was still quite red. There was a sort of mischievous, playful curiosity in his eyes. He was carrying a can of Diet Dr. Pepper and, I think, a sidearm under his sweater.

'I see you have a 4700,' I said.

'Yeah. That's a nice tractor. You know something about tractors?'

'I have the same tractor.'

Alan seemed very pleasantly surprised.

'You do?'

'Yeah. And I can see you're having some problems with the seat. The weather kills those plastic seats.'

'I stopped ordering the damn seats. I just put a pillow on there now.'

'These tractors are covered in plastic. But the mechanics is pure art.'

'I'd have to agree with you,' he said. 'I couldn't have a piece of property like this without a tractor.'

'Sure is beautiful here,' I said.

'I used to have a lot of animals. Now I just have these dogs and a couple of ducks. This small dog is blind but he sees with his nose.'

We talked about John Deere tractors for a good deal of time, and then he told me that he once had several goats.

'Goats? I had goats.'

'Those goats are crazy,' he chuckled.

'What kind of goats did you have?' I asked.

'Saanen,' he said. 'Big white Saanen goats.'

'That's what I had.'

'They're pretty smart goats,' he said.

'If they had hands, they'd be dangerous,' I said.

And we shared goat stories with each other, trying to out strange each other and doing a good job of it. Anybody who has harbored goats for any time will do this, and the stories seem to become more strange over time.

'I had a goat who walked on his hind legs on a full moon,' I told Alan.

'Yeah, I've heard of them doing that,' he said. 'You like Dr. Pepper?'

We walked into his house and into a cavernous room covered with music memorabilia—framed photographs and gold records and posters. From Otis Redding to Sam & Dave to Lynyrd Skynyrd to The Allman Brothers Band. I sat down on the couch and Alan went into the kitchen to retrieve a couple of cold Diet Dr. Peppers. The walls told me that this Alan Walden had a story to tell. I've seen some good walls in my time, but this was certainly the best.

Alan and I talked about tractors and goats for an hour or so. Neither of us mentioned anything about his history in the music business. We had work to do first. We had to learn to trust each other. And sometimes that takes a lot of conversation. And, frankly, that's the way it should be.

SOUL OF THE SOUTH
ACT ONE

OTIS, JOHNNY, AND ME
SCENE ONE

When I get to heaven, I want to see Otis Redding, my family, and then my horse, Johnny. I hope horses are allowed in heaven. Johnny was the fastest horse in Macon, Georgia. Johnny and I raced everything—fifty-five Fords, Chevys, chopped rods, and Harley Davidsons. One day, Johnny and I left a modified Cushman Eagle in the dust, gasping for air.

Johnny was a gelding but very much a stallion at heart because he didn't get cut until he was six, so he had a lot of wildness left in him. One time, a stallion got loose from another property and came after Johnny, who was tied up to a fence, and he started pecking at him and biting all over his ass. I looked out the window and yelled, 'Get him, Johnny!' and Johnny turned around and took that stallion to the ground—stomped him good—and that stallion never bothered Johnny again. All Johnny had to hear was my permission to take that stallion down. Johnny fought like a stallion because he had the heart of a stallion. Johnny could climb a bank almost straight up like a surefooted goat, and I could ride him right off of a damn cliff.

Johnny also helped me with the girls. I'd ride him over to Wesleyan College and canter around in the field outside of the women's dorm. We were quite a sight.

I had a paper route, and we went out every afternoon together. He'd pull up to the paper tube and stop, and he knew the paper was in the tube after he heard it thud, and then he'd take off in a gallop. One time I was in a race with a friend, and Johnny and I were running down the road real fast. When we got to a tube on my old paper route, Johnny stopped and ran over to the paper tube. He wouldn't budge. I didn't have any papers to stuff into the tube, so I just slapped the tube and Johnny took off, and we still won that race.

I could also do trick riding. I could stand up on his back and ride. I could crawl around his neck in a full gallop and jump up from behind, like the Range Rider did on television. I did that Pony Express bounce—bouncing off the ground and back up onto the saddle. I rode bareback every race so I could shed the weight of the saddle.

Johnny never kicked me and he never bit me—not like a lot of people in the music business tried to do. I could walk out into our twenty-five acres of pasture, give a certain whistle, and Johnny would come flying across that pasture. Johnny was a special beast that craved and adored attention from me. My mother would walk out the door with a carrot, and Johnny would come up to her and eat it right out of her hand.

Johnny came out of a wild horse herd from Gray, Georgia, where Otis would ultimately build his Big 'O' Ranch and I would have my log cabin right next door. The previous owner used wired hackamores to try to break Johnny's spirit, cutting three deep scars into his nose, which indicated his abuse. I paid a grand total of thirty dollars for him, equivalent to about two hundred and eighty-five dollars in today's money, plus ten dollars to have him trucked to the Walden Ranch.

Eventually, when the ranch was sold, Johnny was forced into a horse stable. One weekend while I was home from college, I visited Johnny at the stable, only to find him with no water, no hay, and swollen ankles. I knew that if I wanted to save his life I would have to sell him, which I did. A hard and heavy decision I still feel regret from. It was one of the saddest days of my life.

I tried to track Johnny down later, but there was an absence of sales records. To this day, I can still hear the rhythm of his hooves pounding away on red clay while I sang 'Go, Johnny, Go!' patting his neck down to his hind right leg.

Some years later, I picked out Otis's horse, Comanche. I picked him out, bought him, had him delivered to the ranch, and rode him for the first week he was there to break him in. Otis fell in love with that horse. He had so much peace of mind riding Comanche all through the woods. But Otis was inexperienced with horses, and the first time he rode Comanche he went across the field with his arms flapping, looking like a pelican trying to get airborne. One of the happiest moments of Otis's life was when he finally won a race between himself on Comanche and me and my new horse, Dynamite. When he passed me on that dirt road, I saw every tooth in his head—the biggest smile I had ever seen. I'll never forget that smile.

A SIMPLE MAN FROM MACON
SCENE TWO

I have been a simple man all of my life. I grew up in the country and was very proud of it. I love the country. I love everything about it. I moved back to the country after my success. I like to think of the song 'Simple Man' by Lynyrd Skynyrd, and that kind of describes me.

And be a simple kind of man,
Oh, be something you love and understand,
Baby be a simple kind of man . . .

I am an honest, simple man, and definitely a loner. I love spending time alone. Unlike Al Green's great song 'Tired Of Being Alone,' I never grew tired of it.

I'm surprised I'm still here. To be the oldest Walden in history just blows my mind, because I was always a sickly child. Being sickly taught me how to live and to appreciate every moment. I had asthma, and I was determined not to live my life sitting in a chair and being still. I never let asthma get in my way. I guess I was like Teddy Roosevelt—he never let asthma get in his way.

I thought in my high-school years about what I would do with my life after I got out of college. I wanted a job where I could wear blue jeans. I wanted to be a landscaper or a mailman or something that was outside—maybe a telephone lineman or a forest ranger. I wanted to be outside in the fresh air, and around nature.

I never dreamed in my early years that I would end up in the music business. But a man never knows where he's going to land. Little did I know what was coming. I didn't know I was to be so blessed and woven into the fabric of the quilt of R&B and southern rock 'n' roll—didn't know I was going to ride on up that mountain. It's a rough climb to the top of the mountain and, I discovered, even rougher trying to stay up there, because once you're up there, you have to hold it.

Behind the glitz and glamor—behind the stars and fame—there I was, a simple man from Macon, Georgia, who, along with my brother Phil and Otis Redding, tried to make sure the great music all came together. We tried to ensure that the wonderful talents got what they deserved and gave all of us what we desired. Rock on.

Macon has always been a hub of southern music. When a band came down south, they stopped in Macon to see the Walden brothers. When they got to us, we offered management and publishing and booking dates and travel for the musicians. We tried to make their jobs and lives as comfortable and easy as possible. Memphis, Tennessee; Muscle Shoals, Alabama; Macon; Hattiesburg, Mississippi; New Orleans—that was our beat, but we took acts as far north as Detroit and as far west as L.A. and east to New York. We worked from the Apollo to the Whisky—from London and Paris to the jungles of Africa. We would try to help those who came to our shop. Sometimes there were problems, but we did the best we could.

I love Macon. I moved away from here one time for five months. And I would have crawled back if I had to. I was never so miserable in my whole life as when I was away from Macon. I like to think I had a hand in building up Macon. Life was easy for us after we got over the integration issues, and after they got over us bringing the longhairs to town. Phil went to Nashville and Atlanta, but I always wanted to stay in Macon. I was offered work in California but I didn't go. I am not crazy about traveling. Once you've seen a city numerous times, they become kind of boring. I became more aware of flying after Otis's death. Then, after Bill Graham and Skynyrd's plane crashes, I became more paranoid.

For the most part, I always kept my life real simple—kept everything the way I could understand it. When I was in a conversation and someone started using big intellectual words, trying to see if I knew the meaning, I would say, 'Excuse me, I don't know what that word means.' I wasn't embarrassed to ask what the word meant. I've always tried to learn as much as I could from every situation, and from the smartest people in my life.

The smartest one of all was my brother, Phil. He was brilliant. Nobody could negotiate a deal like my brother. Phil made one of the smartest deals of all time. He got all of his masters back for everybody that he had recorded at Capricorn. He walked into Polydor and walked out with his entire catalogue. I was a good negotiator, but I couldn't make some of the deals he made.

Years later, Phil was one of the most important people in Jimmy Carter's campaign—that's how smart he was. It has been said that Carter would not have been president if it hadn't been for Phil Walden. We energized rock 'n' roll for Jimmy Carter. We opened the doors to the entire stable. After he got elected, everyone wanted something. When it came to Phil, he told Carter that all he wanted was for him to be the best damn president ever to hit the White House. Phil wanted Jimmy Carter to be Thomas Jefferson.

Phil was smart, and I learned everything I could from him. We made things better for artists. We were the ones who got the Black artists paid. Phil and I were the first ones who started accounting for Black artists directly, and they trusted us because of that. Black artists were getting ripped off all over the place, but not at our shop. I kept very detailed books and knew what every artist got, and every artist knew what he or she got. I worked for one solid week of the month on all of the statements and got them square before I got them to the artists. If they had any questions at all, we answered them. If they weren't happy, we'd make it right. It was a lot of work, but integrity sometimes takes work, and it's important.

I created simple statements that were not hard to read. The artists could read them and know exactly what they made and how much they were spending. A lot of companies would get the artists flashy suits and nice cars, but that was just an illusion of making money. A lot of these guys and gals came from nothing—the children of sharecroppers, dirt-poor preachers, and bootleggers—from bare feet to alligator boots. Most of them traveled a hard road. We didn't want to be part of that hard road. We wanted to be a smooth road and a safe road—a road protected from thieves and robbers.

We felt if we prospered our Black entertainers, the world would become a better place.

Otis was one of the smarter artists because he cared about the promoters. Many entertainers use the promoters and make money off of them and forget about them. Otis would go to a promoter after a show and ask him how it came out—did the promoter make money or lose money? If the promoter told him he'd lost money—say four hundred dollars— Otis would whip out two hundred and give it back to the promoter.

'I want to be the guy who makes you money,' Otis would tell the promoter. 'I want you to book me all the time.'

That was smart. That was good business.

Otis was business conscious. He thought about money a lot. The last thing Otis said before he got on that plane was, 'Man, I never missed a gig in my life. I gotta make that dollar.' And then he headed for Madison. That's what he was thinking about. But he wasn't thinking about 'making that dollar' for himself. He was thinking about 'making that dollar' for his family and his home.

The promoters fell in love with Otis because they knew he wouldn't stiff them—and they knew *we* wouldn't stiff them. He carried on an excellent relationship with promoters. I never saw him disrespect anyone.

Otis told me to book him seven days a week. He didn't want to be off, and he didn't want the band to be off because he didn't want them to get into trouble. He didn't want any idle time in the hotels because it bred dissension and carelessness. The band guys were always getting into trouble when they had nothing to do—drugs, booze, and women are a deadly cocktail on the road. It was usually something wild, and he didn't want that happening. He wanted them to concentrate on work. Many of his band members were very young—some still in high school—and didn't have a lot of life experience. A few of them had a good deal of it.

Otis Redding was all about the work. That was the name of the game. It was always 'take the stage'—take command of it and rule while you're up there. Own the performance and be professional all the time. Don't be up there cracking jokes. Hit them with music and soul. That's what the people are there for.

My father is the one who taught me how to work hard. Before I had my own paper route, he had a rural paper route and I was the collector. I didn't realize it at the time, but that knowledge was going to be very helpful in the music business. I was taught how to approach people directly for the money they owed. The thing I didn't like about that job was the damn biting dogs. It gets kind of tiresome when the dogs keep biting you, with the owner sitting up on his porch trying to assure me that 'that dog won't bite!' and the dog with my leg in his mouth.

I got up at 1am—that's about four hours before a rooster—to go pick up our newspapers and throw them until six, go to bed at six-thirty, wake up at seven-thirty to catch the bus at eight. When I got out of school, I had to run and meet my father for the afternoon route. We'd ride a hundred and ten miles in the morning and a hundred and fifteen at night. Seven days a week. I don't know when I slept.

WHERE I CAME FROM
SCENE THREE

My father was C.B. Walden. His actual name was Clemiel Barto Walden. He was known as Pops to all of the musicians, but I called him Daddy. If I could talk to my father again, I would say, 'I love you. I sure am proud of your transformation. I'm proud of you and how you came back to life to help us. I even appreciate your arguments. One thing I know is that you loved me, and I certainly loved you with a passion that goes a little bit stronger than most son's and father's relationships.'

On the day my father was born, his daddy had carried his eldest son, my father's oldest brother, in from the field where he got his neck broken under a wagon wheel and died. Daddy's family were sharecroppers in Redan, Georgia, and they worked the land and gardens all the time, so he grew up pretty hardscrabble—not unlike Otis Redding's father. My father managed to stay with his grandaddy a lot, and because he was his namesake he got to ride on the wagon when all the other boys had to walk through the fields, so he was his grandaddy's favorite. I think there were eight or nine children in his family.

My mother, Carolyn McLendon Walden, was sophisticated. She went through LaGrange College, back when hardly any women went to college, and graduated the highest in her class. She was artistic and loved to paint. She had an excellent, educated vocabulary, and she was very, very much a Christian woman. My mother was the one who first told me all about God. She kept us all on the straight and narrow.

If I angered my mother, she wouldn't say too much. She'd wait until my father came home. 'Alan needs a whipping,' she'd demand. And my father never said a word to question her authority—didn't ask the reason for my punishment. He'd just take off his belt and whip my ass.

Growing up, I knew about being different from Black kids. I knew about that from seven years old. Before that, I had never heard 'Black man' or 'Negro.' I didn't think I was any different and I never felt any different. Maybe because, in my soul, I knew I wasn't any different.

When I was a bit older, I was with my father and I went into a store to get us a cool drink. A mature African American lady let her change slip from her hand, and it scattered all over the floor. I got down and helped her to pick up the change. I got up all the change and handed it to her. She thanked me and I went out to the car.

'What in hell took you so long?' my father griped.

'There was a lady in there that dropped her change, and I was helping her pick it up,' I told him.

'Was she that old Negro woman who walked out?'

'Yep.'

'Alan. You don't call a Black woman a lady,' he said. 'You just don't do that.'

We used to get our haircuts in a barbershop in a building we eventually bought. The barbershop was across the way from a hotel that catered to prostitutes. There wasn't any air conditioning in the hotel—or anywhere else for that matter—so they kept the windows and curtains wide open to get air. It was pretty difficult to concentrate on anything but what was going on in that hotel. That was the red-light district, and the 'B girls' were standing out in front on Broadway and Poplar, enticing men to go into the bars with them to buy drinks.

Not too far from there was the Douglass Theater, founded by Charles Douglass, a vaudevillian and theater impresario. Charles was also the first African American millionaire in Macon—the son of a slave from Virginia. From slavery to great wealth and influence in one generation. The Douglass had a very cool chronology going back to the early twenties, when it was a venue for great jazz and blues acts— from Bessie Smith and Cab Calloway to Duke Ellington and Otis 'Rockhouse' Redding.

There was the Ritz Theater on Cherry Street, a place my mother deemed 'off limits'—there was a pool hall next door. You could go into the Bibb on Saturday morning and see a live teen show and a movie, but that was kind of boring for me. Also, we had the Rialto and the Capitol. The Grand Opera House on Mulberry Street was a classy venue that started showing films in 1936, and in the forties was owned by Paramount Pictures. You might want to head out to the 41 Drive-In Theater with your gal, or maybe the Moto Vue, though I frequented the Dixie Drive-In, and I would go early to secure a place in the back row, where we could have the most privacy and steam up the windows.

Before the show, we'd hit the Pig 'n' Whistle and order burgers from the 'curb boys'—African American hops who took our orders. Of course, you'd want to take your date and cruise the drag on Cherry Street to start the night off.

DO YOU HEAR THE MOCKINGBIRDS?
SCENE FOUR

In the early sixties, while my brother Phil was at Mercer University, he started booking Johnny Jenkins & The Pinetoppers for high schools and fraternity dances. Otis Redding was the featured singer, but Johnny was the undisputed star of the show. I first met Otis at one of these dances. Otis was always so friendly—he spoke to me first, and I liked that.

Phil booked the Pinetoppers all over Alabama, Georgia, Mississippi, Louisiana, Texas, Florida, South and North Carolina, and even up to Virginia. Johnny was very spectacular onstage. He did a little rhythm with his body and the women went wild. The son of a laborer, Johnny was a good-looking guy, and very well-manicured.

Johnny grew up poor and put his first guitar together from a cigar box and rubber bands, as did many great guitarists like Eddie Lang, Pee Wee Clayton, and Carl Perkins. Johnny turned into one of the top guitar players of all time. He could make a mistake and cover it before anyone picked up on it. He was that fast.

Johnny was a left-handed guitar player and one of his fingers was double-jointed, and his hand was all over that neck. He'd pick that guitar behind his head and duck and slide across stage. God, that man could play guitar. He was a natural entertainer—a *born* entertainer.

My father worked at Gay's Clothing Company over on Third Street. It was owned by his brother, Roy B. Walden Sr. All of us Walden boys— Phil, Blue, and me—worked there at one time or another.

One Friday at the clothing store, I addressed a Black man as 'sir.'

My father took me aside.

'You don't call a Black man *sir*. You call them *customer*.'

Macon was still very segregated, though less so than other parts of Georgia and the South in the early sixties. African Americans used to come in from the countryside on Friday and Saturday to spend their money at Adam's Lounge, Club 15, Red Rooster, the Douglass, or Peyton's Place—Peyton's Place was the first integrated nightclub in Macon. Nighttime was the most lively time to be downtown. Macon was exciting and alive. You could hear it and you could feel it.

My father wasn't happy that Phil was spending all of his time and money on shows and neglecting his studies at Mercer. Both he and Otis's father had their doubts about their sons' interest in rock 'n' roll.

Otis's daddy was a pastor, and early on in their relationship he ordered Phil away from the property. He didn't want his son to sing any rock 'n' roll. Otis's mother, Fannie, was always real quiet about it all.

'We don't want you here anymore!' he shouted at Phil.

Of course that didn't stop Phil and Otis. They just kind of kept it away from him. I think Otis's father really meant that he didn't want his son to sing rock 'n' roll and forget about singing in the church. That was his fear. He really meant that. In those years, some people—mostly white people—thought that rock and blues and even jazz, the most popular music, was the 'devil's music.' They considered the music to be sexually suggestive and dangerous. Some believed that the music would literally drive the young mind insane, which naturally led to drugs, drink, and illicit sex.

I was working at the store one morning when I was probably sixteen. My father told me that I needed to run an errand. Turned out he was sending me over to the courthouse to pay Otis Redding's fine. He knew Otis because of his working with my brother, Phil. Otis had been in jail for a couple of nights for selling a car that he hadn't paid for yet. The fine was about sixty-five dollars.

Otis was tall and lanky, with the biggest smile and a great personality. When he came out of that jail, he just stood there and smelled the air and took these big whiffs of the afternoon of Macon.

'What are you doing, Otis?' I asked him.

'Man, smell that fresh air. Look at the trees. Look at the sky. I hear birds singing,' Otis said. 'Do you hear that? Do you hear the mockingbirds singing?' It was the most beautiful description of downtown Macon I had ever heard.

Otis appreciated life. He was thankful for life. He went over to the store and thanked my father. I think that's the day Otis and I became friends.

Otis was a decent young man. He rose above anger. He transcended anger, unless someone tried to hurt his family or friends. He was probably the best-natured man I ever knew in my life. He taught me how to make more friends. I was already good at it, but he taught me how to reach for the stars.

'Dream a little, Red,' he told me. 'Let's dream.'

You felt that when you were around him—that it was okay to dream.

One semester, Phil didn't have his tuition, and my father wouldn't give him any more money, because at that time he was mad at Phil for spending all of his funds working with the Black bands. Otis dropped by to see Phil and saw that he was upset and asked what it was about, and Phil told him the truth. Phil had spent his tuition on promoting the bands. Otis left and came back later that afternoon with a paper sack, and he took that paper sack and dumped it out onto Phil's desk. It was dimes, pennies, nickels, quarters, fifty-cent pieces, dollar bills— nothing bigger than a five.

'One of us needs an education,' Otis said.

It was enough to pay Phil's tuition. Otis had gone out and he must have asked every person in Macon for the money in that bag.

SEPARATED BY RACE BUT NOT FROM SOUL
SCENE FIVE

In the late fifties, my oldest brother, Blue, went to work for Motorola in Indiana, and, when he returned home, he had a pile of records of Black artists. Phil and I listened to them over and over and over again. It went all the way with us. We fell in love with Black music—Etta James, Sam Cooke, Lloyd Price, Ruth Brown, and so many more. Some of the artists on those records would become associates and friends. 'Tutti-Frutti' changed our whole lives. Phil thought it was the most exciting music he ever heard.

During those early years, Phil and I would head over to the Douglass or to the Macon City Auditorium. One night at the City Auditorium, we saw Hank Ballard & The Midnighters—Hank did the original 'The Twist' in 1959, before Chubby Checker took it over the mountain in 1960—and we also saw The '5' Royales, who had released 'Dedicated To The One I Love' before it was covered by The Shirelles and then The Mamas & The Papas. I sat in the balcony with all the other white kids. Back then, we weren't allowed to mix—separated by race but not from soul.

Not only were the bands exciting onstage but it was my first exposure watching African American kids dance and dress up and have fun. It was something I had never seen before. It was something I will never forget.

Back when Phil was the president of his fraternity at Lanier Senior High, he got Percy Welch & His House Rockers to play at a party there. Percy had recorded 'Back Door Man' and 'Nursery Rhyme Rock' on Fran Records, out of Louisville. Percy and the House Rockers were the first Black band to play a white fraternity in Macon. Percy showed up without any PA equipment, but the date was a huge success.

Musicians helped each other around Macon with a heap of southern hospitality. When Percy died in 2004, Little Richard spoke to UPI about how Percy had given him clothes and the keys to his car so he could make it to his first Apollo Theater performance in 1956: 'I didn't have clothes, my mama had twelve kids, my daddy was a bootlegger, and the boot was empty that day.'

Little Richard was born in Macon, Georgia, and he always very proudly referred to his roots in Macon. The truth of the matter is, Little Richard had been run out of Macon—not because he was homosexual or for walking around town carrying a red parasol, but because one night he was cruising on Main Street in a convertible with a nude woman in the back seat. The authorities gave him two days to get out of town.

Some of these entertainers were truly tough and came from hard upbringings, full of struggle and angst. Little Richard's father was shot and killed outside his bar in Pleasant Hill, an African American neighborhood in Macon, settled after the Civil War.

The college students loved the Black bands, and everybody started calling Phil. Phil started doing these shows, and I would help out by selling soda or doing anything I could to make things run smoothly. That was me, always behind the scenes.

Phil started booking African American acts at local colleges and high schools. The kids dug the music, and they couldn't get enough of it. Fraternities wanted to know where Phil got these bands. We didn't realize it at the time, but we had begun to spread the word. Something big and important was happening in the South, and the embers were catching hold of the tinder in Macon with enough fuel to ultimately set the world ablaze. A fire that would never be extinguished.

Phil quickly realized he was getting enough calls to possibly make a few bucks, so he started booking Percy more. Percy would give him a price—maybe three hundred dollars—then Phil would add a hundred, and he would make that.

We started looking for more bands to book. Maurice Williams & The Zodiacs were the most popular college band there ever was—them and Doug Clark & The Hot Nuts. Maurice had a big record, 'Stay,' on Herald Records. He was super nice and a very smart guy who came out of the church life in South Carolina. So many of the great Black singers got their chops in the church choirs. Almost everyone sang gospel at one time or another. Church was a great place to stand up in front of people and learn how to sing and to deal with an audience.

R&B dates back to the church and the choirs and those old soulful melodies. That's where soul music came from. I would say ninety percent of the R&B artists had a relationship with gospel somewhere along the line. Everything was gospel-influenced, and a lot of songs were lifted right out of those hymn books and carried down from the 'Negro spiritual' on the plantations. Otis started in the choir, as did Aretha, Sam Cooke, Ray Charles. Sister Rosetta Tharpe and Mahalia Jackson brought the spiritual right up to the mountain.

Maurice had a manager who ran that band like a machine. The Zodiacs were always on time and always dressed beautifully. They never had a complaint. Truly professional. Maurice is still singing today, and he sings for the same people he sang for in fraternities. His audience may be older, but they are all still very much in his groove. Back in 1957, he recorded a song he wrote called 'Little Darlin',' back when The Zodiacs were The Gladiolas, and which later became a smash hit for The Diamonds, out of Canada—technically a white cover, but it connected, and I understand that Maurice thought highly of The Diamonds' version.

Doug Clark & The Hot Nuts were right up there with Maurice Williams & The Zodiacs as one of the most popular college bands. When Phil brought them to Macon the first time, the police threatened to put us in jail if he let The Hot Nuts sing dirty songs at the show.

The Hot Nuts sang a lot of songs that were very racy and blue, and the college kids ate them up faster than pizza and beer—'Ding-A-Ling,' 'Roly Poly,' or 'Bang Bang Lulu.' The law made it perfectly clear that if they sang one dirty song, our asses were going to jail and the show was going to be shut down.

Doug performed a great, raucous, non-blue set. The crowd was so orderly that a policeman who was listening to all the songs and waiting for something to pop came up to me.

'This crowd is really well-behaved,' he told me.

'We run tight shows,' I told the policeman.

'I'll tell you what,' the policeman said. 'I'm going to walk outside and get a little fresh air and have a smoke, and I'll probably not be able to hear what the band is singing.' And then he walked outside.

I ran to the stage, shouting 'Give them "Hot Nuts"!' The band broke into 'Hot Nuts,' and the crowd went wild.

'Hot Nuts' was one of Doug Clark's most popular songs. It was a modified version of a song called 'Get 'Em From The Peanut Man (Hot

Nuts),' recorded by Lil Johnson, the dirty blues singer from Chicago, in 1935. Not many people remember Lil Johnson, but Little Richard did. He did another song recorded by Lil, 'Keep A-Knockin' (But You Can't Come In).' A lot of people don't realize that the first lyrics of 'Tutti-Frutti' were also a bit indelicate: '*If it don't fit, don't force it / You can grease it, make it easy.*'

A few years later, I brought the Hot Nuts back and we grossed six thousand on their return! I've heard that Otis Day & The Knights, who were featured in *National Lampoon's Animal House*, were inspired by Doug Clark. Makes sense. That's what the scene was like.

Bobby Marchan was a great singer—in fact, he was sometimes the lead singer for Huey 'Piano' Smith & The Clowns. They had some big records in the fifties, like 'Rockin' Pneumonia & The Boogie Woogie Flu.' Bobby made it to #1 on *Billboard's* R&B charts in 1960 with his version of 'There's Something On Your Mind.'

Bobby was gay and didn't believe in hiding it one bit, at a time when a young gay man—especially a young Black gay man who sometimes performed in drag—could quickly get himself hurt or killed. He did a lot of fraternity house parties, and someone from the crowd would invariably holler, 'I got a big dick!'

'Bring it on up, darlin'!' he'd yell back. They loved him for that. I think they loved Bobby's honesty, like they loved Little Richard's honesty. There was a lot of pushing the moral envelopes in the Black entertainment community.

Little Willie John was one of Phil's favorite singers. He was originally out of Detroit, and he was a master showman. He was the brother of Mable John, who recorded a lot at Motown and Stax, as well as backing big artists like Ray Charles as a member of The Raelettes—Mable was the first female signed by Berry Gordy. Willie had hit after hit, including his monster recording of 'Fever' in 1956—Peggy Lee covered it a couple of years later, and The McCoys hit with it in 1965.

One night, Willie was performing at the Apollo, and he showed up wearing nothing but a dirty T-shirt, Bermuda shorts, and flip-flops. He was sent out to get a new wardrobe, and he returned with a shaved head and a dress. He knocked the place out, performing in drag. Unfortunately, a few years later, Willie was convicted of manslaughter and died in prison. I went to his funeral in Detroit. Berry Gordy was there, and Aretha Franklin sang, along with Mable.

Willie made it to the Rock & Roll Hall Of Fame in 1996, and he deserves to be there. So many of these performers have been forgotten about. These were the guys and gals who laid the foundation blocks of what we see as cutting-edge today—most of it happened more than sixty years ago. God bless them all.

The Instigators, out of Albany, Georgia, were Black singers with white musicians. They were out in Tuscaloosa, Alabama, to play at the University of Alabama, and the Ku Klux Klan made an unscheduled appearance, but not because they dug the music. The Klan cut a hole in the top of the band's van with a torch, poured gasoline in, and lit it on fire. The band was playing for a fraternity who got afraid and put them out to fend for themselves. That's when the Kappa Alpha fraternity—they are known as the KA's—faced down the Ku Klux Klan. They took the band into their house and blocked the doors to prevent the band from being harmed.

'You're going to have to burn us out. We're not going to turn these guys over to you.'

The experience was so traumatic for the musicians that they broke up. They really thought they were going to be killed that night.

That was a picture of the South in those days. There were weak people, there were strong people, and there were heroes. Every time we went into a filling station or a restaurant to get some food to take out, you just never knew how things were going to land.

Some years later, myself and a group of us—Rodgers Redding, Carolyn Brown, Kay Brenda Stephens, James Ross—were over at the Black Elks Lodge in Barnesville, Georgia, to listen to some music. I was the only white person in the crowd, so we turned out to be the targeted group. And then the guns were drawn at our backs. Those guns were law enforcement. We were led out at gunpoint and put into the car. They followed us to the city line, and we all held our breath until we cleared Barnesville. We did what we were told, and we never looked back.

All of this went down because I was the single white boy in the Black crowd, listening to Black music and hanging with Black friends. In my late sixties, when I was attending the Barnesville Blues Festival with Rodgers, we were presented with a key to the city jail and a formal apology.

THE POWER TO MELT PREJUDICE
SCENE SIX

Otis Redding had an infectious, optimistic personality, and it opened my father's eyes. He loved Otis so much that he slowly became aware of how he was being treated by some white people, and that made him feel bad and remorseful—then renewed his spirit. Otis turned him. Otis softened his heart. He got into seeing how all Black people were treated and saw how it affected Otis. That's when he really began to question the morality of segregation of any kind, and to understand integration.

Pops got a lot of teasing from the locals about his position on race and his associations with the Black entertainers.

'You still in the nigger business?' I heard one guy say to my father.

'Let me tell you something,' Pops told him. 'When I'm sitting across the table from Otis and we're drinking a good bottle of wine and we're eating a big thick steak, you'd be surprised how white he is.' Most didn't like hearing that.

I used to get phone calls at the office all the time. Somebody would call me a 'nigger lover' and hang up.

That was the culture my father grew up in, and it was the way things were. Say what you will and take what you will. Even when the Civil Rights Act of 1964 was passed, it was still hard for Otis Redding and a lot of people. But Otis was the kind of man who could melt the cold hard steel of deep-seated hate and suspicion. He melted my father's heart. I think Otis Redding had the power to melt prejudice.

As my father spent more time with Otis, he changed. My father loved Otis and Otis loved him. He became slowly aware of how unfairly Black people were treated. He saw it and didn't like it one damn bit.

My father hired the first Black man, Robert Cumming, to work in a clothing store in Macon—a job that required a suit and tie. African Americans could be janitors or laborers, or they could work in their own communities at various jobs or in Black-owned shops with a Black clientele, but not as a salesman where they had to deal with white customers. My father was the first to do that in Macon. This was all because of the effect Otis had on him. He grew to love Otis like his own son.

On a cold winter night, when Phil and Otis were in the very early days, they played the Royal Peacock in Atlanta. It was the main club in the city—one of the first integrated clubs in the South. It was probably the most important club on what used to be referred to as the Chitlin' Circuit. These clubs and theaters were mostly in the south, east, and north, and as far west as Texas, where Black entertainers performed in front of Black audiences. A lot of the clubs were owned by Black entrepreneurs.

The Peacock and the Apollo in Harlem were two of the premiere venues on the circuit. On any given night you could see acts like Fats Domino, Wilson Pickett, The Four Tops, or The Drifters.

The Peacock was rocking that night, for sure. It was way early on, and Otis was still with Johnny Jenkins & The Pinetoppers, but he had begun to mean something.

On the way back to Macon, heading home with Phil riding with the band, they broke down about sixty miles out of town. The night was wickedly cold. We may be in the South, but nights get cold in Georgia.

They got out to walk to a filling station, but when they walked inside to make a phone call to my daddy to tell him to come get them and stood around the heater for a bit to thaw out, they were told they had to leave the filling station. The man working there strapped on a pistol. Phil made the call, and as soon as they were outside, the guy locked the door and drew his pistol to 'protect' his filling station from these dangerous killer musicians. That's how things happened. And they sucked it up, because if they started trouble, they would have been blamed for that trouble, for sure. I heard my daddy talking to Phil, and I could tell it was trouble. Daddy woke me up and explained the situation. And then he called Blue.

'I'll get Blue. We need to be there as fast as we can,' he told me. 'Phil and the boys are in trouble, and I hope we can get there on time.' So Daddy called Blue, and we roared off into the night.

Blue—his real name was Clark—grew up in the street-fighting school with some tough-ass Macon boys, so he had to fight. And he could fight. He would tear your ass up unmercifully. He once hit a man so hard, he knocked his eye right out of its socket. You think that would end the fight. My brother continued to pound his face in the area where the eyeball dangled. Blue had a bull neck and was built like a side of beef. When he hit you, he'd bust you up. I saw him hit a guy and break his jaw in three places with one punch.

Another time, I witnessed Blue putting a guy down and then stomping on him. I tried to get him off the man by wrapping my arms around him.

'You've got to stop. You're hurting him too bad,' I begged him. 'You're going to kill him!'

'If you don't turn me loose, I'll break your ribs,' Blue threatened.

'I'm your brother and I'm trying to help you.' And wham! Blue got off the guy and hit me so hard, I went down on the ground and didn't think I was ever going to get up. Phil came in, and Blue went after the guy again. Phil drew back and slapped Blue in the face real hard, knocking sense into Blue and bringing him back from wherever he was. Phil knew how to handle Blue. He knew how to handle anyone.

By the time my father and Blue arrived at the car where the band was waiting, Phil's lips had turned purple. The musicians had all wrapped themselves in their sweaty performance clothes, which probably made them colder. Blue went into the service station and taught the guy who wouldn't let them stand around the heater a hard lesson. I don't know what kind of lesson it was, but Blue was a pretty good teacher, and you remembered his lessons.

The only one I ever saw get the best of Blue was my goat, Stinky. I taught Stinky that if someone kicked him, to rear up and butt the shit out of them. He was able to stand up on his back legs and throw all his weight into a headbutt. Blue did make the mistake of kicking his foot at that goat. Immediately, Stinky rammed Blue's ass to the ground. Blue flipped the goat over and was about to nail him with a fist when I managed to stop him and explained that I'd trained the goat to do that. Blue never bothered Stinky again.

Stinky would stand up and lick my lit cigarette out of my mouth and swallow it. Then he learned to grab my pack and run away to the barn. I loved that goat like anyone would love their dog. I would even let him into the house, and he'd never trash anything or lay a pellet. At night, Stinky would come up to my window and gaze in to watch television.

My daddy was always there to get Otis out of any trouble. Herbert Ellis—whose brother, Jack, would become the first Black mayor of Macon in 1999—was a friend of Otis. During the early sixties, Herb and his girlfriend had gone to a stump whiskey house, which is a place where you buy bootlegged moonshine. Stump whiskey is a damn strong drink to run through your guts, and sometimes it makes a person crazy. It was called stump whiskey or stump hole whiskey because moonshiners used to hide their operations in holes under tree stumps so the government men wouldn't find them.

When Herb was in this stump house, the moonshiner started hitting on the girl.

'Hey, man,' Herb told the bootlegger. 'You're not going to mess with my lady.'

The bootlegger and his son beat the hell out of Herb and threw him out onto the street.

Herb went and got Otis and two of Otis's friends: Sylvester Huckabee, known as Huck, and Bubba Howard. Huck looked out for Otis, and Bubba Howard helped out Huck, though Huck didn't need any help. He was the baddest cat in Macon and maybe Georgia. He served in numerous prisons, he was a master thief, and it was rumored that he had killed nine men. Huck has been referred to as Otis's occasional road manager, but he was his bodyguard—for Otis and for me, when necessary.

Bubba Howard was a racist. He didn't like me one bit.

'I hate your fuckin' guts, Alan.'

'Why do you hate me Bubba?' I asked.

'Because you're white.'

'I guess I have to accept your answer, if that's the way you feel.'

It did amaze me how Bubba cleaned his life up—not only by becoming deacon of his church, twenty-five years later, but also because he was nice to me!

Huck would hit a man and knock him into tomorrow. A detective went to arrest Huck one night for something, and Huck beat the shit out of the detective right on the street.

Huck had a little grocery store in Bellevue, which was the toughest side of town and very dangerous, and it didn't make a difference if you were Black or white. Some of those people over in Bellevue were angry and some were just mean. And Huck was the King of Bellevue.

Huck would stock maybe one can of sardines and some sausage, and maybe a bag of sugar and some mustard. The scales were there so he could weigh out his marijuana—and he was running it right there at the entrance to Bellevue. Huck put guys on bikes selling pot. He had all these teenagers out riding bikes selling pot all over Bellevue, like Fagin had pickpockets in Dickens's *Oliver Twist*. Keep in mind that just having a joint of marijuana back then could mean serious jail time. If you were Black, you'd probably wind up on a road gang. Huck didn't care about jail. He had been in jail many times and considered it his 'reading' time. He mostly read books about how to break out of jail.

During a fuel shortage, Huck was stealing gasoline trucks. He would get a bulldozer, dig a hole, drive the truck into the hole, and cover the truck up. After a while, he'd dig it up and sell it. Huck and his pals hijacked truckloads of electronics, guns, and everything else. I remember him coming to my office with a diamond ring.

'You like this hot ring?' Huck asked, thinking I might be interested.

'How hot is it?'

'They don't even know it's gone.'

'How'd you get it?'

'I walked into a jewelry store and had him lay out a bunch of rings. I had an apple and put it on the counter. When the jeweler wasn't looking, I pushed the ring into my apple and then just kept on eating the apple and walked out with this.'

Every time he showed me something like that, I told him to take it back. He'd shrug his shoulders and then just walk away, kind of dejected. Just one time I wanted a gun for my personal protection. He showed up at the cabin—he always showed up in the middle of the night. I went outside and Huck had a pistol for me. It was a .22 caliber long rifle mounted on a .38 frame with a big pistol grip and nine shots—completely modified. I loaded nine hollow points into the cylinder.

'Is it accurate, Huck?'

He took five old shotgun shells and threw them out onto the yard. He fired five shots and hit them all.

'Let's see you pick them up,' Huck said, handing me the iron.

I shot and picked up all five.

'Damn, Alan, you can shoot!'

Huck, Otis, and several other friends all loaded up and slammed down in front of the stump house and started blasting the place and shooting up some of the people in there. The bootleggers started firing back, and Otis wound up with a leg full of birdshot—ironically from his own gang. Otis and Huck hauled over to our house, where my father, Huck, and I picked birdshot out of Otis's leg. But a few other people were shot as well as Otis, and someone said Otis did some shooting.

'I'm afraid I'm in trouble, Pops,' Otis said.

'You are in serious-ass trouble, Otis. The police are going to come and get you for sure.'

The next morning, Pops went down to City Hall and got the Solicitor General and figured out a way to reduce Otis's charges from possibly attempted murder to just paying a settlement of thirty-five thousand dollars—to be paid to the people who were shot. Pops convinced the solicitor that Otis wasn't involved in the shooting and that he was hiding behind the car, and that those lowlifes at the stump house were lying. The police liked Otis and they liked Pops, so they believed the story. Or, I should say, they accepted the story, and preferred to believe that version rather than the moonshiner's version.

Otis was a tough guy. He had been raised on the poor side of town. He was very brave, and he had more friends in the police department than anyone ever thought possible. One night we were riding up the hill and I said, 'Hey, Otis. Be careful. There's Oscar Levrette.' Oscar was the biggest ticket writer in Macon, Georgia. He'd write you a ticket for anything. If you had a loud muffler, he'd give you a ticket.

Otis went running up to Oscar's motorcycle.

'Hey, Mr. Levrette. How ya doing?'

'Hey, Otis. How ya doing?'

And then Otis gave Oscar a few dollars for breakfast. We got back into our car—a Ford convertible with four on the floor. Otis popped that clutch and peeled rubber all the way down the street. Oscar Levrette didn't do a thing—didn't even look up.

Sheriff Holmes Hawkins in Gray, Georgia, where Otis later had his ranch, was a very prejudiced sheriff. *Prejudiced?* It was rumored he had a noose hanging over his desk to intimidate African Americans. If you were Black and you were caught speeding or anything else in Gray, you were in trouble.

People like Sheriff Hawkins are why northerners were afraid to drive through Georgia back in the day, and it is how a lot of rumors spread up north. A lot of northerners were petrified about driving through the South—mostly because of people like Sheriff Hawkins. They showed no mercy back then. And so, after Otis had already bought his place and we had gone through the thirty days to protest against him buying the house—Pops had written it into the deed that if any white neighbor objected within thirty days, the sale would be null and void, which kind of made everyone out there feel comfortable—and after we knew the house was his and we were going to be there, Otis paid old Sheriff Holmes Hawkins a visit.

'Mr. Hawkins. I know that you and your wife can't go to dinner with me, but I would like to treat you to a dinner on me.' Otis gave him a hundred-dollar bill. And that hundred-dollar bill made Otis number one with Holmes Hawkins—number one with a bullet. The whole time we lived there, we never had any problems with the police. They always treated us with respect.

YOU'LL SING WHEN I TELL YOU TO SING
SCENE SEVEN

One time, when Otis was already known, he was driving a new white Cadillac down in North Florida. It was running hot, so he stopped at a service station, and he saw the owner strap on a gun when he pulled up to the pumps. When the guy came out, Otis started doing a parody of what he thought the man with the gun wanted to hear, knowing full well that his mission was to get home to his family safely.

'Lord have mercy, boss man, can you help me? My boss man's car is running hot and he's going to take a stick to me, sure as hell.'

The man heard what he wanted to hear. 'I'll help you out, boy,' he told Otis, who was acting the part of a 'compliant Negro.'

Otis got his car fixed and got it filled up. 'We'll come back and see y'all,' he said.

Otis could go that route if that was what it was going to take to get the job done. It was about survival, and that's what you need to understand. Otis wasn't ashamed of this story—if he had been ashamed, he wouldn't have told me it. That is confidence, and that was a man who was secure.

Contrasted to that, we did have one situation in Asheville, North Carolina. For some reason, the promoter, who had been real kind to us, went sour one night. Otis wanted to get paid before he went onstage, which was not unusual, since that's how we always did it. The promoter went and got a couple of hoodlums and barged into the dressing room. One of them took out a knife and cut off Otis's tie. Not a smart play.

'You're going to sing, baby. You'll sing when we tell you to sing.'

Otis hit the man so hard that he almost broke his wrist—knocked him against the wall, grabbed his own pistol, and pinned all the thugs against the brick in the dressing room. On that night, he was definitely not a 'compliant Negro.'

All of a sudden, a policeman comes in with his gun drawn and points it at Otis.

'You're under arrest.'

'You're going to arrest me for defending myself against these hoods here?'

'Otis. I'm arresting you to get you out of here safely. They've already busted all the windows out of your bus, and your tires are cut. We need to get you out of here to save your life, and that's what I'm trying to do.'

Otis went along with the arrest and got safely away.

YEAH, MAN, THE
SOUTH WAS JUMPING
SCENE EIGHT

We had music happening everywhere in Macon, Georgia. You could go to many nightclubs and bars to see different acts. Over on Broadway was Anne's Tic Toc Lounge. Little Richard sharpened his early chops singing there, along with James Brown and Johnny Jenkins, featuring Otis. There was Adam's Lounge out on the Old Gray Highway, a club where I put on a lot of shows on Sunday nights during the early sixties. My father didn't want me hanging out and working over there, so I told him to join me the following Sunday, and if he thought it was a bad idea, I wouldn't go work there.

Heck, I'd be mounting shows with Joe Simon, The Impressions, Rufus Thomas, and Inez & Charlie Foxx, the great sister-brother act, who hit with a wonderful song called 'Mockingbird' in 1963. Pops went to one show with me and didn't say a word. The following Sunday, my father asked, 'What time is showtime?' He wound up really digging it. In fact, he started taking the tickets at the door and counting the money. He was very happy because a lot of the men who shopped at his store on Friday and Saturday nights were his customers digging the scene.

The Adams brothers had another club called the Ebony Lounge in Milledgeville. I did a few shows over there, but I didn't feel safe. They were real wild country folks over there. There was another juke joint called Club 15. That was tombstone territory. You go there and you better be packing some iron.

One night, The Pinetoppers were playing with Otis and James Brown, and the Flames came in and started blasting the place. James was gunning for Joe Tex—he wanted to scare him or kill him all over some lady. Apparently, James was doing dance steps while he was shooting, according to my brother Phil, who was there at the time. James spread some cash around and took off, and that was the end of it. That was a dangerous club.

There was a place over in Atlanta called B.B. Beaman's Ballroom. I had done a lot of business with B.B., but on this night the manager was in charge. After 'Soul Man' broke in 1967, Sam & Dave were scheduled to perform two shows within a four-hour period. I was there with Carolyn Brown. At a bit passed midnight, during 'Soul Man,' the manager cut off the sound. He told me that he was paying for a show that lasted until midnight, and he wasn't going to go any further. The crowd started to get very angry.

'You see that man who took your money?' Bo Anderson, Sam & Dave's road manager, told the crowd. 'He's the one who cut the sound so we can't sing.'

The crowd went crazy. People started to tear the place up. We escaped to the dressing room as the place was being ripped apart. Someone lit a fire outside our dressing room and smoke started to pour in. Outside, someone shot out the windows of our bus. People were fighting each other and smashing everything in sight. When the police arrived, they led Sam & Dave out. They didn't care if I got beat up or not. They figured I was a white guy with a Black girl in a Black club, thinking that Carolyn was my date and I deserved to get knocked around.

PHIL AWAITED THOSE ORDERS AND HE AWAITED THOSE ORDERS AND HE AWAITED THOSE ORDERS SOME MORE
SCENE NINE

Before Phil went into the army, in 1962 and into 1963, we were doing pretty good. Phil wanted to record Johnny Jenkins's 'Love Twist' with The Pinetoppers, along with 'She's Alright' and 'Shout Bamalama.' 'She's Alright,' written by Otis and James McEachin, had been originally recorded in Los Angeles while Otis was visiting his sister, Louise. It did okay regionally, but nothing more than that. But Johnny's 'Love Twist' did get the attention of Joe Galkin, Atlantic's main promotion man in the South—Joe would later become my dear friend and one of my guiding forces in the music business.

Otis was an occasional driver for Johnny Jenkins, and they drove up to Memphis so Johnny could record some songs at Stax—songs that didn't really impress Jim Stewart or anyone else. Jim, along with his sister Estelle Axton, had founded Stax back in 1957—they took over the old Capitol Theater.

They had some extra recording time while they were up there, and with the encouragement of Al Jackson of the M.G.'s, Otis cut a couple of tracks: 'These Arms Of Mine' with Johnny Jenkins on guitar and Steve Cropper on piano, and 'Hey Hey Baby' with the M.G.'s. Steve Cropper and Joe Galkin got Jim Stewart to sign Otis to a recording contract. Jim Stewart wasn't too impressed with the work and later gave half of his publishing on the songs for hardly anything to John Richbourg (John R.) of WLAC in Nashville.

Steve Cropper was on guitar for a lot of songs with Otis at Stax. And he co-wrote a lot of songs. Duck Dunn was usually on bass, Al Jackson on drums, and Booker T. Jones and sometimes Issac Hayes on keys. When Otis recorded at Stax, he would sit down with Steve Cropper and give Steve what he wanted for guitar, and then he would tell Duck Dunn what he wanted for bass—then Booker T. or Isaac Hayes.

Booker T. & The M.G.'s were the best band I ever worked with. These guys could catch on to a hit and take it with a run. It was fun making records at Stax. You just went from one song to the other, and if you made a mistake, you started over. You did it over and over and over until you got it right.

Al Jackson was the best drummer I ever heard—better than Ginger Baker and all the guys who really made a name for themselves. He didn't do fancy rolls and solos, but he was steady as a rock. Otis would be there, and he'd explain to all the musicians what he wanted and what he heard in his head—humming out the parts. They would pick it up right away. Then he'd turn around and look at Al and tell him, 'You just stay with me,' and that's exactly what Al did. Then there were Floyd Newman and Joe Arnold, Wayne Jackson, Andrew Love—The Mar-Keys were basically the studio guys at Stax.

Thanks to John R. and Hamp Swain at WIBB (The King Bee), Otis's 'These Arms Of Mine' got to #20 on *Billboard*'s R&B charts. 'Hey Hey Baby' was the A-side, but it sounded too much like Little Richard. The record was put out and nothing happened with that song. So Hamp and John R. decided to flip the record and play 'These Arms Of Mine,' and then it started selling.

Otis wanted Johnny to work with him, but Johnny had a resentment toward Otis because Otis was getting some success. Otis cared a lot about trying to help Johnny. But Johnny was one of those guys with an arrogant side to him, and you couldn't talk any sense to him. I know because I've listened to a lot of Johnny. But 'These Arms Of Mine' was a legitimate hit.

Interestingly, I was away at college at the time, and I remember some of my friends laughing when I told them that Otis had a hit record. They did not believe it was real and went as far as to say, 'I like Otis, but I don't know if he can really sing!'

I gave an interview with Michael Buffalo Smith on Swampland.com, and I told him that Johnny Jenkins did not like to fly, and there was a split between the band and Otis. During this time, Otis traveled solo and rehearsed with local bands early in the afternoons in each of the cities where he performed. Deep down, he always wanted that same steady backup band. He met this great band from Newport News, Virginia, that had a great horn section, full rhythm section, a male singer named Roy Hines, and a female singer named Gloria Stevenson. Thus, the Otis Redding Show & Revue was born. Their first transportation was a 1949 Flexie tour bus, not in very stable shape, but Otis made it keep rolling, and the show expanded the concerts even further across the country, moving from town to town almost every day.

If you graduated from college and you had an ROTC scholarship, you had to go to the army—even Elvis had to go to the army in those years, though he was drafted. Phil was contractually bound to the army because he accepted the scholarship and owed a few years of military service.

Phil had declared a hardship case because of my father being ill— Phil was really the only breadwinner at the time. My father had some sort of mysterious illness—he collapsed while drinking a beer near the clothing store. The doctors could never come up with a name for it, but it took him all the way down to being totally paralyzed—it was a stroke, more or less. He stayed in the hospital for months before he came home, and for some reason his testicles swelled to the size of tennis balls.

Uncle Sam sent Phil a telegram saying that he was to await orders for his military duty. So he awaited those orders. And he awaited those orders, and he waited some more. Phil awaited those orders for a hundred and eight days, which made him AWOL from his two-year commitment over in Germany. This was good fortune for Phil, because the Vietnam War was heating up, and we would eventually lose over fifteen hundred Georgia boys in Southeast Asia.

Phil sent a telegram to the army informing them that he would be more than happy to report for duty but had not received any orders. He immediately got a phone call, ordering him to be on a plane at 4am the following morning.

Phil and I got together at 4pm. I had twelve hours of training as Otis Redding's manager and running my brother's booking agency. Phil told me he had left the company with five thousand dollars in the bank, which would have been great, but he didn't tell me he had ten thousand dollars' worth of debt. So, from the first day of my job, I was working with what seemed to me as insurmountable debt—bills that we needed to pay to stay open. We were desperate from my first minutes running the company.

Phil had loaned his father-in-law, who was a very wealthy man at the time, fifteen hundred dollars, and that was from Otis Redding's royalties! *Man*, was I pissed. His father-in-law's business went broke, so I paid back Otis's royalties by borrowing money from relatives. Waldens always pay other Waldens back, in one way or another. Otis trusted me totally with money because of decisions like that. I was so mad at my brother I wouldn't answer his letters when he was in Germany. He left me to take care of the company and didn't tell me the truth about the money he owed. It was a hard lesson—and, I think, a valuable one.

There were some tough times, but we endured them and continued to work hard and were determined not to let the office be closed. We were going to keep it open until Phil's return. The fact that he was so late leaving for the army was a bit shocking to me. We had no time to do any real training. I just kind of stepped into the office and had to take it all alone, since Otis was on the road most of the time.

Thank goodness we had Carolyn Brown. Carolyn worked sixty to seventy-five hours a week for twenty-five dollars—sometimes we were there all night. From these humble beginnings, she went from that twenty-five dollars a week to being the highest paid female in the state of Georgia. She was making great money and driving a Bentley and all of that, but she worked harder than any other woman in the office. She was one of the smartest ladies in the whole state of Georgia. She ended up running Phil's publishing companies, and she did all of my copyrights. She ran that office and I loved her. She was like my sister.

I remember Tyrone Davis coming into my office some years later. Tyrone wanted to see me, and he felt like he was pretty damn important. He got as far as the reception area and he cussed out Carolyn Brown.

'You got to go. We don't need you around here,' I told Davis.

'Hey, I'm Tyrone Davis.'

'I don't give a damn who you are. When you come in here, you treat these ladies with respect.'

We treated our people right, and they worked hard for us. They liked working hard. I had the first integrated staff in Macon, Georgia. It was just Otis, Carolyn, and two secretaries, Sherry Emmet and Angela Corbet, and sometimes Bobby Marchan.

I used to go to work sometimes at six so I could be there ahead of everyone and make a pot of coffee and get ready for the morning meetings. I ran four common phone lines and one private—five telephone lines. I knew how to jump from the other to the other. Sometimes I stayed all night and slept on the sofa.

GET OUT OF HERE
YOU SON OF A BITCH!
YOU TRYING TO
HUSTLE MY SON?
SCENE TEN

I was a sucker for all the musicians who needed money. I heard all of the stories—the baby needs shoes and the baby needs milk and cry me a river. I had loaned out a lot of money to some of these people who had no intention of ever paying me back, and they never did. I had gotten really down in the dumps and realized I was over twenty thousand in debt. I went to my relatives and my friends and asked for money. In those days we didn't declare bankruptcy—never even crossed my mind. It was never an option, because there was such a negative stigma attached. I called Otis, who was in Baltimore, and told him about the situation and that I may have to close the doors.

'Red. You stay there and I'm going to call you back later. You don't do anything like that.'

Otis didn't call me back. He jumped on a plane and flew to Macon and rushed over to the office. And Otis Redding chewed my ass out. He chewed it out like it had never had been chewed out.

'Phil and I worked too damned hard to even think about these doors closing. If I have to put all of my royalties and all of my road receipts into this company, we're going to keep it open!'

That was the kind of determination and ass-chewing I needed. He knocked the panic out of me and filled me up with optimism. That's the kind of spirit I needed to keep going.

'You talk like that, Otis, and I have to get right with all of these musicians who are conning me out of money. And, with our commissions, we just might be able to keep the doors open.'

'What do you think we need to do?' Otis asked.

'Have somebody here to help me to keep a check on people coming in here so I can concentrate on booking shows.'

'Who do you want to get?'

'The only person I trust on that level is my father.'

'Pops?' Otis asked with a smile.

'Pops,' I said.

'Let's go see him,' Otis said.

'But I think he's dying, Otis.'

'We'll see, Red. We'll see if he's dying. We'll just see about that.'

It was Otis Redding's words that got my father to get out of his easy chair in front of his television with his swollen private parts so big he could hardly walk, and to come to work at the office. I needed as many people as I could who I trusted.

Otis Redding kneeled down beside him.

'Pops. We need you,' Otis said.

That's when the miracle happened. The next morning, my daddy was shaking and weak, but he was at the back door of the house, hardly able to stand but dressed to the nines, waiting to begin his first day at work.

'What time do we open the office?'

We had taken a show with Otis to the University of the South in Sewanee, Tennessee. They did four events a year and let me do all of their bookings. This was the first time Pops went out on a trip. Otis flew, but me and Pops hit the road. We did the show and started back that night.

Pops wasn't in great shape. He could walk but he was still partially paralyzed. We attached a suicide knob to the steering wheel, so he could drive with one hand if needed. I was exhausted driving through the mountains, so I asked Pops to take the wheel. He did, and I went right to sleep. Three hundred miles later, I opened my eyes, and we were a good deal south of Atlanta and almost home to Macon. I looked over at Pops and he was damn happy. He had succeeded at that challenge. That started him. He was back in the saddle. He had the will to live again.

Those early days of having my father working with me were such a thrill—just having him around, with that fighting spirit. One day, some guy came into the office and started giving us crap, and my daddy threw the phone at him. A heavy phone. In those days, if you throw a phone at a guy, you're liable to kill him.

'Get out of here, you son of a bitch! You trying to hustle my son?'

We primarily concentrated on Otis's career, and that's when we started making progress—streamlining and getting rid of a lot of acts that weren't pulling their own and promoting some others. We got out of debt, including the money Phil had 'invested' in his father-in-law's house.

My daddy felt needed. He slowly but steadily regained his health, except for his left arm. I think he got better because he believed in Otis so much. He would do anything for him. That's the kind of love that can make miracles happen.

The next thing I knew, Pops was going out as Otis's road manager. He traveled with Otis and the band members all around Georgia, Alabama, Tennessee, and Mississippi. He wore a turtleneck, and everyone thought he was Otis's personal preacher. Daddy became pretty hip in his old age—though he really never grew very old.

My daddy came into the office one night while I was smoking a joint, and man was he upset.

'Red! Oh, no! No, no, no! You can't smoke that pot! You're going to become a drug addict!'

'Daddy, I'll make a deal with you,' I suggested. 'You sit right here with me and smoke some of this joint. And, when we get done, if you tell me I've got to quit pot, I won't ever smoke it again.'

I rolled a fresh joint, and he observed the process with curiosity and trepidation. I lit it and we smoked a joint and he didn't feel anything.

'Is that it?' he asked.

'That's it.'

'I need to get a drink,' he said, and poured himself a jigger of Canadian Club.

One night, Otis and Speedo, Otis's road manager and close friend, were smoking a joint behind the airplane before they took off. My daddy was flying with them that night, and he came around to the back of the plane.

'Let me hit that joint thing one time.'

Of course, Otis always had killer pot—both him and Johnnie Taylor. Johnnie Taylor was a real connoisseur. Pops joined Otis and Speedo on this joint. When they were in the air, Daddy fell asleep and woke up afraid.

'Damn, Otis. You just drove through a red light!'

It was just the red lights on the portside wing. I guess when you run into the good pot, you know it.

YOU AIN'T GOING TO MISS THAT GIG, JOHNNIE TAYLOR
SCENE ELEVEN

I loved Johnnie Taylor. He was from a little town in Arkansas, and when he moved to Chicago, he went out on VeeJay Records with a group called The Five Echoes. He sang in The Highway Q.C.'s—a gospel group—and replaced Sam Cooke in The Soul Stirrers. In 1962, Sam Cooke produced a record for Johnnie called 'Rome Wasn't Built In A Day,' but on that song he sounded just like Sam Cooke.

After Sam was murdered, Johnnie made recordings over at Stax. He had his own philosophy and views on different things. He was different. Maybe that's why he was sometimes called the Philosopher of Soul. He had been on the road since he was fifteen, and he was tremendous with women. You'd go to his room and you might find him putting golf balls into a cup.

I was in a studio with Johnnie on one occasion, and I decided to give him a suggestion.

'Hey, Johnnie. When you get to that certain hook there, right after the hook . . .'

Johnnie went from smiles to a look of *I don't like what you just said and it isn't worth shit.*

'Listen, motherfucker, let me set your ass straight. I don't tell you how to manage no damn performer, do I?'

'No, Johnnie. You don't.'

'Well, don't you be trying to help me sing. I can out-sing everybody in your damn stable but Otis Redding.'

I never told him how to sing a song ever again.

Johnnie's résumé included con artist, preacher, gospel singer, and pimp. He would always have a couple of women in the car, and while he was singing, they would go through the audience and sell photos—they all worked for Johnnie, and they traveled with him everywhere. Johnnie had style. He drove nice cars and wore mohair suits and diamond rings. And he could sing.

I think he was right up there with Billy Eckstine—a real good guy when he wasn't intoxicated, but when he was it was only a matter of time before he blew up on somebody—at least once a day. If it was your day, he'd just tear into your ass. He drank a fifth of scotch almost every day.

Johnnie would threaten to cancel dates, and he knew it would just aggravate the hell out of me. He called one night to tell me, 'I got to cancel Spartansburg. I just fired my band and put them out on the street corner.'

Johnnie Taylor would pull that routine so often, I kept two bands for Johnnie Taylor in every city he played.

'No, Johnnie. You ain't going to miss that gig. I got a band already at the theater, ready to play.'

'You sure got me figured.'

YOU'VE GOT BALLS.
WHAT CAN I DO
FOR YOU?
SCENE TWELVE

I had two people that really offered me help in terms of what direction Otis and I should take: Joe Galkin and Joe Glazer.

Joe Galkin was a sort of mentor for me. I nicknamed him Squawkin' Galkin because he was a good talker—he had the gift of gab. Joe was a short, bald, Jewish guy, always dressed in a sharp-looking suit and driving a Thunderbird with a car phone and a couple of diamonds on him somewhere. Joe was a rolypoly guy, but he was one of the best damned promotion men in the world, in my opinion.

Joe would go into a radio station and piss everybody off, and then we'd walk out into the parking lot, turn on the radio, and our records would already be playing! Joe got a lot of my records played. Joe would yell at people and cuss people out, but they always played his records.

When Joe was a teenager, he lived in Macon and had a band, but I didn't know him at the time. Now, Joe came down to Macon a couple of times a month. He had left New York—at one time he owned a nightclub in New York—and became Atlantic's promotion guy in the South.

Joe made Atlanta his home and ended up owning a record distributor there with a lady named Gwen Kessler, and they sold records on top of records on top of records. Joe was a great businessman, and he was very fond of Gwen. They were a powerful team. He was Atlantic's lead promotion man, and he did a lot of work at Stax as well. According to the great record producer Henry Stone, when Joe died he left everything to Gwen.

Frank Sands worked for Shaw Artists, a booking company run by Milt Shaw, who took the shop over from his father in the fifties. After Milt sold the company, he overdosed on heroin. Frank was an Italian from New York. He chose the name Sands so people would think he was Jewish. I guess it helped to have a Jewish name in the music business. The Mesner brothers' Aladdin Records out of Los Angeles, the Chess brothers out of Chicago, Lou Adler at Dunhill, Art Rupe with his Specialty Records—Jews were a big reason why R&B got onto the turntables of white kids and Black kids.

Frank Sands was the one who told me about Joe Glazer and the barrel of acid. A couple of years later, Sol Saffian, the great booking agent, introduced me to Joe, which sent a chill down my back. I had been having trouble getting a license to do business from the unions and was hoping Joe could help.

The union wouldn't give me a license for a booking agency, and the union ran the show. We tried to please them, but they didn't budge. If Phil had a management company and I wanted to open a booking agency, we couldn't do it in the same office because technically, we'd be two companies. There was Redwal Music—one of the first music publishing companies in the South, opened by Phil, Otis, and me — and Phil Walden Artists, which became Walden Artists. We finally physically separated the two companies. We opened another door in the basement and told the union people that we used it every day, so the agency was separated from the management company. Phil was upstairs and I was downstairs. Still couldn't get a license.

I sat down and Joe and I chitchatted. He had one of those little barrels on his desk that when you open the door, a guy's pecker would jump out. Glazer laughed like he had never seen it before.

'Alan. You know, you're an awfully young man to be in the position you're in, with all of these entertainers. You must have a very strong drive to be able to build that in the South.'

'Mr. Glazer, maybe it's time that some of you old farts get out of the way.'

We locked eyes. Neither one of us blinked. We just stared at each other. This goes on for ten minutes, with nothing but glaring at each other. He turned around to Sol.

'I like this kid,' he said. And then turned back to me.

'You've got balls. What can I do for you?'

'I understand you've got connections with the unions,' I said.

'I do.'

'AGVA won't give me a license for a booking agency because our management company is in the same building, and that means me and my brother are running the same business in the same building.'

Joe picked up the phone to AGVA, the American Guild of Variety Artists. Then he called Bob Caruthers at AFM, the American Federation of Musicians, and told him the same thing.

'I've got Alan Walden in front of me who wants a booking license. Please put it in the mail. He's a good guy. Give him a license and whatever else he wants.'

And that was it. When I got home, both licenses were lying on my desk. I had been trying to get them for three years. They were just kept holding out and holding out. Joe got me those licenses. And then he took on the lawsuit when Shaw Artists sued Otis for leaving them early on his contract.

Frank Sands booked all of Otis's one-nighters. Shaw had another guy who booked just theaters. The new owner of Shaw Artists tried to steal Otis. We decided to raid him instead and took all but two of his acts away from him and watched him go bankrupt, smiling all the way through it.

GIVE ME THAT BOTTLE AND LET ME CHUG A LITTLE SOUL
SCENE THIRTEEN

'Security' was my first session with Otis. The Stax Mar-Key horns were punching those sounds off from the beginning. It kicked. It opened up kicking. It wasn't a huge record for us, but that was the first session I went on, and it blew my mind.

Otis and I decided to fly to Memphis. When the plane lifted off the ground, my stomach surged, I was so nervous. Otis was laughing. I turned around and looked at him, and he was smiling and laughing so hard, I forgot all about the plane ride and my upside-down stomach.

When I got to Memphis, I met Steve Cropper, Duck Dunn, Al Jackson, Booker T., Isaac Hayes, and David Porter. Man, I walked in there and I was so shocked because this was one great integrated group of guys drinking out of the same whiskey bottle. I had never seen that in my whole life—give me that bottle and let me chug a little bit of soul. That was unheard of in Macon.

They were like family at Stax. They all loved each other. That was a beautiful and enlightening scene.

When I would go to the recording session at Stax, with the slanted floor and no two walls alike in the whole place, they only had one big space heater to warm that big room. In the winter, when the band was playing, I got to sit on the heater to warm myself up—that was the big thing. Sitting on the heater was a place of honor. When the band took a break, I had to get off the heater and let them warm up. During the winter, the musicians in that studio had overcoats on and big heavy jackets while they were playing, which I thought was unusual—that they could play that good in heavy clothes. That was part of the atmosphere of Stax Records. All of those old studios had a particular sound and vibe.

At Stax, they put in acoustic tiles that had holes so the sound would go through rather than bouncing back. It was a great sounding studio. And the guys were so much fun to be around. I never had any problems. One night Otis and Booker T. got into it, but it didn't last long. They didn't scream or holler. Booker T. made the statement that he could be out playing six-thousand-dollar gigs instead of working in the studio. Otis told him to go make that gig and to bring Isaac Hayes in to do the work. Isaac would be fine with him.

Otis was going to show Booker that he wasn't so powerful and that he could very well do without him. They got over it.

At Capricorn, in 1969, we had a man named Jim Hawkins who came from Athens, Georgia. He built the initial studio. He was the one who put in the baffles to absorb the sound. In the basement we had the echo chambers. Jim built these perfect tiled echo chambers. You could get whatever sound you wanted in that studio. Then Johnny 'The Duck' Sandlin joined us—Johnny produced The Allman Brothers Band and was a very good engineer and session man, and he and my friend Paul Hornsby were the real technical geniuses of the studio. Paul was also one of the top producers and engineers at Capricorn, and he remains one of my closest friends today.

Johnny had contractors go in and remove some of the support beams of the building to eliminate vibration coming off the street, which was a hundred yards away. Downtown Macon is all concrete and brick, and Johnny felt there was too much vibration from the eighteen-wheelers hauling through town. And those trucks were going to rattle the beams and rattle Johnny until they were cut. We were going for the dead sound. We got it so you could clap your hands and nothing would travel. Totally dead sound.

SHOOTOUT AT THE OK CORRAL
SCENE FOURTEEN

We were at an Otis Redding fan club show at a venue called the New Look Club, which was on a second floor—a little club, but it could accommodate our crowd. I was with Otis, Huck, Bubba Howard, Carolyn Brown, and my date, a very attractive African American young lady who could carry her own in any situation. She was there to help me run the door and count the money.

Carl Thomas and his band, The Roller Coasters, were playing. Carl was like Johnny Jenkins—he was manicured and good-looking. Women were crazy about him and he always had a beautiful girl on his arm. Now, on that night, Huck told me that if I ever felt that I was in any sort of trouble, to hold up one finger in the air and he'd be on it. Well, as sure as the world, I got into an argument with a guy at the door who started giving me crap and my girl reached into her purse and pulled out this big-ass .38 and held it where the guy could see it. I held up my finger, and Huck jumps over the balcony and lands right in front of this guy. One punch sent the guy down a flight of stairs. Huck then dragged him off and beat the shit out of him. Then the fellow, knocked to pieces, apologized to me and my girl. Apology accepted.

The Roller Coasters had played for free as a favor to Otis and me. After the show, Carl walked out onto the street with a gorgeous girl on his arm and was approached by Bubba Howard.

'Hey, baby,' Bubba said to Carl's girl. 'You don't need to be with his ass. You need to be with me.' Then Bubba tried to pull the girl away from Carl.

Carl wasn't much bigger than me, and Bubba was a big man.

'You ain't gonna take my lady away from me,' Carl warned Bubba.

That's when Bubba took out his pistol and hit Carl in the face, knocking him down to the ground, and stuck the gun into Carl's mouth.

'Listen, nigger. You're fixin' to have your brains splattered all over the pavement,' Bubba threatened.

'Please don't kill me,' Carl pleaded to Bubba. 'Don't kill me.'

So Huck was there, and Bubba was there, and Otis and me. Carl ran up the street with The Roller Coasters, and they got guns out of their cars—shotguns, rifles, pistols—and they started walking down Cotton Avenue, about seven or eight of them. Then we looked down the other way, and another group was coming up behind us. *Where in hell did all of these guns come from?* We're in the middle, and everyone is armed and ready to go and start shooting.

I ran out in between the group coming down the hill and I'm begging them to stop.

'You don't want to do this, man. This is stupid. Someone is going to get killed! Don't do this shit!' I shouted.

Finally, The Roller Coasters went back up to talk it over for a minute, and I went back to where Otis was. I hopped into my car and pulled up next to him.

'You get your ass in this car! You can't afford this,' I pleaded. 'They're going to send your ass to jail this time. They won't care who you are.'

City Hall was right across the street from where we were, with all of the police department right there. We got a group coming up the street and another coming down the street. I'm sitting in the car, trying to get Otis in the car.

'Red, I ain't running from shit,' Otis said. He was standing his ground.

'Get in the damn car, Otis! You know I love you! We don't need this trouble!'

I finally got him into the car and got him out of there as fast as I could. Then I came back and started talking to the band, because they wanted to find Otis and shoot him. I ended up at their house, trying to talk sense into them. The guys in the band were still convinced that they wanted revenge, but I got them to calm down, and that was it. That was the end of it.

The Roller Coasters were a great band. I'd book them and they made every date right on time. Truly a professional band. They ended up in New Jersey, trying to get a break in the North. They sent me a demo one time that was very similar to 'Sweet Soul Music,' and I sent it to Atlantic and it was turned down. That ended my relationship with them. They didn't send me anything after that.

NIGHT RIDERS
SCENE FIFTEEN

Otis and I had a lot of experiences driving around the South. One night in Alabama, a couple of guys pulled up beside our car pointing a shotgun at us and fixing to pull the trigger and shoot—or so we thought—and there was no reason to think they wouldn't. So Otis let down the window to speak to them.

'It's Otis Redding.'

The fellow with the shotgun turned to his pal.

'It's Otis Redding! What are you doing in Alabama, Otis?'

'We are on our way to the studio to record.'

The next thing you know, we're in a parking lot drinking beer with two guys who were going to shoot us five minutes earlier. Otis had the spirit to turn people around.

Otis knew how to handle people from all walks of life. He could almost sense everyone's personality. Most of the time, he'd shake hands—he had a very firm handshake and a million-dollar smile. (You did judge a lot on handshakes back in those days. Someone gives me that fish handshake and I don't bother with him.)

I don't care if a person was a total racist, they would be impressed that Otis was so outgoing and friendly. We broke through the color barrier. With music, we brought more people together than all the sit-ins and the boycotts and everything else. We preached love like Dr. King. Otis said it at Monterey—we all love each other, don't we? He spread joy. This was a good guy who helped his family and friends, and many times people he really didn't know very well. It didn't matter who a person was, he treated them like the most important person in the world. Otis made everyone feel special.

I had been out on the road with Otis for about eight days. We were in Raleigh, and we were in the hotel together. We were always in the same room. I told him that I better head back to Macon and check with the office and see what was going on and catch up with calls and everything.

'Okay, Red.'

I was called Red because I had red hair. I wouldn't let anyone call me Red outside my family and Otis, and maybe a couple of Blue's friends.

'But Red. If you're going home, you need to use this,' he said, handing me a brown bottle. 'You need to take a bath in this.'

'Why?'

'Because some of these nightclubs we've been playing in and some of these hotels have lice in them.'

'Crabs?'

'Yeah. So you need to bathe in this before you go home, so you don't take them home with you.'

'But Otis, I've never had crabs in my life.'

'You can't be too sure, Red. They might be hiding in your cracks and crevices.'

So I poured the bottle of this stuff into the tub and sat in it for about an hour, scrubbing every part of my body—including the cracks and crevices.

When I got out of the bathtub and walked into the room, Otis turned around and started laughing.

'Good God almighty, what's happened to you?'

'Nothin'. I just took a bath and put that stuff in the tub.'

'How much did you put in there?'

'The whole bottle.'

'You're supposed to put in a capful. You're all red!'

I rushed to the mirror and it looked like the worst case of sunburn I had ever seen on a human being. I was red!

'I wanted to make sure I would kill all of those crabs,' I told Otis, who was laughing uncontrollably.

'Well hell, man, I think you did.'

Living out of a suitcase is hard. No telling what you may face. When we drove through Alabama or some other place in the boonies with musicians, I took up the floor mats in the back seat and opened up the drain plugs so the band could urinate into a funnel onto the road. I tried not to stop because if you did, there could be trouble. Every time you go into a filling station or any kind of restaurant—even takeout food—there might be a problem. People today can't imagine how rough it was and how dangerous it was. It was easier to stop at 'colored only' motels. If we could find a place for 'colored only,' we'd check into a couple of rooms and sleep four or five to a bed.

DON'T BE WRITING
ABOUT DOM PÉRIGNON
WHEN ALL YOU KNOW
ABOUT IS DRINKING BUD
SCENE SIXTEEN

When you were around Otis, you felt that he was going to come up with something good. And, sure as the world, someone would throw out a phrase and he'd take it up the mountain.

Keep it simple. Do what you love and it's never work. Write songs about the things you know in your life. Don't be writing about Dom Pérignon if all you know about is drinking Bud. If you're a southern redneck, be a southern redneck. Be honest.

We knew that the secret of success was having our own songs. They flowed out of Otis. Once he was on a roll, that song would be written right there in twenty minutes.

We thought about songs all the time. Anything that sounded good for a possible song title, we'd keep it and suggest it for a song. All of us—Speedo wrote songs, I wrote songs, Phil wrote songs, Zelma wrote songs. A girl I don't know wrote 'Security' and gave it to Otis and he re-worked it.

Speedo—Earl 'Speedo' Simms—was the road manager for Otis Redding, and he also opened for him on occasion. Speedo was a very close friend to Otis and a wonderful man. He road managed Arthur Conley, Johnnie Taylor, Betty Harris, Bobby Womack, and Percy Sledge, and he later worked for The Allman Brothers Band as well. Speedo was also a songwriter and wrote for Eddie Floyd and Arthur Conley. Speedo did everything, and he could count money faster than anyone.

Speedo's ex-wife wrote a few lines and the title for 'Respect,' or so the story goes. I know Otis didn't write all of that song. According to Speedo, he was going to record the song, but since his voice was hoarse, Otis did it instead. Speedo said in an interview with Otis Redding III that Otis was going to buy him a house for the song, but the plane went down before that could happen.

During one of our Apollo shows, Otis and I were sitting in the hotel and we were waiting for Speedo to show up. He had driven straight through from California, which is about three thousand miles. Speedo arrived at the hotel and we were happy to see him, and Otis asked him if he wouldn't mind going out and getting him some ham and eggs.

'I am a little tired, Otis. I just drove three thousand miles.'

'Okay,' Otis said. 'But I sure could use some ham and eggs.'

So Speedo went out and got those ham and eggs for Otis. He loved Otis that much.

Everybody around Otis thought in songs. We were always trying to come up with a title for a song that would knock him out. I actually co-wrote a few songs with Otis, but I never received any writer's credit except the last one—I never asked for it. I was doing a manager's job, but I was also learning how to write. I co-wrote 'Your One And Only Man,' 'Chained And Bound,' 'Mr. Pitiful,' 'Ton Of Joy,' 'Love Comes And Goes,' and my big one, 'Champagne And Wine,' for which I did get a credit.

'Champagne And Wine' was supposed to be a re-write of '(Sittin' On) The Dock Of The Bay.' Otis came up with a new melody for that song on the way to Memphis. I probably wrote eighty-five percent of the lyrics.

It was fun writing songs. I still every now and then attempt to write a song. I found that the average guy can write a song if he concentrates hard enough on it and pays attention to what has been written before and what is going on in that particular time.

The song is the backbone of the artist. If the artist doesn't write songs, he's always going to be dependent on other writers. What are you going to do when those writers become drug addicts or alcoholics and disappear? All of a sudden, you've got an artist without songs. It was a constant search to place the right song with the right artist. If you can't find the song, the hits will dry up.

If I was giving advice to young people coming up in the management business—I've always enjoyed helping the younger artists—the first thing I would tell them is, don't sign an act that can't write songs. Pick a band or artist who writes and is supporting their music with their own writing and you'll make a lot more money.

You can take a song like 'Free Bird' or 'When A Man Loves A Woman,' and people remember where they were when they heard it, who they were dating, and what was happening in their lives. They are relating to the song on a very deep level. 'Dock Of The Bay' will flash you back immediately.

I was able to tell the difference between a hit record and just a record. I wasn't always right. But I was right a lot of the times. I had a better average than most of the record guys and gals.

Otis and I worked hard when he came off the road. He and I would get in that office, and he would be on one line and I would be on the other, calling disc jockeys all over the United States. 'How you doing, and how about a date?' We took care of a lot of business.

We developed reputations real fast. We treated our entertainers right. We got them paid. Other agents and promoters and managers *showed* them the money. We *got* them the money. We brought respect to the African American artist in America. We brought them prestige. We really cared about our artists and those who worked for us, and it was obvious because we fought like hell for them. So when you listen to some of that music today—an Otis Redding record, or Percy Sledge, or anyone from our agency—you're not just hearing music but also the sound of iron being hammered and bricks being laid for those, especially African Americans, who are in the business today.

We started making more and more white friends on the road. When we first went out there, his audience might be ten percent white. But for his last tour that he did, the audience was more like forty-five percent white. And it had grown that big, and Otis was the main one they would go see in those years—Otis and James Brown were the two favorites of the white audience, with James Brown over Otis. We just reckoned we'd get James the next year. James was always our target competition.

Our early years together were just so much enthusiasm and so much fun. Otis made work fun. When I was out on the road, he'd tell me to go out and party—that I stay in at the office all the time. It was true. I worked every number and made the books square.

I was never afraid of being in an all-Black audience. I didn't fear anybody in those days. Otis Redding was one hell of a street fighter. When he was by my side, I didn't worry about anybody. He looked after me. He also promised that to my mother, and he always did.

PHIL COMES HOME
SCENE SEVENTEEN

When Phil came home from Germany, the family picked him up in Atlanta—my father, my mother, and myself, and my wife and Phil's wife, Kathy. When we got in the car and we were riding back to Macon, Phil started telling me to tell Otis to do that and this and all kinds of orders. He actually had a list for Otis.

'I'll tell you, Phil. Things have changed a little bit since you left. We don't tell Otis what to do anymore. We suggest it.'

My father backed me up. 'Red's right. We suggest things to Otis, and so far, he's accepted all of our advice. We had to adjust to that with respect. You had been used to telling Otis what to do.'

I got a lot done when Phil was in the army.

By the time Phil returned from Germany, Otis and I had a string of hits. 'I've Been Loving You Too Long' was in the Top 10 of *Billboard*, and 'Respect' was already in the can! Phil congratulated me on what a good job I had done and wanted to know if I wanted to stay on and work or go back to Mercer. He really wanted me to go back to college.

'I want us all to be educated, Alan,' Phil told me.

But I told him, 'I can't see going back to college where I could learn how to make less money.'

We immediately began an even stronger push to expand. We decided to buy a building on Cotton Avenue. This building had been a chicken slaughterhouse: they raised the chickens in the basement and slaughtered them upstairs. When I swept it out the first time, I swept chicken heads out onto the street. Very crude. We didn't have a lot of trouble gutting it because there wasn't that much to gut. We remodeled the upstairs into three offices. Phil and I shared an office, Otis had his own office, and the secretaries were in the front. We put in wall-to-wall carpeting and nice tiles, nice furniture—decorated it real well.

We were doing pretty good. Otis was getting two thousand a night, and that was good money in those years. *Otis Blue* was killer. *Otis Blue* was Phil's 'welcome home' present. It was the first session Phil went to when he got back from Germany. Otis showed him what he could do. We had already cut 'I've Been Loving You Too Long' and 'Respect' in mono, but a stereo version was needed, with a new board.

Being in the studio with Otis on the day he recorded 'I've Been Loving You Too Long' and 'Respect' was the most exciting session I ever went on. He knocked both of those songs out on the same day.

Otis Blue remained the favorite for most people for years and years, though some of the others may have outsold it after his death. People are funny. When a singer gets killed like Otis, the public will run out and buy his albums right away.

There was a white girl on the cover of *Otis Blue*, and we caught a lot of flak about it from the African American community. They didn't like Otis having a white girl on his album cover—especially a blonde. Atlantic made the decision to do that, and when they put it out, the DJs started to complain, and then some of the public started to complain. According to several sources, the model is either Nico— Andy Warhol's protégé and singer for The Velvet Underground—or the German model Dagmar Dreger. But the actual photo was not commissioned. It might be a stock photo shot by Peter Sahula. The Otis Redding Estate thinks that the model is Dagmar.

Otis Blue started a long and successful relationship with the legendary producer Tom Dowd. Tom would produce tracks with Arthur Conley, The Allman Brothers Band, Lynyrd Skynyrd, and a number of artists and bands for Capricorn. Tom was a wonderful human being. This man had the most outgoing personality. He was the kind of producer who told you what to change and then explained why he wanted you to make that change. He would explain it very well and the musicians would understand him. And the musicians liked Tom.

Tom was so smart. He went to Columbia and trained as a physicist—he worked on the Manhattan Project, developing the atomic bomb with Robert Oppenheimer. Tom was brilliant and a great communicator. He could get more out of musicians than anyone. I think he was the best engineer and producer I ever knew. He did them all—Eric Clapton, Ray Charles, The Drifters, John Coltrane, Rod Stewart, Bobby Darin. Tom engineered so many hits. And he was always there for me. Tom also consulted us on building the studio. We bought one building, and Tom's first impression was that the ceiling was not high enough.

'We've got twenty-five-foot ceilings, Tom.'

'Not high enough.'

Some people would have listened and then done what they wanted to do to save money. Not us. We listened to Tom.

It was cheaper to buy a building next door than to gut the ceiling—cheaper to go two doors down and buy a furniture store that was closed, with very high ceilings.

With Phil back, we launched immediately into expanding new territories. In those days, I'd spend many nights on my office sofa because I worked so late. It didn't make sense to come back to work in an hour or two. We lived our business. Phil would work seven days a week, but I used to try to be home for the weekend, to spend a little time with my wife. I would close all the drapes and park three blocks away from the house and make it look like I wasn't home. Phil was divorced at the time, so he wanted to go party.

We had a good staff in those years. We had a number of good agents—Terry Rhodes, Rodgers Redding, Zelma Redding, Steve Cole, Allen Osborne, Jerry Womack, and more. I moved the booking agency downstairs, and we had a conference room and a snack bar and four offices, and a big open area with three or four secretaries. There was always someone to get us lunch and drive us to gigs and all of that. It was very simple.

The office looked good. It was clean. It was new. I had a stockroom about as big as a large closet that I put a cot in so I could take a power nap. I could lock myself in, take an hour nap, and get up and start booking again. The whole staff was close. We were all close to each other. We treated each other with respect.

WHEN THE WOMEN FAINTED, THEY FELL BACK, AND THEIR HEADS WOULD SMACK ON SOLID WOOD
SCENE EIGHTEEN

I never had been to New York in my life, so I was excited to go there to accompany Otis. I landed at the airport and there was nobody to pick me up. Here I am in New York City, and I don't know where to go. I was completely lost and confused, but I figured it would be okay as soon as I got my bearings.

Otis had a phone in his car, but he was rehearsing at the Brevoort Theater in Brooklyn. The Brevoort Theater was in the African American neighborhood known as Bedford–Stuyvesant. It was one of those old theaters that had been open since the silent film days, and it really did go note for note with the Apollo, with performers such as Jackie Wilson, Otis, James Brown, and Gladys Knight & The Pips. Everyone played over there at one time or another.

Speedo finally showed up, and I was damn happy to see him. I hopped into the car and we headed over to the theater, but Speedo had smoked some grass and we got lost. I don't blame him. We could have gotten lost even if he wasn't stoned. We got to Brooklyn and we drove around quite a bit—going around in the right neighborhood but not hitting our mark.

Once we got there, Otis wanted to get a bite to eat. We wanted to find a restaurant that was close by and smelled good and eat there. We walked up the street with a friend of Otis named Gene Lawson. Gene was a gangster—a professional gangster, not just a tough guy. He just loved Otis. He never hit on him for money. He would show up at different parts of the country, just as friendly as could be. He always had some weed with him.

We smelled the food cooking in front of one restaurant and decided to go in. We got a table, and when the waitress came over, I asked for a ham sandwich.

'We don't serve ham here,' the waitress informed me.

'Maybe you got some vegetable soup with a little pork?'

'We don't put pork in our soup,' she said, kind of snarly.

I looked down and her dress was all the way to the floor. No feet showing—her hair was wrapped up. Elijah Muhammad was hanging on the wall and seemed to be looking right down at me, and he didn't seem to be showing me any love.

'This is a Black Muslim restaurant,' Otis told me. I turned around. Everyone in there was looking at me like they wanted to kill me.

'Hey, you guys, I got to go. I can't be in here because people are looking at me hard. It's not good for my digestion. I'll wait on you outside.'

'Drop your napkin, Alan,' Gene told me. 'Drop your napkin on the floor and look under the table.'

I dropped the napkin and looked under the table, and he had a big .45 that could knock out any one of them at any time.

'There ain't nobody going to mess with you in this restaurant.'

I was just too uncomfortable, so I walked outside and walked around, trying to stay out of trouble.

During Otis's performance in the Brevoort, I witnessed women fainting, and they weren't playing around. The women were standing up, and when they fainted they would fall back, and their heads would smack on solid wood. These gals would be out or they would scream, because they hit those bleachers so hard. I've never seen that. I'm surprised some of them weren't killed. When Otis broke into 'I've Been Loving You Too Long'—'*Don't make me stop now / No, baby, I'm down on my knees...*'—it was almost like these women were making love with Otis all at the same time.

We had a perfect show. Gladys Knight & The Pips were on the bill, and they did an unbelievable job. Billy Stewart was on the bill and he had a great show too, coming off of a couple of hit records, 'How Nice It Is' and 'Because I Love You.' Billy was popular because of his unusual singing. Unfortunately, Billy was another talented artist killed in a car wreck—he ran his Thunderbird into a river, killing a few of his band members as well.

In New York, Otis stayed at the Americana, which was the newer hotel in those days, and sometimes the Hilton. Those were the two places we stayed. How times have changed.

While we were working at the Apollo, I connected to Black girls. You didn't see a lot of white girls there—like most of our venues. The hotels wouldn't let me take Black women to the room, but there was no problem with Black men taking white women to the rooms. I'd have to sneak women up the back steps—up the fire escape. I guess the hotel frowned upon the idea of white guys being with Black girls—not that it was any of their business. Different times.

I fell in love with New York City. I loved it. Everyone was so damn frank. They speak their mind in New York, and I appreciate that style, though what they tell you is not always what you want to hear. I had a New York agent tell me, 'You build them in the South and we'll steal them from you when they get up North.' And that guy even courted

Otis. He came down for one of Otis's homecoming shows and played Mr. Big New Yorker, shooting the bull and flashing his New York tough-stuff bullshit. He courted Otis like a prom date—sending him flowers and watches. I made it my personal project to destroy him. I ended up stealing all but two of his acts—Ray Charles and Jerry Butler. I drove him out of business and had fun doing it.

Ray Charles was a class act. To me, Ray Charles and Otis were the best soul singers in the world. I would have loved to have met Ray. I regret that I never did.

Jerry Butler was a true gentleman and a friend. Jerry co-wrote 'I've Been Loving You Too Long' with Otis. He and I loved to play chess whenever our paths crossed. First time I played him, I was sure I was going to wipe him out, but he beat my ass in three straight games. At our second meeting, I beat him three straight times. I loved Jerry. He was always so praising of Otis.

We were booked into white establishments quite often—not as many as the Black clubs, but the Whisky loved Otis. We played the Atlanta Whisky for ten days. Otis played the Whisky in Los Angeles for a week or so, and the movie stars turned out for him and gave him their seal of approval—Julie Christie, Faye Dunaway, Steve McQueen. White girls dancing behind a Black singer was prestigious.

We worked hard at trying to add class to Otis's act. We weren't these jive-asses trying to get dope and women and all of that. Also, we were very careful about letting the women get too close. One night during a show, a girl jumped up onto the stage, grabbed Otis's necktie, and pulled it so hard that Otis started choking. He collapsed onstage. Huck had to run out from behind the curtain and cut the tie. Never again was anyone allowed onstage with Otis, except the musicians.

HEY, MAN, YOU EVER HEARD OF MACON, GEORGIA?
SCENE NINETEEN

My brother believed that Johnny Jenkins could have been the greatest name in rock 'n' roll. Had he not been frightened of flying and gotten out there and toured more, he would definitely have given Jimi Hendrix a run for his money. Some years later, Johnny was the first out of the chute at Capricorn with his album *Ton Ton Macoute!*, with Duane Allman on guitar.

Johnny Jenkins was very bitter about his career. He could get bitter and drink stump whiskey. And when Johnny was drunk, he wasn't a guy you'd want to be around. He loved me and he called me 'blessed' all the time—he called a lot of people blessed. I think Johnny was blessed.

In 1966, Atlantic was flipping over Percy Sledge and put together a major promotion plan for him in New York. They were going to have the best promotion men hand-deliver 'When A Man Loves A Woman' because Jerry Wexler endorsed it. We were at a cocktail party in New York City, and King Curtis was backing Percy. I thought I saw Johnny Jenkins up on the stage. But how did Phil get Johnny out of Macon if Johnny wouldn't fly?

I went up to the stage to say hello to Johnny Jenkins to find out what was going on, and then getting a bit closer I realized that it wasn't Johnny Jenkins at all. The guitar player looked exactly like Johnny. He tuned his guitar like Johnny, wore his bouffant hair like Johnny. The guy turned out to be Jimi Hendrix. It's funny, Hendrix became so big, but he was all but lost the night he played with Percy.

When they took a break, Jimi walked by my table.

'Hey, man. You ever hear of Macon, Georgia?' I asked Jimi.

'What you going to do, tell me about Johnny Jenkins?'

'I sure am.'

GOT TO GET DOWN
IN THE SOUTH
SCENE TWENTY

You definitely have to be raised in the South to be a southern man. You can be a converted southern man after fifteen or twenty years, but a real southern man is born in the South, raised in the South, and understands the ways of the South. I have always been true to the South.

Southerners have been knocked down before and got up again, and that's what it's all about. If you're in a fight with somebody, you may just turn that fight around if you keep getting up and keep slugging. You only lose when you stop slugging. All of our great performers— from Otis to Skynyrd to the Allman Brothers to Percy Sledge—none of them ever stopped slugging. They may have sometimes hit the wrong target, but they never stopped slugging.

I remember trying to teach Percy Sledge how to swim at Otis's swimming pool. I had him at the side of the pool and he wanted to jump into the deep end. Well, he didn't swim, and I didn't swim, and if he jumped in, I wouldn't be able to save him. But he jumped into the deep end anyway and started to go down. I grabbed the hook and pulled him back up from the bottom of the pool. If I had jumped in, we both would have drowned. But after he almost drowned—something that would have discouraged most people—Percy stayed in that pool, working it out, until he could at least dog-paddle across the pool. He didn't give up. When we were on the road together—when we stopped at the hotel—he always jumped into the pool.

Percy Sledge became addicted to heroin at one point, and he remained hooked for a while and then dried himself out, cold turkey, all by himself, without going to any kind of detox for help. He did it all on his own. In the studio, he would fall down on the floor, screaming in agony, kicking the junk, but he'd get right back up and start swinging and singing again. That's who he was.

I think southern bands work harder than northern bands. Southern bands have more guts to their music. They *get down*. They're *funky*. They put the grit to it. I didn't care too much for male performers with high voices. I want that deep *growl*—that *growl* that comes out of the guts—that is born in the soul.

Southern bands have more pride in their work. When a southern band gets on the stage, they *slam* you and they *hit* you—they come on after you. Charge all the way! Take no prisoners! Kill! Stomp 'em into the ground!

Otis Redding *stomped* it out. Otis put the *grit* in it and rocked the house.

Otis wasn't afraid to drop to his knees and plead and beg the audience. That made him more vulnerable, which made him more powerful. Skynyrd were like that. They would go up on the stage to play against some other band and they were the showstoppers, man. Skynyrd could stop the show in a split second and nail you and punch into the spirit of the Southland. Southern guys—James Brown, Little Richard, Otis Redding Lynyrd Skynyrd, The Allman Brothers Band, Booker T., Molly Hatchet, The Outlaws—so many great bands that came out of the South understood that you *got to get down*!

Otis Redding was a southern man. When Otis got successful, he was offered James Brown's house in New York and all of this to sign with another agency.

'What do you think of me living up in New York in that house, Red?'

'I think you ought to stay in the South where you got your break,' I told Otis. 'I think you ought to stay with the people who got you started and be loyal to your fans. This is where you are from.' And that's what he did.

Southern hospitality is very real. The southern man acts so different than the northern man. Southern people are friendly and show hospitality. They make people feel welcome. I have great pride in being a southern man.

When Phil and Otis and me sat down for a meeting, we had a triangular brain. We had three different personalities. We all had our own little special thing. But when we put our heads together with a common goal, we did what we needed to do. For us, there was no turning back. If we were told to walk through a wall, we'd figure out how to do it. That's just how determined we were to make things happen.

We did our jobs very, very well. We were the top managers of our time. We were knocking them out left and right.

I considered those very special times in my life because I would be amazed at the results that we got once we came out of a meeting. I don't know of a meeting where we didn't succeed at completing our mission. We didn't hit like The Beatles, but we were steadily climbing all the time, trying to get hotter and hotter and hotter and expand to the white audience and capture the whole world.

Those were some very strategic meetings when we actually had the plan laid out, and each one of us knew what area we were going to specialize in. I had this country personality—I didn't twang when I talked or anything like that, but I wore blue jeans and T-shirts and tennis shoes to work. And I came on to you very sincere and open. People trusted me. I wasn't bullshitting. That was me.

It was fun to feel the power, and that was kind of an ego thing. By 1966, we had the largest roster of Black talent in the world, and right out of Macon, Georgia: Otis Redding, Sam & Dave, Percy Sledge, Clarence Carter, Johnnie Taylor, Eddie Floyd, Arthur Conley, Joe Tex, Booker T. & The M.G.'s. Albert King, Willie Mitchell Orchestra, Joe Simon, the Fiestas, Bobby Marchan, Hank Ballard & The Midnighters, James and Bobby Purify, Oscar Toney, Eddie Kirkland, Wilbur Harrison, The Ovations, James Carr, Dave Baby Cortez, Alvin Cash & The Crawlers, The Van Dykes, Albert Collins, Clarence 'Gatemouth' Brown, Ty Hunter, Otis Clay, The Precisions, The Kelly Brothers, Lee Dorsey, The Meters, Ruby Andrews, Maurice Williams & The Zodiacs, Kris Kenner, Ernie K. Doe, Roscoe Shelton, Big John Hamilton, Lattimore Brown, The Wallace Brothers, Bobby Womack, Al Green, Tyrone Davis, Etta James, Mable John, Jimmy Hughes, Z.Z. Hill, Arthur Alexander, O.V. Wright, and Candi Staton soon signed with our organization. At one time, we represented forty-five Black recording artists.

Etta James was my baby, and I managed her for a time. Etta was the roughest, toughest-talking woman I had ever met in my life. She'd out-motherfucker you in a minute. She was a big woman, sometimes called Big Red. You didn't mess with Etta James because she could fight like a man. She was a street-raised woman, and she had been on the road since she was in her young teens, and she had some great records—she had 'Roll With Me Henry' (later changed to 'Wallflower'), 'That's All'—'At Last' is an iconic jewel today.

The problem was, during the mid-sixties, Etta had a heroin habit. She came into Macon one night in real bad shape. She was completely strung out on drugs and was desperate. She asked me if I could find her some heroin or some pain pills—anything to get her through the night. So I sent her to my friend and he rustled her up some codeine just to straighten her out a bit.

Etta James had her problems, like a lot of people do, but she was a beautiful woman. My biggest achievement in life was quitting drinking. That was the smartest thing I ever did—and the hardest thing. I always thought if I drank beer, I wouldn't be an alcoholic—but you can become an alcoholic on beer. That was one of my major, personal achievements. My father was an alcoholic, my brother Blue was an alcoholic, and Phil became addicted to cocaine. We all have our struggles with demons, so, when someone asks me about Etta, I tell them that she was a beautiful woman.

Etta James was the first act that I went to see in a Black nightclub, before Otis. I went to see her at Adam's Lounge. I introduced myself and we hung out a bit. She was super nice to me. This was my first spin into a Black nightclub, and there I am, hanging with Etta James, and man, she treated me like I was somebody—she had the ability to see not what I was but what I wanted to become. She made me feel real important, and she liked me a lot. And I liked her a lot.

Etta and I talked, and I stayed all the way until they loaded the equipment and went on to the next town. She treated me with respect. We became friends, and whenever she was out on the road and ran into someone from Macon, she would tell them to make sure to say that she said hello to Alan Walden.

Otis worked with Etta on 'Security' over the telephone, and he was a tremendous help to her—he and Rick Hall both—Rick being the owner of Fame Studios in Muscle Shoals, and sometimes referred to as the Father of Muscle Shoals Music. Etta put my song 'Champagne And Wine' on her retirement CD. I wrote that song with Otis and Roy Lee Jr. Johnson, a few nights before Otis died. I respected and loved Etta James.

Wayne Cochran, the White Knight of Soul, played bass on 'Shout Bamalama' and 'Fat Girl' for Otis in 1961 and they became great friends. Wayne wrote and recorded a song called 'Last Kiss' in 1961. The song was about a girl who got killed near his house in Thomaston, Georgia. J. Frank Wilson and the Cavaliers took it to #1 in 1963. It was a huge song and became an iconic song for that early sixties scene:

Oh where oh where can my baby be
The Lord took her away from me
She's gone to heaven so I got to be good
So I can see my baby when I leave this world.

Wayne would pass through Macon four or five times a year. He had more soul than any white boy and more than a lot of Black boys. Wayne knew how to shake it and get down. He danced on stage as good as any of them and that's why people like James Brown and Otis respected his talent so much. He was for real, and with his horn band, C.C. Riders, he could kill an audience. Jackie Gleason caught him in a Miami club called the Barn, one night and put him on his television show and Wayne's star really took off. He had white skin and the biggest bleached white bouffant hairstyle you ever saw on a man. Otis and I ran into Wayne one time walking through the Atlanta airport with a wildcat on a leash. He sure knew how to work it.

With his revue, he had become a huge star in Las Vegas and was a favorite personality on the talk shows. He never held anything back and was never shy about pressing his faith—he wound up pastoring a large church in Florida and still sang and danced, though from the pulpit, bringing his congregation to their feet every time. Wayne was a good old country boy with a heart of gold. We remained great friends right up to his death.

Oscar Mack replaced Otis in Johnny Jenkins & The Pinetoppers. He was the featured singer in Johnny's band that I reinvented after Phil went overseas. Oscar Mack was the lead singer. We cut a song for him at Stax called 'Dream Girl' and Otis is singing the background. When you listen to the record, you are aware of the richness that Otis adds to the song.

Oscar was a great showman, but he had one big problem—his hygiene. He could enter the front door of my office and I could smell him three stories up. Riding with Oscar in a car for three hundred miles was almost unbearable.

Otis suggested we hire Oscar to introduce Gladys Knight & The Pips, which we did, although one night he accidentally called them The Pimps. The Pips told Oscar that he was either going to take a bath or he had to go. There was a tub in one of the bathrooms, and they shoved him in there. They listened and heard the water and splashing and then decided to peek in. Oscar was just sitting at the edge of the tub, splashing the water with a towel.

James Carr had 'The Dark End Of The Street.' He sounded so much like Otis Redding—he was definitely working in Otis's vein. James loved smoking weed. He carried a pipe around, and everyone thought he was smoking tobacco. In those days, everyone hid when they smoked marijuana, but James smoked right out in the open. Eventually, he went nuts. He came to Macon to go over his career plans with me, and I sat there for an hour and a half talking, laying out the whole plan.

'What do you think, James? What do you think of the plan?'

He had been asleep behind his sunglasses the whole time I was talking.

'I'm sorry Alan. What did you say?'

Something was wrong with James. He went to Miami and covered up all the mirrors in the room and said there were two-way mirrors and people were studying him. I had him committed twice to a psych ward.

'I can't book you anymore unless you get me a letter from your psychiatrist and he tells me you're mentally able to go on the road.'

He called me one time from Alabama and told me he could not make a show in Louisiana.

'You already got a couple of strikes against you. You better make that damn date.'

'I can't, Alan. There is a huge snowstorm.'

'There ain't no snow. You get in that car and you go on to that date.'

'The state troopers are blocking the roads.'

'That's all in your mind. Get in your car and drive!'

And James Carr did drive. He went on to the gig.

Clarence Carter walked into my office that same day. He was heading into Macon from Alabama.

'Man, I didn't think I was going to get here. The damnedest snowstorm hit Alabama and Mississippi, and traffic is stopped all the way through both states!'

Poor James Carr drove in that snow and made the show. It wasn't in his mind.

Clarence Carter was one great entertainer. He gave me three gold records—'Slip Away,' 'Too Weak To Fight,' and 'Patches.' All three were million-sellers. And we had lots of other hits as well.

Rick Hall asked me to get involved with Clarence. He was my Redwal client, instead of Phil Walden & Associates. Part of our deal with Otis was that we were going to start putting other artists into Redwal Music. Otis was becoming a bigger partner in Redwal, and we had dreams.

Otis had dreams that one day our two families would work and live together, including his brother, Rodgers. We would all stay on a big property. I've read in other books that Otis was so dissatisfied with Phil and me that he was trying to always get rid of us. That upsets me. That's not how it was.

Ben E. King was special. A special person. He had been with The Drifters and had so many hits, and he had such a beautiful voice. He also had hits on his own—'Spanish Harlem' and 'Stand By Me.' He was a perfect gentleman. Otis played with him at the Apollo Theater—the first time Otis ever made a live album.

Otis came back talking about Ben E. King's spins and turns and just how he did his arms. Otis ended up incorporating a lot of Ben's moves into his shows—he was that impressed with him.

We all liked Ben. Gary Donehoo and I had gone up to Lake Sinclair, which is a retreat about forty miles from Macon, to spend a weekend. I met Gary when he came down here to book one of the high-school fraternity parties around 1969. I just liked him automatically. I had a dream about opening my own company, and Gary was a workhorse and the best friend and partner a man could have.

Gary didn't have but one album in the whole house, and that was a Murray The K album that had a cut of 'I Who Have Nothing.'

'We've got to find Ben and sign him.' And we did.

He'd had a beautiful career but Atlantic had let him go, and now he was signed to Crewe Records—Bob Crewe out of New York. Bob wasn't really into R&B, but he was a hugely successful producer and writer—he co-wrote some of The Four Seasons' biggest hits, like 'Rag Doll,' 'Walk Like A Man,' and 'Silence Is Golden.' He had hired Larry Maxwell, who was the promotion man for Motown.

I flew to New York and met with Bob, and the next thing I knew, Ben and Noreen were sitting in my office ready to sign a contract. Ben and I were friends until he died.

Lee Dorsey had 'Yah Yah'—*Sittin' here la la | Waitin' on my ya ya | Uh huh*—'Ride Your Pony,' 'Get Out Of My Life Woman,' 'Working In The Coal Mine.' He continuously came back with hits. He'd have a hit and then a couple of misses, and then come back with another hit. His producers were Allen Toussaint and Marshall Sehorn, and they were in New Orleans. Allen was one of the best pianists I ever heard. A real nice guy.

Lee and I did one album on Polydor. He had a song on there called 'Yes We Can.' The Pointer Sisters cut it, and it was a smash hit for them.

The Meters were Lee Dorsey's rhythm section in the studio. They were The Neville Brothers—primarily an instrumental band with a unique beat. They were hot, instrumentally. They were a very good band, but when I had a gig set up for them in Jacksonville, they told me I had to cancel the date because they had done research and discovered they traveled so many miles for so many years and they had worked out the math and had decided that this was the trip they were all going to be killed in a car wreck. A premonition of death? I told them that I'd heard everything, but a premonition of death? That's crazy. That philosophy is crazy. But they believed it.

'Those Black Muslims aren't going to be very happy.'

'We've done the math, Alan. We'll all be killed.'

'You'll be killed if you *don't* show up.'

They didn't show up, and I couldn't book them anywhere—I didn't want to book a band who couldn't show up because of premonitions.

The Meters were the first outside band to record at Capricorn Records. We brought them in when we were testing the sound. Marshall Sehorn had been a longtime friend of mine: he'd had some success in the business, but I kind of brought him back to life. He and I hit it off real well.

THE RANCH
SCENE TWENTY-ONE

Otis had moved from an apartment off of Lyndon Avenue to a house on Commodore Drive, which was in a nice African American neighborhood, but he was still not happy with his lack of privacy, so he got my father to look for a house.

My father picked out the Big 'O' Ranch. It did Otis a world of good. We ended up in the Round Oak section of Gray, Georgia. Otis and I pretty much ran our section of Round Oak. We could handle most things. And the sheriff did let us handle most things.

I bought a log cabin about a mile from Otis's. It was a part of the old Continental Can woods, where they owned a lot of trees for pulp. I had just gotten out of the hospital from a horse falling at a full gallop and rolling over me when my father wanted to show me this piece of land and the old cabin he had purchased, way out at the end of a dirt road. As soon as I saw it, I fell in love with it.

'Pops. This *was* your house,' I joked.

He loved me and he let me have the cabin.

My little log cabin was like heaven out in the woods. It was frontier all the way. The logs had been pulled from the woods with mules and laid by a common eye, not a leveler. That cabin was forty-nine years old when we got it, and that was about fifty years ago. And it looks good even today.

I also loved it because no two walls were alike, because the logs were all shaped differently, like the walls at Stax. It had a big stone fireplace that was a great place to listen to music. I would have a lot of entertainers out there—Duane and Gregg Allman, all of the guys of

Skynyrd, Percy Sledge, Clarence Carter, Boz Scaggs—they all hung out at the cabin, kicking back and picking guitar around the fire.

Some of the happiest years of my life were spent in that log cabin next to Otis's ranch. Boz Scaggs and his beautiful girlfriend at the time, Carmella, lived there for five months too. Later on, Gregg Allman wanted to buy it. The cabin had so much privacy you could sunbathe nude without a worry in the world if you wanted.

Otis never took musicians to his house except for members of his band, close friends, and on special occasions. I remember one party out there around early 1967. Otis was trying to get his swimming pool done. I don't recall the circumstances, but a few Black Muslims came down from New York. A lot of Black performers and sports personalities were getting interested in that movement in those days. Otis decided to feed them barbecue. Otis decided to cook six whole hogs—six whole hogs on the spits, with people poking them and managing their progress. He worked so hard at this party because he was proud of his ranch, and he wanted people to have a good time.

Aside from the Muslims, there was a pile of promotion and radio people. Six Greyhound buses showed up and everyone piled out. Everyone was impressed except the Muslims, because they don't eat pork, and right in front of them were six whole, very large roasting hogs, the fat dripping onto the fire.

Otis couldn't even walk. He was exhausted. People got up to sing and play music, but Otis just sat there on the stool, shaking hands. That was the most tired I had ever seen him—more tired than any post-performance. There was something going on in his head that day. Something deep. Something he was not willing to share.

Otis and I bought a buggy and a buggy horse, and we figured we'd take the families on Sunday afternoon rides on the dirt roads. I had never connected up a buggy and neither had Otis, so we just kind of pieced it together the best way we could. We hooked the horse up—we thought right—and we started down the road. We headed up an incline for a bit and decided we didn't want to go any farther— we turned and headed for home. The buggy started to roll down the hill faster than the horse could trot in front of it, which was very dangerous, because the horse couldn't outrun the carriage he was pulling, and unless the road flattened out that horse or we were bound to get injured or killed. The front of the carriage started bumping the rear of the horse, so it started bucking and kicking and going wild. It looked like we were all going to turn over. Everybody was screaming, and I managed to get control as the carriage hit a flat section of road and slowed to a stop.

Otis and I got out and managed to calm down the horse, who was just about ready to have a heart attack. We unconnected the horse and let my wife and Zelma lead the horse back to the barn while Otis and I pulled the carriage back—pulling it like a couple of mules down the dirt road. He rode in it again later on, but that was the only time I rode in that buggy.

Otis loved that ranch. He loved sleeping in his own bed because he spent so much time on the road.

One time, Otis was out on the road and I was sitting in my log cabin and I looked up and saw this young man named Junior ride up on Otis's horse, Comanche. Junior was from a local neighborhood near Otis's ranch. Comanche was ringing with sweat, and he had been running way too hard.

Junior got off the horse and started telling me about some guys who broke into the barn to ride the horses. 'They are riding up and down the road and when I told them to stop riding Otis's horses, one of them kicked me in the ass,' he told me.

I grabbed my pistol and I looked up, and another damn guy was riding *my* horse very hard into *my* yard. It was a hot day in the summer, and the horse was sweating. A horse can drop dead when ridden like that. I went across the yard and did one of my Range Rider maneuvers and knocked the bastard off my horse. Then I whacked him across the face with my pistol.

'If you want to keep your brains, you do as I tell you,' I told him. I got him to get up and take the saddle off of my horse and carry it all the way to Otis's barn, which was about a mile in the heat, and a saddle gets heavy in the heat. I got into my Thunderbird, peeled out in the dust, and headed to Otis's, and all of a sudden here comes another one of these clowns riding Zelma's carriage horse, and the horse was sweating and in a near panic state. I drove up, put the Thunderbird's door into the horse's chest, and made the horse rear up. When he did, I pulled that knucklehead down by his shirt and slapped his head with my revolver. I told him to take the saddle off and head to the barn. I wanted to see what kind of damage these guys had done.

When we got to the barn, there were three more! I recognized these guys from Bellevue. Someone had thrown the reins in Junior's face.

'Which one of these boys kicked you in the ass?' I asked Junior, and he wasted no time in pointing him out.

'You go over there and you put your foot up his ass and bring him off the ground,' I told Junior. 'And if you don't put a foot up *his* ass, I'm gonna put a foot up *your* ass.'

Junior went over there and kicked that boy and raised him at least a couple inches off the ground. The other guy decided to jump me, which was a mistake, so I pistol-whipped him halfway down to the lake. And I wouldn't let up on him. Every time he started backing up, I started on him from the upside. I had a bad-ass pistol in those years, and I was pissed. I made the guys go back down and repair the barn, and they spent hours cleaning the horses up and grooming them and drying them off.

'Don't you ever be seen out here again. You scared Zelma half to death.'

The next day, Otis called.

'I heard about you, Red.'

'What did you hear?'

'I heard you had to put those boys off the horses and off the property. When I get home, we're going to Bellevue, and we're going to finish the damn job.'

'Finish the job? Otis, I've been brave enough. I'm going to let it lay where it is. I don't think they are going to come back and mess with your property ever again.'

Otis had planned to build a landing strip at his Big 'O' Ranch so his plane could land and take off right at his house. After a trip, he could be dropped off, and the plane could then go to Macon to be properly serviced. On the way to a gig, he could be picked up. Ironically, construction for that strip was to start on the Monday after the Sunday he was killed. That landing strip would have been such a joy for him. When he had to go to the Macon airport, he still had to drive another forty miles to get home.

Otis had held out on getting life insurance. African Americans had a feeling that if a white man bought insurance for him, he'd get mad at him and kill him for the insurance. That's how it was back then, and that's all there is to it. Take away what you will.

'I just don't feel comfortable with everyone owning insurance on me,' Otis told us.

A week before he died, we all bought insurance. Otis bought his. The company wouldn't give him double indemnity because of his flying. They wrote him a whole-life policy, but they made up for it by a fifty-thousand-dollar accidental policy. We did this on a Wednesday or a Thursday.

'If I walk out this door tonight and I get killed, am I covered?' Otis asked the insurance man.

'Yeah. You're covered right now, Otis. All we need is the check.'

Well, Otis got killed on Sunday, and the accidental insurance rejected him on Monday. We sued and we lost. All because we were rich white kids with Cadillacs and telephones in our cars and all of that. The opposing attorney made us look so filthy rich and just living a life of excess. The judge looked at it like, this poor man is selling life insurance, he goes to church, and he is a good and decent man. His wife was even reading the Bible in court. They literally tore us apart. Made us look bad in front of the jury, and the jury made the decision and ruled in the insurance company's favor. I developed a horrible attitude toward insurance companies. Had I recorded the agent making the statement that Otis was covered, we could have won the thing. I think about these things from time to time.

When Otis and I were hunting the week before, we were walking toward the lake, pointing to a place in a little clearing. Otis stopped and stared at the beautiful location. He was quiet for a long time, and then he spoke—quietly and sincerely.

'Red, if something happens to me, this is where I want to be buried.'

'Okay, Otis.'

'You'll make sure that happens?'

'Yes, Otis. I will.'

And he was killed the next week. And I had him buried right where he wanted, and he's still there.

I think in some ways, Otis had a premonition of his death. Maybe because of the insurance and pointing to the ground where he wanted to be buried. And then I took him squirrel hunting, and we were coming back to the house. I had five squirrels that I killed.

'How many did you get, Otis?'

'Red, I couldn't shoot 'em. I don't want to kill anything anymore.'

Keep in mind that Otis was the kind of guy who would shoot a sparrow out of the air. He loved shooting. But he had changed his mind about hunting. Sometimes that happens. One day a fellow hunts, the next day he doesn't. You listen to a couple of his songs and it makes you stop and think—like 'Nobody's Fault But Mine.'

One day I got to pay for my mistakes, y'all
It's gonna carry me straight to my grave.

I remember once booking Otis on a plane out of New Orleans. The plane went down over the Gulf of Mexico. I turned on the television as the list of names scrolled across the bottom of the screen. The phone rang and I figured I was going to hear confirmation of horrible news. Then I heard Otis's voice.

'I betcha thought I was dead, didn't ya?'

I couldn't believe it.

'Otis?' I cried.

'Yeah, Red. It's Otis, and I'm not dead. I missed the flight that went down.'

Otis had been working with Dickie Doo, a hot disc jockey in New Orleans, who made him late for his flight by thirty seconds. He saved Otis's life that day, much to my happiness.

WE GOT THEM WHAT THEY WANTED AS LONG AS THEY WERE PLAYING OUR RECORDS
SCENE TWENTY-TWO

Payola definitely existed, and we definitely did it. If a disc jockey wanted a payment for a television or maybe a new refrigerator, or a car payment or a house payment, or cash, we got them what they wanted, as long as they were playing our records. It was definitely against the law, though after 1960 it was a misdemeanor. But I could have gotten into trouble. Payola ruined Alan Freed after he was hauled up in front of the Congressional Payola Investigation.

Alan Freed did not believe in playing white cover versions of Black songs—Pat Boone's 'Tutti-Frutti' from Little Richard's version, or The Crew Cuts' 'Sh-Boom' from The Chords—and I respected him for that. But as Roger Schlueter of the *Belleville News-Democrat* wrote,

'It didn't take long for these sanitized versions to lead music fans to discover the more earthy originals that are beloved today. By 1958, the cover era was over as black artists became stars in their own right.'

Freed also did a lot to integrate audiences at his shows. Maybe that had something to do with him being the scapegoat. Maybe because he was Jewish. Maybe he was a little rough around the edges. Maybe white parents were afraid that he was destroying the fragile minds of their children? Dick Clark was certainly involved, and he testified, but he was a 'fine young man' according to Oren Harris, the committee chairman.

From Lydia Hutchinson in *Performing Songwriter*, 'Why did the committee single him out? Freed was abrasive. He consorted with Black R&B musicians. He jive-talked, smoked constantly, and looked like an insomniac. Clark was squeaky clean, handsome, and polite. At least on the surface. Once the grilling started, Freed's friends and allies in broadcasting quickly deserted him. He refused—on principle—to sign an affidavit saying that he'd never accepted payola. WABC fired him, and he was charged with 26 counts of commercial bribery. Freed escaped with fines and a suspended jail sentence. He died five years later, broke and virtually forgotten.'

Everybody was involved with payola. We had to do it. James Brown was doing the same thing. Everyone was. Since we were trying to catch James Brown, we were convinced that we had to do what he did to keep the same type of relationships going. I could palm a twenty or a fifty or a hundred in a minute. I'd shake a DJ's hand and he would rake the grease right out of my fingers.

In those years, disc jockeys only made a hundred or so a week and that was not a lot of money for them—especially the ones with families. They also had to buy nice clothes and drive cool cars to keep up appearances, and that took money and plenty of it. Their audiences expected the DJs to be celebrities and hip—wanted them to be stars— but most of them were always broke, so every bit of payola they could get was a big help. A hundred dollars was a nice gift.

The disc jockeys would wait on you when you came to the stage. They were definitely not scared about asking you for some money— or anything else for that matter. But I insisted I see the numbers. I wanted them to show me some numbers on the charts. I wanted to see the Top 10. I wanted to see three or four of my songs in there—not just Otis but all of the acts that I was handling. I wanted to see what I was paying for. I wanted to make sure we were getting something for our payola.

In the case of radio promotion, you could piss off a disc jockey real easily by not handing him enough payola or not fulfilling his wish list. We were probably one of the few management companies that checked the numbers. James Brown and us—checking the lists and checking the plays.

I remember going into Atlantic Records one time to see Jerry Wexler, and he had piles of cash on his desk and was stuffing it into envelopes and writing names on the envelopes—a huge pile of cash. And he sent those envelopes out every month. That way he didn't have to do a lot of salesmanship. Basically, the radio stations would play your records for money. The record couldn't be a complete dog, but sometimes they were, and they were forced down the throats of the unsuspecting teeny bopper.

It was Jerry who came up with the term 'rhythm & blues.' Before that, records by African Americans were referred to as 'race records.' Out of all the record executives that I've known, Jerry Wexler was probably one of best. He was a super nice guy and he supported us Waldens immensely. It was nice to be able to call Atlantic and get Jerry on the phone rather than go through secretaries for twenty minutes, although his secretary, Noreen Woods, was a sweetheart, and she would find answers for me right away if Jerry was not around. She was the girlfriend of Ben E. King.

Otis did payola when he was on the road, and I did it from the office and the road. We promised people dates. We had a lot of disc jockeys who liked to promote shows, and they would make a lot of money on these shows—to emcee the show in conjunction with the radio station. We'd give them a date and make sure that they made money on those dates. Otis would go out sometimes on the weekend and sometimes return without anything. He'd do a date for a radio station and he'd pay his own expenses and then he'd pay the DJ. He was that kind of guy. He knew the value of that radio station. All of them. Any type of station.

Black and white radio stations were separate. When Hamp Swain was on the air, he was initially on a white station. WBML gave him a show, but then he moved over to WIBB, which was all Black. Hamp Swain was the King. He was the nicest disc jockey in the whole world. This guy played every record I took to him—good or bad. He only borrowed money from me one time. In those days, when you handed a disc jockey money, you could kiss it goodbye. Most of them had the image of being stars, and they were, to an extent but they were often poor and always struggling. After Hamp borrowed fifty dollars, he was at my office at the door the very next day to pay me back.

Our Otis homecoming shows at City Auditorium were always a success. It was the talk of the city in June or July—one of Macon's biggest annual events—and it was always sold out. Everyone looked forward to these shows—white and Black kids mixed very well. I remember the first year that the white kids started coming downstairs from the balcony. We didn't know what was going to happen, but it all worked out great.

We gave Hamp a percentage of the homecoming shows, so he ended up getting about a thousand dollars a year out of it. But he was a nice guy. He taught us about promoting, and all the tricks to promoting. He taught us how people would slip into side doors of shows, and how even cops slipped people into shows for money—at the same time as trying to keep people from sneaking in.

There was a Black promoter in town, and I don't know how he survived. He'd let the police be there and they would walk the other way, and then the door would be unlocked and thirty people would run into the auditorium. A ticket wasn't any more than two-fifty. Tickets were very reasonable, and you'd see five or six acts for a couple of bucks. You'd get your money's worth, for sure. There was corruption everywhere, but working with disc jockeys and radio stations was all very important—a necessary ingredient for success.

SEEMS LIKE I'VE BEEN LOOKING FOR TALENT MY WHOLE LIFE
SCENE TWENTY-THREE

When I first started working with Phil, I was lucky if I was able to take home twenty dollars a week. I remember when I got it up to fifty dollars and I thought I was in big money. But it made me appreciate what I had. When you work and earn your way, you definitely appreciate what you've done a lot more. I was young and energetic, and anxious to go to work. And I dove into it at full speed.

Bobby Marchan tied in with Percy Welch. Percy owned a little Black hotel in town. He rented the rooms by the hour. Each room had a little bell; when the hour was up, he'd ring the bell, and you'd have to pay for another hour. But he would let entertainers stay there in the hotel at a discounted rate—and longer than an hour. All night, in fact. He kept Bobby Marchan, Eddie Kirkland—known as the Gypsy of the Blues—and Arthur Alexander there.

Eddie Kirkland had been John Lee Hooker's guitar player for thirteen years. I loved booking John Lee Hooker. We would speak on the telephone a lot, and he stuttered real bad—sometimes he could barely speak. But when he got out onto the stage, he didn't stutter at all. Once he rolled into 'Boom, Boom,' it was all pure heaven. John was fun and easy to work with—a true professional. I booked him everywhere.

In 1963, Phil sent Eddie over to Stax to record a song called 'The Hawg'—a pathetic record, really, but it played well on the blues stations. Eddie wound up as an auto mechanic, but then he picked things up again and became a legend. Even though Eddie was forty or so, he'd do flips on the stage. One time he jumped off the side of the balcony onto the stage, doing a flip on the way down.

Eddie stayed in Macon for quite some time. He did all right. He made it to eighty-seven and was killed in a car crash in Florida.

Arthur Alexander was one of the first acts I booked. He didn't have a particularly strong voice, but he was a brilliant songwriter and stylist. Arthur was produced by Rick Hall at Fame Studios in Muscle Shoals, and he had written and performed iconic hits like 'You Better Move On' and 'Anna (Go To Him).' Great acts like The Beatles and The Rolling Stones covered his songs—so many of the cutting-edge blues and R&B from England was birthed in the South. Arthur's manager owned a drugstore, so he was constantly giving Arthur all these pills—jars full of them. Arthur would take those pills to the fraternity gigs and, after he played the gig, he would sit around and sing a cappella in the fraternity house and share his pills.

Rick Hall was one of the best producers in the world. He would work a singer until he was so hoarse he couldn't talk—trying to find out what the singer's range was, what his limitations were, what he was truly capable of. Rick and the great writer/producer Dan Penn, and Rock & Roll Hall Of Famer Spooner Oldham, were all over there at Fame, and we were there quite often. Rick and Dan were real country boys. When Rick was a boy, he was dirt poor and slept on hay. Before he died, he gave away millions of dollars.

Over at Muscle Shoals Sound, they'd have Wilson Pickett, The Staple Singers, Bobby Womack, Bob Seger—even The Rolling Stones went there and recorded. The 'Pickers' were something else. If you could set the groove, they could lock in faster than anyone.

Dan Penn and I spent lots of time together in the R&B days. Dan is a wonderful writer—song after song after song. Rick Hall had a habit of putting his tongue in his cheek—'What do you think, Dan?'—and Dan would say, 'I think you should try it one more time.' Together, Dan Penn and Spooner Oldham were Rick Hall's right arm. Spooner is the one who put the fantastic keys on Aretha Franklin's *I Never Loved A Man The Way I Love You*. He and Dan were usually part of all aspects of the production.

At Muscle Shoals, if you could show that you had talent, the musicians would lock in behind you and stay on you and never let you out of their sight. They played on everybody's records. Rick Hall had over three hundred gold records, and Jimmy Johnson at Muscle Shoals had hundreds more.

Muscle Shoals had the Muscle Shoals Rhythm Section, and it was the second best studio band that I ever worked with: Jimmy Johnson, Barry Beckett, Roger Hawkins, David Hood, along with Tippy Armstrong, Pete Carr, or Wayne Perkins on guitar—great guys and great sounds.

Jimmy Hughes, Percy Sledge's cousin, was working with Rick Hall at Fame. Jimmy had a hit over there called 'Steal Away':

I know it's late but I can't wait
So come on and steal away.

I loved 'Steal Away.' I heard that Jimmy was performing in the area and I wanted to see him, but when I called Rick Hall to find out about Jimmy's gig, he told me that Jimmy was home in bed.

'Well, somebody better get down here, because a phony Jimmy is performing in Macon.'

'I don't know who is performing, but it sure isn't Jimmy Hughes.'

So Jimmy hopped on a plane and came out to Macon, and we went over to see who was imitating him. Turns out, some amateur had been doing a show, imitating Jimmy Hughes. Jimmy approached the guy and held a picture of himself to his face. Jimmy then sang 'Steal Away' to please the audience and clear his name. While Jimmy was in Macon, I signed him to a booking contract.

Rick Hall expressed that he really wanted to get into soul music.

'Man, I've got some soulful acts,' I told Rick. 'We'll bring some soul over to Muscle Shoals.'

I went up there with Otis and Arthur Conley, and the end result was the million-selling 'Sweet Soul Music.'

Otis and I first met Arthur in Baltimore, Maryland. We used to get suits up there. For twenty-five dollars apiece, we could get real nice sharkskin and mohair suits straight out of the factory. While we were up there, we met Rufus Mitchell, who also owned a small booking agency and booked Otis around Baltimore on occasion.

Rufus had a little demo called 'I'm A Lonely Stranger' by Arthur Conley & The Corvettes. Man, he played that song, and both Otis and I were super-impressed with Arthur's voice.

'Man, this guy can sing,' Otis said.

When we re-signed with Stax in 1965, part of the deal was that Otis could produce for Jotis Records, which stood for Joe Galkin and Otis.

Phil had brought Billy Young from Germany over to Stax. He was on the USO show that Phil produced for all the soldiers. Billy was a very soulful guy. We got him over here and we cut at least three songs for Billy, produced by Otis, but they didn't do very well. One of Billy's records, 'The Sloppy,' was written by Otis.

One day, Otis and I were sitting around and talking about how much of a shame it was that Arthur wasn't selling.

'This is a shame, Red. Why don't you call and book a studio? I'll produce Arthur Conley.'

'Sounds like a winner to me,' I assured Otis.

The first session I had with Rick Hall was with Arthur, Otis, his band, and a singing group called The Epsilons, who became McFadden & Whitehead.

Phil was at a record convention, so Otis and I went up to Fame with Arthur. The first song we cut was 'Sweet Soul Music,' written by Otis and Arthur, and it sold a million copies right out of the box. Sam Cooke's name was later added because it was determined by a lawsuit brought about by J.W. Alexander, Sam's manager, that 'Sweet Soul Music' sounded very much like Sam's 'Yeah, Man.' Tragically, Sam had already been murdered in California in 1964—the world lost one of the greatest soul singers of all time that day. Sam was a big influence on Otis, especially his *Live At The Copa*.

The opening horns on 'Sweet Soul Music' are from Elmer Bernstein's score to *The Magnificent Seven*, the great, popular western from 1960. But they were also used in a Marlboro cigarette commercial. That's where Phil first heard them and mentioned them to me.

'Sweet Soul Music' had a lot of inspiration. The lyrics really tuned into a time and place. This was our lives, our joy, and this is what we lived for.

Otis thought he was making Arthur sound too much like himself, so we started thinking about another producer for Arthur. When Otis got killed, Tom Dowd took over producing Arthur.

We were always looking for talent—seems like I've been looking for talent my whole life. And, man, I found a lot of it. Arthur was one. He didn't smoke, didn't drink, and didn't know how to drive. And he could dance his ass off. He was as sweet as a dream.

I purchased a Lincoln for Arthur, but he neglected to tell me that he didn't know how to drive. He drove that Lincoln from Macon to Atlanta, not knowing how to drive—that's about eighty-five miles without knowing how to drive. How does a person do that? Determination, I guess.

Arthur Conley never got over the death of Otis Redding. He moved to the Netherlands, changed his name to Lee Charles, and lived a quiet life, singing occasionally. He died in obscurity in 2003.

They did a lot of overdubbing at Fame in Muscle Shoals, doing the rhythm tracks first and adding tracks. I'm used to doing things over and over again until I get it right. Man, those Muscle Shoals 'Swampers' were the perfect studio band. They are on hundreds of million-sellers. Rick Hall probably had four hundred million-sellers.

WE JUST WANTED TO FIND OUT WHAT IT FELT LIKE TO HANG A WHITE BOY OUT THE WINDOW
SCENE TWENTY-FOUR

Phil met Sam & Dave in Miami and convinced them we needed to be their managers. Phil did that very well—convincing people they needed to do what he said for their own good. Jerry Wexler had just made Jim Stewart a gift of Sam & Dave at Stax.

I didn't meet Sam Moore and Dave Prater until they got to Macon. Before they got out of control on cocaine and all of that, they were absolutely double dynamite. They once held me out of a hotel window by my feet.

Johnnie Taylor and Sam & Dave were playing over at the Apollo, and we were at the City Squire Hotel down near Times Square. They all were pretty tooted up on cocaine, and Johnnie was drinking heavily as well. Sam & Dave and Johnnie got nuts and grabbed me, shoved me to an open window, picked me up, hung onto my feet, and hung me *out* the window, laughing it up and telling me that they wanted to find out what it felt like to hang a white boy out of a window.

I was petrified. I had never been more frightened in my life. One of my shoes could have come off. All I could see was a sidewalk seven stories below, and the only thing separating me from certain death was the grip of three coked-up guys.

I usually had a great time working at the Apollo Theater in New York. I'd always give Eddie, one of the backstage men, a bottle of wine, because he was kind and helpful to us. Frank and Bobby Shiffman, the owners of the Apollo, always took care of us—we brought them some of the top acts in the world.

Back in the sixties, the neighborhood around the Apollo was very dangerous. The alleys were full of junkies and thugs. It was hard to get a cab to the theater.

'Take me to the Apollo.'

'I don't go up there,' I would often hear from the cabbie.

I was in the dressing room and some gangsters kicked open the door, holding a machine gun, all set to sweep the place. They weren't looking for me, but just in case I got in the way, I jumped out onto the fire escape and crouched down in the darkness. The show was being emceed by a popular DJ named Rocky G. on WWRL. They had him in an alley on his knees with a pistol to his head, threatening to kill him if he didn't get his ass out of Harlem. I worked my way around to the front of the theater to try to get a cab. One stopped, and a very big man stepped in front of me and the cab.

'I'm taking this cab.'

'Okay,' I said, more than willing to oblige.

This very old junkie woman approached me for a cigarette—there was something wicked about her. As I was lifting one smoke out of the pack, she opened her other hand and she had razor blades taped between her fingers.

'Keep the pack,' I told her.

Sam & Dave had one of the best choreographed shows of any duo ever. You would think that they spent hours and hours rehearsing their act, but they didn't. It came all on impulse when they got on the stage. And they would repeat the good things that went over on another show—swinging their coats at the same time, and being in perfect step with each other, bobbing off and feeding off of each other. After the drugs got involved, they became unmanageable. That's the only way I can explain it.

On another outing, I was in Chicago with Sam & Dave, performing at the Regal Theater. Everybody played the Regal—James Brown, The Supremes, The Temptations, Gladys Knight & The Pips, Jackie Wilson, everyone. I was told and warned about a gang called the Blackstone Rangers who controlled the streets around the theater and not to go near them. Everyone was warning me about how bad they were.

The female side of the Rangers had, prior to this night, pushed their way into the Regal and poured lighter fluid into a girl's hair and then lit her hair on fire for no other reason other than to show everyone how bad they were. And they were bad. The poor girl ran out of the theater with her head on fire. And that was the female side of the gang! The male side of the gang was just tough and bad, or that was their image. Some people say they helped the neighborhood, but that was not my business. It was their side of the street. I wasn't up on the public-relations side of the Blackstone Rangers.

Sam & Dave took the stage. And when they *took* it, brother, they *took* it. I decided I needed some fresh air, so I went outside in the alley to get me some. This African American guy, maybe eighteen or nineteen, dressed in black leather and looking like he had been hurt so much he couldn't be hurt anymore, comes up to me while I'm standing on the steps in the cool, Chicago night air.

'Give me ten dollars,' he said.

I looked at him. I look around and he's got seven more right behind him. And there's only one of me. Even if there had been more than one of me, it seemed that I was, without a doubt, in the wrong place at the wrong time—or at least in the right place at the wrong time. And just by looking at him I knew he could probably beat my ass, let alone whatever the rest of them could do. But a guy like that wouldn't beat my ass, he'd just shoot me or stab me. So I reached into my pocket and got my ten-spot out and handed it to him.

The Ranger looked at me for a long time. I don't think this was the kind of guy who did too much talking. I am sure when he walked into a room, people probably avoided his glance.

'If you happen to get some booze, I sure could use a taste,' I said.

And they just walked away and didn't thank me for the ten or tell me to kiss their ass—just walked away and, frankly, I was glad to see them go. Those guys really put the buzz on me.

I was upstairs in the dressing room and the show was still going on. I decided that I was never going out into the alley ever again, just as the backstage 'doorman' hollers up to the dressing room.

'Hey, Alan. Your buddies are back.'

'Who?'

'Your Ranger buddies.'

'Tell them I'm not here.'

'Alan. You don't understand. We don't mess with the Rangers here. They'll come in here and get you and help themselves to anyone else they want while they're in here.'

So I went back outside, and there were the same eight guys.

'Hey. You wanted me?'

The Ranger opened up his coat and pulled out a bottle of cheap bourbon. Well, I hated bourbon from getting sick off Early Times in high school, and I never drank it after that. But on that night in

Chicago, I chugged it down faster than Johnny Jenkins chugged his stump shine. I drank it until it came out of my nose and ears.

'Thanks, man,' I told the Ranger. 'I needed that.'

The Rangers walked away. Never said a word to me. I was probably one of the luckiest white boys ever to be in the Regal Theater. That was sheer luck. Maybe they could tell I was soulful. I had heard they had beat up a cop on one corner while another cop turned his back. They were part of Chicago. They were tough. I was tough too. Just not that tough.

I always spoke to the major radio stations in the North, including WVON-AM, which was partly owned by the great Leonard Chess. So, while I was in Chicago, I decided to go by the radio station and take Sam & Dave over there for an interview.

Sam & Dave went into the interview, and I walked into the station manager and introduced myself.

'I'm Alan Walden.'

'Hell, we know who you are and we know what you do.'

'I'm glad you know who I am and I'm glad you know what I do.'

'We play a lot of your records.'

'I know you do, and I appreciate it.'

'If you send us a decent record, we'll play it.'

I made friends up north: people like Moses 'Lucky' Cordell, 'The Baron Of Bounce,' and E. Rodney Jones, 'The Mad Lad,' in Chicago; Hoyt Locke, known as 'Dr. Bop,' out of Milwaukee: '*This is Doctor Bop on the scene with a stack of shellac and my record machine. A little country boy from across the track, so down with it, baby, that I'll never go back.*' Those guys helped the Waldens a lot. They kept our music playing a long way from Macon.

YOU'LL NEVER GIVE ANOTHER ENEMA AS LONG AS YOU LIVE
SCENE TWENTY-FIVE

Percy Sledge had a heart of gold. I received a call from Rick Hall over at Fame Studios, and he was telling me about a demo that was sent over to him. I discovered Percy Sledge by hearing the demo of 'When A Man Loves A Woman' from Rick over the telephone—the version recorded by Quin Ivy and Marlin Greene. I immediately booked a flight, contracts in hand, and went to Muscle Shoals to find Percy.

I met Percy at Colbert County Hospital in Sheffield, Alabama, where he was working as an orderly and had just given someone an enema. Before he worked as an orderly, he had picked cotton and sung in his church choir. Like most of the African American singers of the day, he had come off of a hard road.

'Are you Percy Sledge?'

'Yes, I am,' he said, and he walked over to remove his gloves and wash his hands. 'You'll have to excuse me. I just gave someone an enema.'

'Percy Sledge! You are going to be a star!' I said, to which his first reply was, 'Do you think I can quit this damn job?'

'I do not believe you will give another enema as long as you live.'

I played 'When A Man Loves A Woman' for Phil, Otis, and my father. Phil said the song might be a Top 70 and Otis figured 60, but they both dug the hell out of the song. It would grow on Otis even more.

'Take that damn funeral march off the phonograph,' my father said.

Three weeks later, Percy Sledge was making over ten thousand dollars a week. Quite a jump from a hundred and twenty-five at the hospital. Percy and I hit it off right away, and we signed a contract later on in the afternoon I met him in the hospital—with his lawyers and his producer, Quin Ivy, present. The song went to #1 and sold one million, three hundred thousand copies in ten days—my first #1 song.

'When A Man Loves A Woman' was originally recorded in Quin Ivy's cave-like studio in Sheffield, Alabama. It was literally rugs and egg crates nailed over the walls for acoustics. The whole board was just four big knobs. Spooner Oldham was on the organ, Marlin Green and Jimmy Johnson on guitars, Albert Lowe on bass, and Roger Hawkins on drums. The horns were supposed to be redone because they were out of tune, but that version is what was released. The record came out, and that's what you're hearing.

When Jerry Wexler first heard the song, he pointed out the horns were out of tune. So Quin and Marlin overdubbed new horns and sent the master copy to Atlantic. Ironically, the two tapes ended up being mixed up, and Atlantic put on the out-of-tune horns again by accident. There is beauty in imperfection, like in those Persian rugs.

Percy Sledge had a unique voice. Nobody sounded like him. He put his heart and soul into his music. Percy Sledge was my second favorite R&B singer. He and I never had an argument. Ever. He trusted me totally—he even had me sign his checks. He was one of the most humble guys you ever wanted to meet.

In 1966, Percy performed at the Hollywood Bowl, at The Beach Boys' Summer Spectacular, along with many of the top groups, including The Lovin' Spoonful, The Byrds, Chad & Jeremy, and Neil Diamond.

Otis went to Percy's dressing room, and Percy was very frightened of performing in front of so many white people.

'I hear you're scared, Percy.'

'Well, Otis . . . I actually am. This is the first time in front of a white audience this big.'

Otis hammered down the courage and inspiration in a way that only he could do.

'If I had that damn song of yours, Percy Sledge, I'd be out there pouring my heart out and loving it. You *got to* just get on it.'

Percy listened and he went out there and he charged the stage and started dancing.

Percy Sledge was not a fantastic, tricky showman—he didn't swing the mic like Joe Tex or James Brown, didn't walk like Otis. He just did his own little dance steps, and they were all very simple—he was perhaps more of a country singer than a true soul singer. But, man, he was really something.

Percy didn't write songs, so he was dependent on songwriters. I was with him at the Apollo one night when Leon Hayward came backstage. I had been talking to Leon about representing him. I introduced Leon to Percy and Quin Ivy. Leon told us about a song called 'Warm And Tender Love,' written by Bobby Robinson and Clara Thompson.

Bobby was a major force in Harlem and the R&B world, and definitely a hit with Atlantic—Bobby brought Gladys Knight to New York from Atlanta when she was still a teenager. He had a record store called Bobby's Happy House on 125th Street, and, as reported by Douglas Martin in the *New York Times* at Bobby's death, 'Old Timers remember James Brown's limo parked outside, and people breaking into a happy strut as they responded to the music tumbling onto the street.'

There was a story floating around—it is not verifiable, but it was told to me—that Bobby got angry at a fellow one time for counterfeiting his records. Bobby took the guy and stuck his hand under a record pressing machine and turned his hand into a 45.

Phil and I understood exactly how to follow up with the next record. We knew that sales would deteriorate, and that would get the DJs to flip to the B-side, and then the next move was to come out with a new record right away. It was all about the timing. Records came out fast in those days. You couldn't spend a year in the studio working on a song or two. Time was very valuable.

I JUST HEARD LITTLE RICHARD WAS AT THE PEACOCK
SCENE TWENTY-SIX

Twiggs Lyndon was the best road manager of all time. He was a legend. Twiggs and I were in high school together. One weekend I wanted to get out of Macon, so my friend Bobby Ellerbee and I decided to check into the Holiday Inn at Atlanta, which was one of the nicest hotels in the area back then. When we got our dates squared away in the rooms, we met up at the Coke machine to compare notes.

'Hey, man. I just heard that Little Richard was at the Peacock,' Bobby said.

'You got to be kidding me. What are we gonna tell the women?' I replied.

We decided to tell the girls we could only get two tickets.

I knew that Twiggs was with Richard as his road manager, so we went over to the Royal Peacock. That night, Twiggs was making sure Richard put on one hell of a show. Of course, he would have anyway— I've never seen him do anything less.

Henry Wynn owned the Royal Peacock. He was the South's biggest Black promoter. He owned his own cab service in Atlanta. He was also heavily involved with the numbers racket. Occasionally, Henry would ask me to package his shows.

Henry would tell me that he didn't care if he made money, he just didn't want to lose money. I think music was only a front for him.

We were having fun backstage after the show, and Twiggs and I had a chance to talk. After a show like that, it is almost impossible to have a conversation, but Twiggs and I found a little quiet space.

'I'd like you to come by and see me sometime, Twiggs. Maybe we can work together—you being with Richard and me being with Otis, Johnnie Taylor, Percy Sledge, and all. We ought to be able to put something together.'

And he did come over to see me. When he came by, he was very interested in what we were doing. Twiggs started spending more and more time with me, and then, after Richard came off the road, he came home and settled back into Macon.

Twiggs went out with Percy Sledge, Arthur Conley, and Johnnie Taylor. And, man, he had those guys trained so well. He had strict rules and took his job very, very seriously. And the musicians respected that ethic and depended on it.

Later on, during his Dixie Dregs run, Twiggs built a hidden

compartment in one of equipment trucks that you entered by going down under the truck and then climbing up—a little room where they could have a couch and where people could get stoned and sleep and not have to worry about police or anything. I never rode there.

When Twiggs went to England, he met a British road manager, and this fellow taught him about itineraries and all sorts of efficient ways to handle and organize road receipts and finances. Twiggs came home with an arsenal of management tools, as well as a very distinctive beard, several tweed sports coats, a cap, and a vanity cane. But he was carrying that style out much further, and he made it his own.

Twiggs looked after the performers so good that when they got off the plane or bus at a gig, he gave each one an individual envelope. Inside that envelope, along with the keys to hotel rooms—who was in what room; all pre-checked, of course—was everything they needed to know about the city, the hotel, the venue, the potential problems and cautions—where the women were, and which ones to look out for. To avoid arguments and conflicts, he separated the musicians who needed to be separated. All they had to do was read the sheets—setup times, soundchecks, schedules; even the layout of the venue and the stage, where each amp would be and each trash can would be; where the beer went and where the wine went; the bathrooms and changing rooms.

Twiggs did everything. He believed strongly, as I did, in limiting your risks as much as possible to avoid failure, ensuring a successful show. And he wrote the most bulletproof riders in the business. Promoters were terrified of his riders. He had total control of the gigs—not only on the performing side, but on the venue and promotion side.

One night, Twiggs was with Percy Sledge and they arrived late in Virginia, and by the time they arrived, the promoter had already filled the club with people. Twiggs kept the band parked out front and wouldn't let them get out of the bus.

'Looks like we're going to have to empty your whole club and let them come in again for the count,' Twiggs said. 'That's in the contract.'

'We can't do that,' the promoter complained.

'Okay. You keep everyone in their seats, and we'll go in and count them.'

Twiggs got two or three guys with little counters, and they went through the club and counted every damn person in the club. Twiggs wouldn't let Percy and the band into the club without being paid up front, using his count.

Another time, Twiggs was out there in Mississippi, and he pulled in for gas with a band. The owner of the station came over to the car and stuck his racist head right in the window.

'Boy, what you doin' with all these Black folks?'

'You know, I have the hardest time. More people think I'm white than you can ever imagine.'

The man looking at him like he had just been smacked over the head with an axe handle.

'You're Black? Damn if you ain't the lightest one I ever saw.'

Twiggs liked to have fun on the road. He was also excellent at lining up women. He collected hundreds and hundreds of groupies' phone numbers, and he had a book of information that was something else— their ages and their likes and dislikes. He was truly my right arm. I loved Twiggs dearly and he loved me.

In Alabama one night, we were done with the Percy Sledge homecoming show in Sheffield. It was a huge crowd. There were as many people outside as inside. The word was out that the side doors were going to get kicked open. Twiggs and I got hip to the plan, and we would have to deal with it. We both carried pistols in those days, and Twiggs had a hair-trigger on his that didn't make me feel too comfortable—a trigger so sensitive that the gun would go off just by touching it.

A bunch of guys broke open the side door, and Twiggs and I locked arms and charged straight into about fifteen of them. We managed to push their asses all the way out the door—I still don't know how we did it. Then we drew the iron. When the crowd saw those pistols, they started moving away from us fast. They could have easily beat the shit out of us, but we weren't scared in those years. We ran top shows. You didn't let people in the side doors. It was the Old West. We all carried guns and knives, and we weren't afraid to use them.

There was a club down in New Orleans that had a ticket box by the door. The promoters would drop all the tickets, and then they would count the tickets and pay you the percentage. Twiggs got word that they were taking tickets out with a little trigger-release: when the box filled up, the trigger would be hit, and the tickets would fall onto the floor below. We got paid on the tickets in the box, so the guy was robbing us by dumping tickets out of his special box.

Twiggs pretended to do a soundcheck and rigged the box so the door wouldn't open, and then he sat there across from the promoter, smiling at him all night, while he was trying to get the trap door to open without Twiggs getting wise—Twiggs having the best time watching someone trying to screw him and who was intending to screw him but failing with great frustration. That's the kind of fearless detail man Twiggs was. Twiggs loved his work, and we had great fun along the way.

YOU NEED TO LET A THIEF STEAL EVERY ONCE IN A WHILE TO KEEP HIM HONEST
SCENE TWENTY-SEVEN

I used to work the balcony at the Otis homecoming shows. It became a prestige thing to sneak into the show. I hired police to watch the doors for fire laws. Then we had to hire our own people to watch the police, because the police would let the people into the side doors. Then, just to be sure, we walked around and checked on them. I found out that Huck was letting people in at another side door and making fistfuls of cash. I went up to him.

'Huck? This ain't right. I need to set you straight here.'

'Let me set *you* straight, Alan. You ain't going to set me straight.'

'I'll set you straight or Otis will set you straight.'

'Well, you better let Otis set me straight, 'cause you sure in hell ain't going to set me straight.'

So I walked into the dressing room to let Otis know about his pal, Huck, who was stealing from the hand that fed him.

'You're not going to believe who is letting people in, Otis.'

'Huck?'

'He probably let thirty or forty in already,' I complained.

'Alan. Huck's a thief.'

'Yes, I know.'

'He's a natural born thief. You've got to let him steal a little.'

'Why, Otis?'

'You need to let a thief steal a little once in a while to keep him honest.'

Otis didn't fuss at all, but Huck did stop letting people in.

So Otis was right. Maybe Huck needed to steal to prevent him from going crazy. People would climb a high-powered tower in the back with signs all over it, warning them to beware of high voltage. They were climbing up that damn thing to get onto the balcony. I used to sit out there with a pistol. I faced down a few nuts crawling on that tower.

'I'm gonna tell you something. You better start crawling back down.'

People even crawled through the air-conditioning tunnels, which had big fans that could chop them up. They'd crawl up the side of the building using ropes, garden hoses, or anything they could find.

At the end of the night, since I didn't look like the big money man, I was elected to take the money out of City Auditorium in a paper sack. I just walked out like I was gathering tickets, got into the car, and took off.

One year, the guy Otis was in the shootout with rounded up his friends and put the word out that they were going to shoot Otis on the stage if he performed. These weren't idle threats. These guys were killers. So, when Otis came onto the stage that night, Huck appeared from stage left, Bubba Howard from stage right, and some others—we had about six guns—behind Otis, in case anyone started to shoot.

I had my gun loaded and hidden behind the curtain. It was tense. We almost had more people with guns on the stage than musicians. These days, it's hard to wrap your head around a scene like that. Very, very tense. Right in the middle of the set, somebody lit a cherry bomb and rolled it onto the dance floor, and people started to panic and run toward the doors.

'Kick open the door and let them out!' I shouted. 'They're going to trample each other to death!'

Some did get trampled and hurt. They were in that big of a hurry. We almost had a riot when they charged the doors and all of those people who were trying to get in ran in. All those people who were fearing for their lives ran out. Regardless, it was still a great show.

In 1966, my father was doing a show with Otis in Baton Rouge. Huck and Speedo were with him. The promoter and my father checked out the box office to make sure all the money was there—about twenty-seven thousand dollars. My father gave Otis the word to go onstage. When Pops went back to collect the money, he opened up the box office and the promoter along with all the money was gone.

My father was a pretty hip street person. He studied all the people backstage and spotted one guy who looked like a hustler, who kept watching him.

Daddy walked over to the man.

'I don't know how much they're paying you to watch me, but I'll pay you double if you can show me where that money went.'

The guy led my father and Huck and Speedo into the ghetto of Baton Rouge in the middle of the night. They went up to a little house and the promoter was sitting in his kitchen, counting his money. The three of them didn't knock, they just walked in.

'You thought you were going to get away with this,' Daddy told the guy. 'You could have had half the money, and now you're getting none of it.'

Huck had a look about him. He had killed nine men, and my father let the promoter know that. One more wasn't going to make a difference to him. They relieved the man of all of the money and left, and that was it.

That's how efficient my father was. He had great common sense. Great street instincts. He knew how to deal with people, and he knew how to stand up and raise hell if necessary. My father would go into an auditorium or stadium and count every seat in the place. When it was all packed, we knew just about how much money was owed before we went to the box office. Promoters used to roll out bleachers and let more people in, not intending to pay for those extra people. My father spotted it and took care of it. He loved that work.

GOT TO GIVE THEM SOME SATISFACTION
SCENE TWENTY-EIGHT

Around 1966, We were riding five in a Cadillac—Rodgers Redding, Speedo, Otis, William Bell, and me. William's 'You Don't Miss Your Water' was a hit record for Stax in 1961. He hadn't been out of the army for that long.

'Hey, man, what you doing for work?' Otis asked.

'I hardly got anything yet,' William told Otis.

'We can get you on my tour if you want.'

'Sure.'

'Sound good to you, Alan?' Otis asked.

'Sounds good to me, Otis.'

And William rode with Otis the whole tour. He came into the

studio when Otis was doing 'Respect,' and he ended up singing background. He and Otis hit it off good. William Bell is one of the nicest entertainers I ever represented.

I met Joe Simon at the Apollo Theater when he had a couple of records out in the mid-sixties, 'My Adorable One' and 'Let's Do It Over'—those songs were on Vee-Jay records out of Chicago. Joe was a good-looking guy, and he dressed very sharp. When I heard his voice, I thought, *Damn, this guy is like Jerry Butler*. With that voice, he didn't have to do anything but stand there and sing. He was John Richbourg's artist, and I was his agent for probably three or four years.

I loved Joe Simon. When it came time for his contract to expire with Soundstage 7, which was John R.'s label, I shopped around to see what we could get for him. I found him a seven-hundred-and-fifty-thousand-dollar deal from Atlantic Records—that would have been one of the biggest deals of the century. But Joe didn't take it. He went with some guys that owned a label that had never had a hit, I guess because they gave him part of the label's ownership. These guys promised him the world and delivered nothing. He did deliver them some hits, but since he owned a part of the label, he didn't get any advances. Seven hundred and fifty thousand dollars went right out the window. Gone.

I took Joe Simon from a hundred and twenty-five dollars a night to twenty-five hundred, and I did him right. He had a beautiful voice. He was a gentleman. He never cussed. He never drank or smoked. He played his dates. When I handled Joe, he would go to the post office, buy a money order, and mail it to his CPA—a very frugal and conscientious entertainer.

Joe could out-fumble you for a Coke or a cup of coffee. He was the best fumbler in the business. A fumbler is a person who, after dinner or drinks, reaches for his wallet or money and fumbles around until someone else ultimately pays the check. Johnnie Taylor and I were with him one day, and Johnnie suggested that we try to out fumble Joe. So we would fumble and Joe would fumble, and we were all fumbling like fumbling fools, and I finally reached for the check because I couldn't take it anymore. Fumbling takes skill and patience—Joe was the best.

Joe had a truly magnificent voice. I could have gotten him a tremendous deal, and I was looking forward to a commission, but he was a perfect gentleman. We shook hands and I told him I hated to see him leave me, but if that's the way it has to be, that's how it has to be.

'It's the biggest mistake you'll ever make, Joe.'

It may have been and it may not have been. The record label guys wound up with the money, and Joe wound up with ownership that wasn't worth anything. But Joe did hit #1 on the R&B charts with 'The Chokin' Kind' in 1969, and it won a Grammy in 1970 for Best Male Performance. He did all right, ultimately. He's still going strong as a minister.

The first Black artist I ever went to lunch with in a white restaurant was Joe Simon. One of my greatest regrets is that Otis and I never ate a meal together in a white restaurant in Macon. Otis didn't want to cause any trouble. We ate in all sorts of Black restaurants—never white. We were more comfortable in Black restaurants, and the food was more exciting. When we came off the roads, Zelma would put out a big feed for us—turnip greens, candied hams, and pork chops.

Joe Tex was one of the best performers there was onstage. His voice was not real strong like Otis's or James Brown's or Little Richard's, but he had a kind of soft singing voice, and he was a very powerful and exciting performer. He had routines that he did that were just spectacular. He was the first man to polish the performance by using the microphone—throwing it out to the audience but bending the stand-up mic down and stepping on the stand to pick it up or spinning it and sending it toward the audience near enough to scare the crowd. Joe did fantastic splits and spins.

Joe had just as many hits as Otis did while they were both alive: 'Hold What You've Got,' 'I Want To (Do Everything For You),' 'The Love You Save,' 'A Sweet Woman Like You.' Hit after hit after hit. Joe was a tremendous talent. Joe and Otis loved each other, but Joe loved to burn Otis onstage—a great, loving, healthy rivalry.

One time, Otis and Joe were performing together at the City Auditorium. Joe went on first. When Joe came on, he did it all. He was sockin' the fire out there like crazy. He was out to burn Otis a new butt.

'What in hell are you going to do tonight?' I asked Otis. 'Joe is killing them.'

'I don't know, Red. I don't know.'

Otis was wearing his new three-hundred-dollar, custom-made tux—a lot of money for a tux in those days. He walked out onto the stage and raised his hands, and that energy jumped into his life and he went to work. The women screamed at the top of their lungs for Otis Redding. He was doing something new because he was feeling what the audience wanted—hunching over in a pleading way. The women were going crazy. I don't think he did but five songs that night, but he did them extra long—bleeding each one of them for everything they were worth.

When he got into 'Satisfaction,' he started to smoke:

You *got to* have some satisfaction! I *need* me some satisfaction! Everybody *needs* some satisfaction! *Give me* some satisfaction! *Got to, got to* have some satisfaction! *Give me, give me, give me* some satisfaction! *Give me, give me, give me* some satisfaction! Good God almighty, *I got to, got to, got to.*

He kept that going until the night was his—ripping the hearts out of those gals. The men were going crazy too. I think Otis was giving them strength and heart. This was a magic show. Otis shoved that night right back up Joe's ass. And this was probably the best show I had ever seen Joe do!

I was so proud of Otis that night. He just picked up what Joe had done and took it over the mountain.

When Keith Richards heard Otis's version of 'Satisfaction,' he said that it sounded like Otis wrote the song. Keith was right. Otis did more to those words than any human on Earth.

THE EUROPEAN SOUL INVASION
SCENE TWENTY-NINE

In 1966, Otis went to England and Paris, but I didn't go with him. The package was booked by Frank Sands. My father went in my place because he was in his sixties by this time, and I didn't know how many more years he was going to live. I figured I'd have plenty of times to go over there, so I stayed back to take care of the shop. He had the time of his life. He was getting massages in the hotels and eating pheasant and duck and drinking the finest wines, with a personal driver at his disposal.

The Beatles sent their personal limo to pick Otis up at the airport. Aside from the six or so concerts he did, he also appeared on the wildly popular television show *Ready, Steady, Go!* Otis was on with Eric Burdon, who was good company for him. In 1964, Little Richard considered Eric Burdon and The Animals to be the best band in the world.

The Stax/Volt Review—Otis's European tour—was put together by us. It featured Otis, Sam & Dave, Arthur Conley, Eddie Floyd, The Mar-Keys, and Booker T. & The M.G.'s from Stax—Steve Cropper, Al Jackson, Duck Dunn, and of course Booker T. himself. That tour blew into Europe like a hurricane, destroying everything in its path.

Otis loved the fact that they paid more attention to music in Europe and seemed to know more about songs. The Europeans and the Brits were far ahead of the Americans for their appreciation of the details of the songs, and the technical aspects of the songs—what kind of guitars, what kind of amps, what kind of horns. They got the music on a technical and personal level. The kids would be all screaming and shouting, but they were all into the details, for sure. Americans didn't ask the questions Europeans did. Europeans were more into the deep art of the music.

Once soul music hit Europe, it was a huge thing over there. Otis was bigger overseas than he was here in the States. Otis released 'My Girl,' the song by The Temptations, written by Smokey Robinson and Ronald White. He had a big hit with 'My Girl' overseas. In his version, he makes up some of the lyrics in the middle of it—a couple of times he forgot the lyrics and used his own. He listened to the song maybe two or three times, then went into the studio and knocked it out.

Otis would get super-sexy on the European stages. He had a thing where he'd stretch out the words: 'Been loving you *tooooo* long.' The women would stare at his crotch. He was a real man in those tight pants.

Otis enjoyed Europe, but he did get a little bored because the tour lasted a bit too long. He extended it while he was there, and they got him to go back to certain cities again, but I know that he was anxious to get home. He wanted to get back home to his family and the ranch.

In Europe, Otis was extremely popular. Crowds would mob him wherever he went. Sometimes he was mobbed in America, but not much. Not like Europe. He spoke to the European and British audience—spoke with his heart and soul. He was moving and all of that—there was a lot of sex in his act. Audiences really paid attention to what Otis was doing with his bumps and turning—he was very sexy, and women loved him. But it was his grit and his soul that truly hit home. I think he pushed an audience to an emotional high. He pushed them to feel more alive than they had in a long time.

When Otis dethroned Elvis as the number one male singer in Europe, that was quite an achievement in my life. Three years before, he wasn't known. Otis captured the King.

I hurt tremendously when I heard *Live In London And Paris*. When I heard how good those shows were, I cried and cried. Otis moved me that much. I got into his songs so easily.

Mick Jagger and Keith Richards rode in Otis's tour bus with him, just to be around him. Sam & Dave were with them too. Sam Moore actually slapped Keith Richards in the back of the head because he wouldn't stop talking and asking questions. They told him to 'shut the fuck up.' It wasn't a play slap, either. Didn't matter. Jagger and Richards were taken away with the scene. They really liked Otis. They endorsed him.

We had The Beatles endorsing Otis too. I had always been jealous of The Beatles because they came over here and took command—and made it look like it was easy as pie. I wasn't aware of the work it took to get there. We had been working for years and we hadn't gotten to the Top 10, and here they come with like six #1s in a row. I was jealous of The Beatles, and then they did an interview in Atlanta and were asked who their favorite American singer was. They responded with, 'Otis Redding!' After that, I told my secretary to go out and buy every damn Beatles album there was. I wanted to know about The Beatles.

All of the British entertainers showed up. Rod Stewart was crying in the audience. Tom Jones was backstage. Lots of entertainers. All of the British entertainers turned out for Otis Redding. Who knows how big his next tour could have been?

MONTEREY POP AND '(SITTIN' ON) THE DOCK OF THE BAY'
SCENE THIRTY

The Monterey thing with Otis was actually Phil's big move. He was the one who talked him into doing it, and getting Booker T. & The M.G.'s and The Mar-Keys to back him up. Phil explained to the band that they were not going to get paid anything except a per diem, a hotel, and a plane ticket. He convinced them to go over there for free. That is when I knew that my brother had the suavest way—the smoothest way of getting what he wanted done.

Jerry Wexler was convinced that Monterey was going to be a bad idea for Otis. It wasn't Otis's audience, and it would probably hurt Otis's career. But Phil still booked the show, and Jerry was sitting out in the audience, and Phil sat down and said hello to him.

'Phil, you just ruined Otis Redding's career. This is going to be horrible.'

Well, Otis picked the thing up and took it up the mountain. He took over that whole Monterey Pop Festival and he was the number one man. During his performance, the police threatened to shut it down because Otis's show was making people too rowdy. He was waking people up.

Phil told the police, 'You can shut it down, but the crowd will tear everything up. Let Otis finish his show.' And he did. He finished his show. He only did five songs, but he did long versions. He made a double spread in *Esquire* magazine from that show. *Time* even wrote an article about him. Otis Redding became a household name with the white audience after Monterey. Nothing could stop him. Phil made the right move.

Everybody started paying attention to Otis. He had two movie scripts on his desk waiting for approval. He was just about to explode majorly on the pop scene. He would have been a monster after 'Dock Of The Bay.' When I think of Otis at this time, I think of the song 'Just One More Day'—a prophetic song he wrote with Steve Cropper and McEvoy Robinson:

Ooh, I want just one more day, Lord
And it could be anything that you want it to be

Just one more day. I think that Otis was asking God for one more day of life. I know that Otis always had death on his mind.

I was not on the 'Dock Of The Bay' sessions at Stax. I had been grounded because of my sinus condition. I couldn't fly, and Memphis was a long damn drive. I loved Memphis, but getting there was tiring through those Alabama roads with the twisting and turning. I'd usually go in a day or two ahead to get some rest.

I didn't make any of that week for Otis's final recording of those twenty-six sides. 'Dock Of The Bay' was one of those sides. Otis got to hear the song. Steve had to do the overdubs and everything—the water and birds and all.

Otis was convinced that 'Dock' was going to be it. 'It's going to be my first #1 hit, my first *millyun* seller,' he told me.

So many people had a negative reaction to 'Dock,' including me and Phil. All of us were scared that Otis had strayed too far away from his fantastic, spontaneous 'got to' style and driving voice. 'Dock Of

The Bay' was just as pretty and smooth as could be.

Otis played me the song and another called 'Think About It,' which he had written with Don Covay.

'I would go with "Think About It" over "Dock." It's closer to your style. It's more you.'

That dock was in Sausalito. He was staying on a houseboat when he was playing the Fillmore West. He had a few parties on that boat, but mostly he sat on the dock and rested, *sittin' on the dock of the bay, wastin' time.*

Movie projects, huge concerts, money, fame—none of it really matters without happiness. The line '*I've got nothing to live for*' bothered me, until I realized he wasn't referring to himself but the hippies he was observing.

Al DeMarino from the William Morris Agency wanted to represent Otis. William Morris was one of the most prestigious agencies in the world. They represented the biggest talents. Al came down to Macon, and we drove him around and went over what he wanted for three days. First me and then Phil, and then all together. Then it was time to meet Otis.

We got together with Otis, and Otis listened to Al and took him very seriously. Al was ready to take Otis through the cream tunnel— *The Ed Sullivan Show*, Johnny Carson, Joey Bishop, Steve Allen.

Otis told Al that whatever Phil and I thought, it was okay with him.

When I think about Otis and I think about the ranch, I think about how much peace of mind he found in his country home. He kept it private. He didn't invite lots of people to the house. That was his reclusive place. Not only had he built that huge O-shaped swimming pool, but he also built a pond there on the property so he could fish.

Most southern boys enjoy fishing. There may be some who don't, but I've never met them.

Otis had never caught a fish in his life, and one day he dropped a line in and caught himself a fish. It wasn't a very big fish, but it was a fish. He took that fish all around Macon and showed it to everybody— he was so proud of that fish—as if it were a nine-pound bass. That's the other side of Otis Redding—the side not many were fortunate enough to know.

Otis Redding was a musician, singer, writer, arranger, publisher, producer, but he also took pride in being a farmer. He loved his gardens and grew all kinds of things. He didn't plant and do all of that. He had a caretaker that took care of everything. But he bought all the seeds and hired the people on his land, and it was his garden. He grew beautiful corn, turnip greens, collard greens, butterbeans, and just about anything you wanted.

Otis and I were hunting in the woods between our houses, separated by a couple of hundred yards. I heard two shots and moved through the woods toward the sound. When I got up there, Otis was up in a tree and the gun down on the ground.

'What in the hell is going on, Otis?'

'Red. I shot that son of a bitch deer, and damn, the next thing I knew, he got up and started charging me and I had to climb the tree to get away from him, 'cause he sure looked like he was going to kill me.'

It was a funny sight to see Otis Redding up in that tree. Those moments can never be taken away from me.

Some years later, when Richard Pryor was in Macon filming *Bingo Long & The Traveling Allstars*, Zelma and he became friends. She had a party for him at the ranch, and I was invited over. Richard—who had his grandmother with him—and I got to talking, and all he wanted to do was to catch a fish in the pond. He really wanted to catch a fish, so I got him a spinner and he got into the boat and started rowing out. I assured him that I could lead him to a hole and put a fish on that line.

We went to every hole that ordinarily had bass and didn't get a nibble. After a while he gave up. I actually felt sorry for him because he couldn't catch a fish. Sometimes fish are hungry and sometimes they're not. His grandma went down to the lake and threw out a line from the shore, and in a few minutes she caught a six-pound bass.

One time the BBC called and wanted to come to Macon to film Percy Sledge. Phil suggested we could do it out at Otis's ranch and that would be good. Phil assumed that they would shoot Otis while they were out there. But when they got out to the Big 'O,' they only wanted to shoot Percy Sledge—it was during the heat of 'When A Man Loves A Woman.'

Phil laid into the BBC. 'God, man. Even if you don't have any film in the camera, we need to let Otis put a song down, because he's really primed for it and you're going to break his heart.'

They agreed, and they ended up filming the footage for 'Tramp.' Otis was dressed up in coveralls with money falling out of every pocket. We would have canceled Percy if they had not filmed Otis.

On a quiet autumn night, Otis and I were sitting out in front of his house. I cherished times like this. Otis took out his acoustic guitar and started picking. He then went into 'Respect' and 'I've Been Loving You

Too Long.' He was singing 'Respect' as a slow ballad and 'I've Been Loving You Too Long' as an up-tempo. They were beautiful and they were gentle. I think I was the only one to hear them. All I could do was close my eyes and dream.

IF YOU LET ME HAVE ANOTHER DAY
SCENE THIRTY-ONE

Otis had been in Memphis recording and was flying to Nashville to do a date at Vanderbilt University. While they were there, they had some engine problems. The problem was fixed by some mechanics, so they flew on from there to Cleveland, Ohio, where they played *Upbeat*, an afternoon teen variety show, and then, that evening, a performance at Leo's Casino—the last stage performance of Otis Redding.

On *Upbeat*, he performed 'Respect' and 'Try A Little Tenderness.' He closed the show with 'Knock On Wood' with Mitch Ryder—Mitch was very soulful. The sound wasn't great, but the performance was a killer. Otis put all of his heart into that little performance—like every performance. It's hard to watch but also beautiful to watch.

Most of the guys and Otis would be dead the next day. They were going to Madison, Wisconsin, and it was freezing cold up there. Otis was advised not to fly. Otis had new deicers on the plane, and he figured it would be safe and the cold wouldn't get them—they had been cleared for landing. Some say he was on his final approach, but he crashed into the freezing water of Lake Monona.

CLOCKWISE FROM LEFT Carolyn McLendon Walden with her sons, Blue, Alan, and Phil; Alan, C.B., Phil, and Carolyn Walden at the family ranch; Phil and Alan in the early days of Redwal Music; Otis Redding (*center*) with Sam Moore and Dave Prater, aka Sam & Dave.

OPPOSITE PAGE, CLOCKWISE FROM TOP
LEFT Alan, Clarence Carter, and Phil;
a Macon welcoming committee greets
a returning Eddie Floyd: Bunky Oldham,
Bobby Wallace, Phil, Eddie, Mayor
Ronnie Thompson, Earl 'Speedo' Simms,
Alan, Blue; Otis Redding on a trip
overseas; Joan Boyette, John Davis, Alex
Hodges, Carolyn Brown, Rose Mary
Chatfield, Sharon Sodeberg, Donna
McMan, Alan, Peggy Thompson, Twiggs
Lyndon, and Phil (*seated*).

THIS PAGE Gary Donehoo, soul vocalist
Denise LaSalle, Alan, singer Bill Coday,
Bill Jones, and Willie Mitchell; WIBB DJ
Hamp 'King Bee' Swain, Otis Redding,
Jimmy Hughes, Carolyn Brown, Johnnie
Taylor, Alan, and Phil (*seated*).

OPPOSITE PAGE, CLOCKWISE FROM
TOP LEFT Rufus Thomas, Alan,
Lucy Bell, Otis Redding, Joe Galkin
(*center*), Al Jackson and his wife,
and Stax Records' Jim Stewart; Alan,
Percy Sledge, and Jack Chisholm;
bass player McEvoy Robinson and
Otis Redding at the Atlanta Braves
stadium; Alan, Jimmy Molten, Otis,
and Phil.

THIS PAGE Crowds gather for
Otis Redding's funeral; Alan,
photographer Dwight, boxing
promoter Don King, Coretta Scott
King, and Andrew Young at an
event for US presidential nominee
Jimmy Carter in Atlanta, Georgia.

THIS PAGE Alan with MCA Records'
Mike Maitland; Allen Collins, Gary
Rossington, Ronnie Van Zant, Bob
Burns, and Larry Junstrom of Lynyrd
Skynyrd (photograph by Bob Johnson).

**OPPOSITE PAGE, CLOCKWISE FROM TOP
LEFT** Skynyrd and friends: Ed King, Gary
Rossington, Ronnie Van Zant, Andea
McGoven, Leon Wilkeson, unknown,
Allen Collins, Billy Powell, Alan, Kevin
Elson, Bob Burns, Dean Kilpatrick; Alan
outside Hustler's Inc. in the early 70s; Alan
shows his support for Jimmy Carter; The
Outlaws show off their gold discs at Arista:
Eric Kronfield, unknown, Charlie Brusco,
Freddie Salem, Billy Jones, unknown, Bob
Feiden, Clive Davis, Monte Yoho, Kenny
French, Alan, unknown, David Dix,
Hughie Thomasson, Judy Thomasson,
Mike Bone; The Outlaws at the gallows:
Billy Jones, unknown, Monte Yoho,
Hughie Thomasson, Henry Paul, Harvey
Arnold, unknown.

CLOCKWISE FROM TOP LEFT Steve Cropper, Alan, and Allman Brother Chuck Leavell; daughter Jessica Walden, actor Billy Bob Thornton, and Alan; Alan, Jessica, Georgeanna, Christian, and Tosha Walden at the reopening of Capricorn Studios in Macon, Georgia; Tosha and Alan.

Otis was struck in the head by something that knocked him unconscious—he was probably unconscious when he drowned, still strapped into his seat. Ben Cauley, the one survivor of the crash, was the only one who couldn't swim, and he survived when the plane broke apart right where he was sitting and threw him into the water, still clutching onto a seat cushion. A couple of the boys came back up, but they couldn't hang on. They sank. If Ben had stayed in the water a few more minutes, he would have frozen to death—rescuers were right on the scene.

Two of the other bandmates—Carl Sims and James Alexander—flew on a commercial flight because of the lack of space for everyone.

The Bar-Kays who died were Carl Cunningham on drums, Jimmy King on guitar, Phalon Jones on sax, and Ronnie Caldwell on organ. Mathew Kelly, the band's valet, also died. Phalon Jones was the oldest—he was nineteen. Just kids. Just very, very talented kids. Otis was only twenty-six, but he sure seemed older.

I was eating dinner with my wife's mother and father at their house. She always cooked broccoli for me, and I was enjoying a plate of fresh broccoli when my mother called.

'Alan. Someone just called and said that Otis's plane went down.'

'I don't believe it.' And I didn't.

'It's true. Otis's plane went down somewhere in Wisconsin.'

In a fit of confusion and rage, I jerked the telephone out of the wall and screamed, 'No! This ain't happening!'

I jumped into the car and sped through the Georgia woods, heading for the ranch to be with Zelma. My mind racing and tears flowing and praying that it would miraculously be all right.

When I arrived, Zelma was hysterical to the point of collapse.

'Alan. You know that Otis is a good swimmer!'

'Yes, Zelma. Otis is a great swimmer. He is a strong swimmer.'

'He's got to be out there swimming,' Zelma cried. 'He's got to show up. I know he's not dead, Alan! I know he's not dead!'

I got a call from the team looking for the plane.

'There isn't anybody alive down there. It's been way too long. Even with an air pocket, it would be gone by now.'

Because I was grounded with blocked sinuses, Twiggs, Zelma, and Otis's father went up to Madison. They didn't find Otis for two days. When they brought him up, he was still frozen and buckled into his seat. *Jet* magazine printed a picture of Otis at the morgue that I detested. Zelma didn't want to identify him. Twiggs and the reverend did that.

OTIS WAS SUPERMAN
SCENE THIRTY-TWO

'Before Otis, I had never loved a man outside my immediate family and relatives. He was the first.'
—Alan Walden at Otis Redding's funeral

We had Macon City Auditorium completely packed and about eighteen hundred people on the outside. That's how many showed up at his funeral. Not one petal of any flower was taken as a souvenir. Everyone gave Otis the respect he deserved.

This was a horrible time in my life. I chose the pallbearers. I picked out the guys I knew really loved and cared about Otis—Joe Tex, Johnnie Taylor, Arthur Conley, Sylvester Huckabee, Earl Simms, Hamp Swain, and my brother, Blue. Blue stood in for me. I just couldn't handle it. Everybody was there: James Brown, Gene Chandler, Percy Sledge, Sam & Dave, Wilson Pickett, Solomon Burke—everyone turned out. We had quite a celebrity audience at Otis's funeral. It was packed to the hilt. Jerry Wexler gave the eulogy. Mayor Ronnie Thompson spoke and called Otis Macon's Goodwill Ambassador.

When James Brown and Joe Tex were leaving, the damn crowd outside went wild. It looked like there was going to be a riot for a short while.

I had to disappear. Go somewhere to be alone. I went downtown, over by the Douglass Theater, where it was quiet. I had to process all of that pain. I didn't know what to do.

Huckabee disappeared into the crowd and I didn't see him for seven years. I heard two policemen at the auditorium talking about getting Huck because he was wanted for some warrants. Huck seemed to know the police were after him, and he slipped away. As soon as the casket was in the hearse, Huck vanished. Now that Otis was gone, Huck had nothing left but crime.

Huck beat a guy up real bad one night, tied concrete blocks to his arms and legs, and threw him in a rock quarry—two hundred feet down to the water. Most people would not survive a fall like that, which was Huck's intent. But the poor kid did survive. Huck went down to see if his work was complete and the fellow was alive, but barely. So Huck dragged the guy to his car and started driving him around Bellevue to show him off to his friends: *Look what I did to this motherfucker.*

That's how mean Huck was. When Huck was finished with his fun, he dropped him somewhere.

One night, a year or so later, the man went to see Huck. Huck figured he was in no danger, so he invited the guy in and headed into the living room. The fellow took out a pistol and put a bullet into the back of Huck's head, killing him.

I wouldn't have shot Huck with a double-barreled shotgun with both barrels at the same time because I would be too scared he might survive. He was that tough and mean.

The police never investigated Huck's death. They just figured someone did what they wanted to have happen anyway. And that was the end of Sylvester Huckabee. The king of Bellevue was dead. Long live the king.

Phil took Otis's death better than me. I was shattered. Three days after Otis's funeral, Phil called the whole staff into the office.

'Okay. I know we're all hurt and we're all sorry, but we've got to go back to work. I'm asking you all to dig in, and let's go to work.'

We needed to get back to work. We didn't have any choice. Phil took on Arthur Conley and I took on Percy Sledge.

Zelma even came to work at the office at one point. Rodgers, Otis's younger brother, worked there as well. Rodgers Redding was one of the best booking agents I ever had and one of the finest human beings in Macon, Georgia.

I remember Otis calling me one time from the road. 'You're not going to believe what happened today. I got hot with Rodgers and went around to his car to give him a whipping, and he jumped out of the car and knocked me onto the ground.'

'What did you do?'

'I said, *Hell, I'm surprised at you, little brother.*'

I was one of the main ones to push for Otis go get a bigger plane because I felt that he would be safer—a Beechcraft H18 with twin engines. It was a dependable aircraft—that's why the military used them. Otis had had a smaller plane before the Beechcraft, and we flew through a tornado in that little single-engine plane. It would fall two or three hundred feet and hit the bottom of an air pocket and it felt like a shotgun blast. And we'd go up over the clouds and it would be the same thing again and again and again.

When we started landing, I felt like someone was driving a nail into my forehead. I thought I was hemorrhaging in my brain. Or I was suffocating. I got out of my seat and was planning to kick the window open to get some air, which would have been the stupidest thing I could have done. The pilot, who had been in the service and had plenty of experience, looked around to see what was happening. He took us back up so I could have the same altitude and it could relieve the pressure on my head. It took an hour and twenty minutes to come down.

Returning home, I went to see my doctor.

'If I were you, I wouldn't even climb a small mountain,' the doctor told me. 'Don't get on any planes. Your sinuses can't take it.'

So I didn't fly when Otis got killed. That would have been my weekend to be with him. My father was down in South America with Arthur Conley, and Phil was in Las Vegas at the Atlantic Records Convention.

We didn't think that Otis would die—that he would ever die. Otis was superman.

My father's health went straight down after Otis died. He got so bad, he'd come into the office and go into the trash for envelopes and mail the secretaries had thrown away.

'Don't throw away these envelopes, Alan. They can be reused!'

Daddy would scold the girls in the office, and he just wasn't a lot of fun to have around. Finally, I had to ask him to stop coming to work. It broke my heart, but it had to be done.

By then, he was a heavy-duty alcoholic. He went through DTs, and I got to see that first-hand. The doctor kept him off of booze for two days, and that was it. Daddy went those two days, and I was his night-sitter. He called me every foul name he could think of. He would make me get him up and take him to the bathroom, and then he couldn't go. I'd put him back into the bed, and a few minutes later he'd want to get up again and start swearing at me. When the doctor came in, I explained that my father was a hopeless alcoholic and that I would rather see him drink than suffer.

'I'll prescribe a fifth of Canadian Club every day. If you can put up with it, I guess it will be okay.'

That gave my daddy an open door to keep drinking, although he never did want my mother to see him drink, so he would keep the bottles out in the backyard.

My mother hated drinking. She didn't want anything to do with a bottle of whiskey. Once, when I was younger, she told me to pee in one of the bottles he hid outside.

When my mother asked me to do something, I did it. I went out there and found his stash and urinated in the bottles.

When my father went out there and pulled it out and took a slug, he gagged and spit it out.

'Who's been messing with my whiskey?' he shouted.

My mother came out and faced down my father.

'I told Alan to pee in that bottle, and he did what he was told to do.'

Pops died in July of 1970. He was only sixty-four years old.

Daddy and I were close. I could talk any way I wanted to around my father. He would listen to me.

I can remember going fishing with him when I was four years old. I went fishing with him every Sunday. That's how he spent his relaxing time.

I still miss you, Pops. I miss you like you just don't know. But I believe you're in heaven with Otis and Blue and Phil and Mother and Johnnie Taylor—and all the people gone before. You probably have a gig tonight, and I hope it goes well.

DREAMS OF MY BEST FRIENDS
SCENE THIRTY-THREE

I would love for Otis to be back here with me. I would give him more hugs than I've ever given anybody. His death affected me horribly. For a hard season, my life was terrible, and it took me a couple of years to stop thinking about suicide. I had beefed up my life insurance to two million dollars and meticulously planned how I was going to be accidentally killed. I figured I'd crawl through a fence while hunting. I legitimately had gone to buy the insurance so my wife would be taken care of after I was gone.

I loved Otis Redding, and Otis loved both Phil and me. He had an undying love for Phil because they started out together. Otis had a great respect for Phil's brain, as I did, but he loved me in a special way too. He would bring all of his personal problems to me. He shared his secrets with me, and he shared his dreams. He shared his fears, he shared his joys. We were a family. I loved Otis as much as I loved Phil, as much as Blue or my mother and father.

Otis believed in God. He and I talked about God quite a bit on the road. We talked about God and heaven and wives and sex and everything else. I don't think there was a subject we didn't cover. We kept each other awake, riding mile after mile along often dangerous country roads. It seemed like people hated us more because we were white and Black together.

We were at the Columbus City Auditorium, where we had a dispute with the club owner. We told the DJ that Otis wasn't feeling well, and after it was announced, everyone went nuts.

Otis and I ran out the back door and headed for a chain-link fence.

'Run, Red!' Otis screamed, as we both jumped over that fence. Then we fled home going ninety miles per hour on those dark, curvy, two-lane backroads.

We were known to make five- or six-hundred-mile jumps—Muscle Shoals was about three hundred and fifty miles from Macon. Stax, in Memphis, was almost five hundred miles. We talked about our wives and our family secrets. We shared everything. Those were some of the best times of my life, trying to keep each other awake.

Otis was an amazing driver. I've been with Otis when our Cadillac would be on two wheels and still make the curve. Sometimes I wasn't sure if either of us were awake. We spent hours and hours riding mile after mile, and we'd keep going. We'd run into some bad situations, and instead of making us do something crazy and end up getting arrested, it would just fuel our desire to make our relationship work more. It just gave us more gas.

And we dreamed. Dreaming was a big part of it and having an imagination. I've always had an excellent imagination.

After Otis's death, I had two very powerful and strange dreams—nightmares, really. In the first dream, I woke up in the middle of the night, and there, sitting at the end of the bed, was my father, with Otis standing behind him. At the time of the dream, my father was still alive.

'Come on, Pops. We gotta go,' Otis said to my father.

'I can't go, Otis,' my father told him. 'I need to stay here and work in the office and take care of business.'

The image of Otis and my father disappeared when I woke up. I felt strange and had to slap my face just to make sure. I called my mother the next day and she told me that my father had had the roughest night ever—that she thought he was going to die for sure.

I think my father actually started dying the minute he heard Otis was dead. He just gave up on life. That's the kind of effect Otis had on him. I do believe that when I dreamed of my father and Otis together, my father was close to death. He was being called to heaven on that very night.

In my second nightmare, Otis had not died in the crash. It was all a big publicity stunt that he had thought up, and he had just disappeared. I was so happy that he was alive, but when he turned around the whole back of his head was crushed, and I knew that he wouldn't ever be able to sing again. I remember thinking, *What will we do with Otis now? He can't sing with a caved-in head. What kind of position can we make for him with a crushed head?*

I woke up trembling.

No other artist ever fazed me like Otis did. None of them. As brilliant and innovative as The Allman Brothers Band were, and as talented as Lynyrd Skynyrd and The Outlaws were, they couldn't match Otis Redding's energy and drive. They did not understand how much energy and how much of his life he gave at every performance— in every note of every song—every moment he was on this earth.

Otis Redding was my partner, but he was also my best friend.

If I could see Otis again, I would say, 'I can't wait to see you out at the ranch. Maybe we could ride the horses? Maybe we could do some shooting, Otis. Let's have some fun. Let's go to Atlanta for the night and have some of those times like we did back in the old days—when we got tired and bored and took off for Atlanta for a night—just you and me. Your charisma attracted attention in every bar we went into. People bought you beer after beer, just so they could talk to you and get close to your cool. Those times were the most wonderful of my life. You taught me so much about life. Not just the music but about life. You had the best understanding of people of any person I knew. You understood things that the average white guy could never understand. Man, they are still playing you today. You changed peoples' lives all over the world, Otis. I have not known anyone to have as much impact on stage as you did. Maybe we can write a song or two.

'And Otis, your family is fantastic. Zelma has done an unbelievable job of raising the kids. And we get along good. I still put flowers on your grave every year on December 10th, Otis. When Zelma lost her leg, I was out there one year, and she was in the kitchen hopping all around and cooking. She was dancing around the kitchen, Otis, and laughing. I told her, You've got the best attitude of any amputee I've ever known, Zelma, and she responded, I lost Otis Redding, Alan. Losing a leg was nothing. That's how much she loved you, Otis.'

AFRICA SCREAMS
SCENE THIRTY-FOUR

Around 1968, I arranged to purchase a house for Percy Sledge in Macon—a house my father picked out, like he did for Otis. The house had huge hedges around it, and no one could see in. It had lots of privacy, with a guest house in the back for his mother.

The night before Percy moved in, some rednecks torched his house and burned the main house all the way to the ground. There was a gasoline trail going to his guest house. Kerosine soaked rags were found inside. Percy, his wife, his kids, or his mother could have been killed.

I was trying to move Percy into Macon to bring more attention to Macon, and whatever bastard set that fire destroyed every bit of that dream. I was even signing Percy's checks for him because he wanted me to help him budget his money. He worked so hard for that house, and he paid cash for it. My daughter Jessica wrote, 'Thank goodness my father had the insight to get enough insurance to the point where Percy got every bit of his money back.'

'Percy, I made a bad choice on this,' I told him. 'I just don't feel confident in handling your money, and with the experience you've been through, I think you need to learn to handle your finances for yourself.'

'It's all okay, Alan,' he told me.

Percy was a sweetheart of a guy. A great guy. I remained friends with him until his death.

When Percy Sledge played Trinidad and Barbados and all through the Caribbean—I think in 1969—he played out in the middle of the jungle. My father was with him as his road manager. He went out into the deep, deep jungle. Nothing but jungle. They drove way back into the jungle, and all of a sudden a field opened up and there's a little pavilion over a stage in case of rain. My father said nobody was there— not a soul around, except for some workers around the stage.

Percy and my father and the musicians did question the decision to play out in the boonies. Then, miraculously, people started walking out of the jungle. Not sure where they were coming from, but they kept on coming. They just kept coming and coming and coming, and that empty field was soon packed. Percy had one of the largest crowds ever in the middle of the jungle. And then the clouds moved in and the sky darkened. When Percy started to sing, the rain started. The rain turned into a downpour. Percy was under the shelter on the stage, and he looked out over the dense crowd of fans. And then he did something incredible.

'If y'all going to stay here in this rain to hear me, I'm coming out there with you,' Percy announced to the crowd. And he jumped off the stage and walked out into the crowd, and he stayed out there with his fans during the rain with an electric microphone. Percy sang out there with the people until the rain stopped. That's the kind of person he was.

One of Percy's biggest achievements was his tour of South Africa in 1970, because there had been a long boycott on Black entertainers playing over there. Percy was going to break it open. Tom Jones's American manager approached and asked me if I would be willing to have Percy Sledge go to South Africa for a show.

'I'd be interested. What did you have in mind?'

'I could pay him four thousand a week.'

'Six,' I countered, knowing that if an offer is made for four, they will usually go higher.

'Okay, six.'

'I want you to meet my other demands,' I told them. 'I want a four-member male vocal group, a four-member female group, and I want a twelve-piece orchestra with reading musicians to back Percy up. I want us to only be responsible for Percy, the road manager, and the orchestra director for the band.'

I also demanded two weeks' rehearsal when he first got there. They had to pay for all of that. Okay. Agreed. Percy opened at the Luxurama Theatre in Cape Town in May of 1970. He hit South Africa so hard that the white people were painting their faces to get into Black nightclubs to hear Percy. This was an indication of just how big this was shaping up to be. There was so much demand to see Percy that he was finally allowed to play in front of white audiences—the first Black man to play in front of an all-white audience. He was the first Black man to ever be admitted into a white hotel in South Africa.

Percy also made a movie over there that outgrossed *Gone With The Wind*, which was a very popular film in South Africa. The film was a documentary about Percy called *Soul Africa*. He had endorsements from Hush Puppies and Pepsi, so the money was rolling in. Percy captured the whole country. From the *New York Times*, dated June 11th, 1970, in an article entitled 'South Africa Relaxes Curb On Percy Sledge Audiences':

> The Government has relaxed restrictions on Percy Sledge, the American Negro singer, to allow him to appear before all-white audiences. The success of Mr. Sledge's South African tour has been so great that white fans have been clamoring to see him. The soul singer was originally restricted to appear before non-white audiences only. Some whites even tried to masquerade as colored in order to slip into his opening night show in Cape Town. On his nonwhite-only circuit it was estimated that Mr. Sledge would earn about $19,000. Now the estimates are doubled.

MACHINE GUN RONNIE THOMPSON AND STARING DOWN LESTER MADDOX
SCENE THIRTY-FIVE

In 1970, when Augusta was burning and rioting, Macon was a bit unhinged. We had a mayor named Ronnie Thompson who always referred to Otis as 'Macon's Goodwill Ambassador,' and I appreciated that about him—he spoke at Otis's funeral. Ronnie was also a popular gospel singer, and he had a gospel television show that was broadcast around the South. During his 1967 run and ultimate victory, he had the full support of Phil and myself, as well as Otis.

Ronnie was known as 'Machine Gun Ronnie' because he fired off a fully automatic machine gun in his backyard late one night. The moniker stuck, and I think he dug it. Definitely an old-school law-and-order man.

Ronnie managed to buy an army surplus armored-personnel vehicle, which was basically a tank, and during the unrest in Augusta, he drove it down Cherry Street to announce that there would be 'no damn riots in Macon, Georgia.' He issued a 'shoot to kill' order on anyone looting.

We didn't have a whole lot of segregation in Macon. We were certainly more mixed than most places in the South. A lot of Black acts came through and visited Macon because of the friendly hospitality there. Many of them moved to Macon. Of course, Percy Sledge got burned out, but that was more the exception than the rule. Macon had pretty good race relations. It wasn't perfect, but it was okay.

During a threat of a downtown boycott by the Black Liberation Front, Ronnie deputized the fire department to protect the stores. That didn't happen, and it sure didn't help race relations.

Ronnie found out there was a train of nerve gas coming through Macon. He felt that it was unsafe because, if the train had an accident, Macon would be dead. He went over to the tracks out near Wesleyan College and stood his ground right on the tracks. 'You ain't bringing that through Macon.' He stopped the train, and they never did come through.

Ronnie loved to hang around James Brown when he came to town. He borrowed James's car one night and wrecked it.

Ronnie would come by the office often, and we all liked him. He was misunderstood, for the most part. He wasn't like Lester Maddox, selling axe handles to beat African Americans. Lester was the governor of Georgia. He had an underground shop in Atlanta where he sold axe handles specifically aimed at hitting Black people. I knew about the shop, and I walked into it one night and just stood there staring at him.

'Can I do something for you?' Maddox asked.

'Nope,' I said, staring at him for as long as I could stand it. I stared at him a little longer, and then just turned and walked out.

Lester Maddox was loved by the rednecks. He remained governor until he was replaced with Jimmy Carter.

FREE AT LAST, FREE AT LAST, GOD ALMIGHTY, I'M SCARED TO DEATH!
SCENE THIRTY-SIX

There was a freedom-themed rally and concert for African Americans held in Philadelphia attended by the most powerful Black entertainers, politicians, and social activists in America. James Brown and Sam & Dave were slated to perform, and since Phil couldn't make it, he asked me to accompany them to the event.

There were only three white people at this show including myself. The singer Len Barry was another. Len had a big hit, '1-2-3,' and was scheduled to perform, but only because the organizers thought Len was Black, which caused great confusion and disappointment. I'm not exactly sure why the promoters didn't know Len was white. '1-2-3' did have a whole lot of soul, and one might think very easily that the singer was Black.

Len and I were the lonely white boys there, and when Len disappeared, that left me in the middle of eighteen thousand of the most angry people I have ever seen in my life. It was not a friendly day. Every step I took, someone wanted to start some shit. Stokely Carmichael was speaking, and I felt like all of those eighteen thousand brothers hated me to my very core.

I wanted to shout out to them that I had spent most of my young life promoting my Black brothers and sisters and that I loved them, and that I was actually *with* Sam & Dave, but I didn't get the chance. The problem was, I couldn't keep up with Sam & Dave. In the confusion, I got separated. They got through security and I was left outside. I didn't have my stage pass, and that was as far as I was getting. I started to panic. They left me and didn't seem to care where I was.

The only reason I brought Sam & Dave there was because they didn't want to perform for free. We had bought a new Cadillac for them in Macon, and their road manager, Bo Anderson, had driven it up. But now I was frightened. It was the scariest event I had ever been to.

I approached a policeman and asked for help, and even they were rude.

'You need to move out of here,' the cop told me.

So I walked into the alley behind the stage, and that alley was filled with people who, I thought, wanted to hurt me.

'Lord, don't let them cut me. Please just let them shoot me,' I prayed.

After the show, I was still looking for Sam & Dave, but they had left me. I thought I was going to be killed. A lot of people had been beat up. I'd hear things like, 'What's this white motherfucker doing here?'

I walked toward where I thought I might be able to get a cab or break loose, and then, miraculously, I heard a guy calling my name—his gold teeth shining in the moonlight. It was Bo Anderson!

I managed to get across the street and he maneuvered his car to me and I jumped in. Bo drove me back to the Ben Franklin Hotel. And even though I had a beautiful suite, I was too nervous and too afraid to sleep.

I went across the street to a bar and played a pinball machine all night just to calm myself down. I didn't speak to Sam & Dave for eighteen years.

I quit R&B after the freedom rally. Then, one day, I came back to assist my replacement settling in and found out the company was losing money, so I started coming to work every day again.

Phil didn't say 'go away.' He was glad to see me back, but we started having more fights over crazy things. I didn't want to do this for the rest of my life. I am not going to be hung out of any more damn windows.

All of a sudden, I was doing business with bad people. The R&B world was turning rotten, and I'm not sure of the reason. I was on the road, and one day I got into an argument with an entertainer, and his road manager threw brass knuckles on the table—the old-school jagged knuckles. The ones that twist and cut your face all up. I guess he wanted to prove how tough he was. I knew he carried a huge knife, too.

I told the singer, 'You really need those to whip me? You outweigh me by twenty pounds.'

He turned over his table of food, slapped the lady that was with him, and I knew it was on. I had my sport coat half off, but my arms were still in the sleeve. We wrestled around and I finally got it off. I grabbed him around the neck. We were in a corner, so I banged his head into one wall and then the other.

He went down to the floor, eyes rolling, and said, 'You are still a motherfucker.'

I said, 'I'm a motherfucker that is out of here.'

I resigned for the second and last time.

Soul music is still in my heart. In the sixties, people had relationships with songs. Soul music comes from the heart. A stone-cold heart. Otis Redding put the *S* and the *O* in soul music. He planted his soul in mine, and it is there where it lives. Otis could walk out in front of an audience, raise his hand, smile, and he had them.

THE PIANO
INTERLUDE
BY S.E. FEINBERG

One night, Alan and I were sitting on the front porch of Rumer and Rob's house—a large southern bungalow on Clisby Place. Otis Redding's upright piano sat in the hallway, and it was hard not to pass it without sitting down and noodling. If you want the Otis Redding vibe in Macon, there are plenty of places to find it—but, in my opinion, there was no better place than at his piano.

Alan took a swig of Diet Dr. Pepper and gave it time to work its way through. During these little conversations, I never knew what he was going to start talking about—a sort of free-flowing stream of consciousness that often produced gold.

Alan took another slow pull on his Dr. Pepper. This time, it seemed to stir a memory or two that may have been hanging around for quite some time.

A MOST SPLENDID RENAISSANCE

ACT TWO

LONGHAIRS, BEER, AND THE HOTTEST GUITARS IN THE WORLD
SCENE ONE

It was a change in season.

Otis would have dug southern rock 'n' roll. He liked lots of music. He would hear something in a singer's voice, and it didn't matter what style it was—pop, R&B, rock, jazz. He didn't care too much for country music. 'Too twangy,' he'd say.

It was after *Sgt. Pepper* that Otis started thinking about 'Dock Of The Bay.' That album was a major influence on him, and it inspired him to change direction in his musical style. And I think Otis would have dug and understood southern rock. Or at least appreciate it for what it was.

The Allman Brothers paved the way for all the southern rock bands. They were the ones who got up there and starved to death and took the heat.

I found out about Duane Allman from Phil. Phil first heard Duane over the phone, playing on the Wilson Pickett 'Hey Jude' session. He was talking to Jerry Wexler, and Jerry wanted to know what Phil thought of Wilson's 'Hey Jude.' Phil thought that Wilson sounded great, but he really wanted to know who in hell the guitar player was. Jerry explained that Duane was doing some things over with Rick Hall and that he was totally different from all the other musicians. This young guitarist was a scrappy hippie living in a tent outside the studio rather than getting a room. Jerry felt that Duane was a genius.

Rick Hall ended up agreeing to do a solo album for Duane. Phil went along with it, and Duane signed with Fame Records and cut about ten or eleven songs. Nobody was really impressed with them—though Duane was brilliant in the studio. Phil ended up buying Duane Allman's contract back from Rick Hall—Phil and Rick were good friends. So, the next thing I know, Phil is raving that he was going to form a whole band around this guy—one of the hottest guitarists in Muscle Shoals. Phil really believed Duane had something special, unique, and powerful. He and I had purchased the building for Capricorn, and we were set to go.

We wanted to get the best people we could around Duane. On drums we got Jaimoe, who had played with Percy Sledge and Joe Tex, and toured with Sam & Dave and Otis. Butch Trucks, Dickey Betts, and Berry Oakley filled out the slate—and, of course, Gregg Allman. Twiggs Lyndon had to be there if the Allman Brothers were to get serious about being organized to go on the road, and to watch over them in general. Twiggs thought the world revolved around Duane—eventually enough to get Duane's face tattooed on his arm.

Duane Allman and I got along real well. I used to let him ride my motorcycle before he got his Harley Sportster. I had a Kawasaki 250—it sounded like a sewing machine, but it was *shit to git.* Duane gave it back after he bought his Harley. I was driving one night, and a cicada bug hit my eye—I couldn't see a damn thing and I almost crashed. Another night, the police were on me, and I lost them on a curvy road. I hit a patch of sand and skidded into a death-defying skid, which headed me into the opposite direction—absolute miracle I'm alive to remember it. After that, I gave the bike to Phil. When Berry Oakley got killed, Phil's wife made him give the bike back to me.

I gave Duane my stereo for his first apartment, and he appreciated that. I think we respected each other. Gregg and I were friends too, and we stayed friends until later on. We used to do a lot of shooting out by my cabin. There was an old dump, and we'd shoot bottles and cans. He wasn't a very good shot, but he had fun. Gregg wasn't a good shot like Ronnie Van Zant. Ronnie knew how to shoot.

When the Allmans settled in Macon, a lot of people looked down on them because they were hippies, though they were redneck hippies. Redneck hippies love to fish. If you don't fish, you're not a redneck. I guess that was the difference between northern hippies and southern hippies, but even fishing didn't smooth the Allman Brothers out with the town right away. Macon was very leery about these strange kids and any stragglers that followed. We were verbally attacked. When the hippies came to town, we were blamed for bringing in drugs and all that goes with that scene. Phil and I were to blame—that's the way the people saw it. At the beginning, people saw us as a threat.

There was some resentment from the old money and the ruling class—the crowd that wanted to keep control of the city and not let these two Walden boys make tremendous money and build up a company that could very well change the face of the town. Forget all of that. They couldn't see that we were bringing money and goodwill to Macon.

What really brought the adults in Macon around were the kids. *Did you know Otis? Do you know the Walden brothers? What were you doing during the years of Otis Redding, The Allman Brothers Band, Lynyrd Skynyrd?*

Some parents tried to fake it and say they liked it, or they were very supportive. The kids would ask questions about it, and the answers didn't match the history, so we became very popular with the young people, especially with all of the free concerts we put on down in the park for several hundred people almost every Sunday—and the shows in Piedmont Park in Atlanta. Phil wanted the Allman Brothers to be 'the people's band,' so that's the direction we took.

Twiggs procured a little two-room apartment in Macon, and The Allman Brothers Band moved in, but to just one of those rooms. The second was used for storage. They all slept in sleeping bags on the hardwood floors. They didn't have a television, so Twiggs showed home movies of us on motorcycles and riding backward on bicycles and such, and they would all get stoned and watch these movies over and over again. This band loved pot and mushrooms, primarily.

On one of the walls, Twiggs painted a large yellow and blue dot. The whole wall ended up being a big frame, and right in the middle was perfect for showing the movies—a kind of psychedelic art. They lived over there for about a year, all of them packed into one little room. Twiggs put in a Coke machine that dispensed cold Budweiser—they could get all the cold beer they wanted, right there in the apartment. That's about all the furniture there was in there.

The police gave us a good bit of harassment at the beginning. Phil and I and the guys were in the studio late. We'd often be there all night, doing one of our 'suicide sessions.' The vice squad of Macon decided to bust the studio, thinking we were all back there, smoking dope and up to no good in general. The front of the building still looked like an abandoned furniture store. I met the cops and locked the door behind me. I told them the door was a deadbolt and I would have to get a key.

The cops gave me thirty seconds to unlock the door or they were going to break it down. So I unlocked the door, knowing damn well we weren't doing anything illegal, and they came in—and man, they were all strong arms and buffalo chests blown out, trying to start an argument with anybody. One cop went up to Phil and laid into him with a major stick up his ass.

'Oh yeah. *Mister* Phil Walden, the music-business big shot in Macon. What are you doing back here, smoking a little dope?'

Phil got as serious as a wounded rattlesnake.

'We're thinking about a recording session.'

'Well, this ain't no recording studio,' the cop said. He didn't realize he was near the entrance to the control room.

'Excuse me, officer,' Phil said, and he lit up the big room.

Boom! Lights up!

'Oh, it *is* a recording studio!' the cop said, very surprised.

'I've had enough,' Phil told the cop. 'We're ready to get back to work. You need to leave here.'

The cops reluctantly left and went outside but they hung around, leaning against the trees—all around the building and the street. We got a little scared and figured they were interested in grabbing us one at a time to rouse us up a bit. I did remember I had some pot on me— they could have busted me at the door and got what they were looking for—so I slipped the bag to my wife, and she stuck it down her pants. We decided to get out of there one at a time.

One of the Allman Brothers roadies jumped on his motorcycle and took off, which pissed off the cops for some reason. A cop fired a shot at him—the roadie kept going. That's what we had to deal with around Macon. It was hard going.

A photographer came down to take pictures of The Allman Brothers Band—this poor northern boy out in the Georgia woods with this wild southern rock 'n' roll band. He wanted a photo of the band sitting naked in a creek. But they said if he was going to take their pictures nude, he had to be nude as well. So he stripped off his clothes and shot the session—the photographer and the band naked.

At some point during the session, Dickey Betts decided it would be a good idea to steal the photographer's clothes and hide them. This poor guy was in the woods, scared and naked. They told him they were going to leave him out there, and he was almost in tears before they gave him his pants back.

That was one hell of a day. They were supposed to be taking a bubble bath in the creek, but the water was moving so fast, the bubbles washed away—they just wound up naked in the creek, sitting there like a bunch of raccoons.

COVER OF ROLLING STONE?
SCENE TWO

I call Boz Scaggs the Sinatra of rock 'n' roll. He's got one of the mellowest voices I've ever heard in my life. I love Boz. He came to Macon pretending to be a writer for *Rolling Stone*, and I spent three days wining and dining him, thinking I was getting close to *Rolling Stone*.

By the third day, I thought I might make the cover, I was that excited. Then Boz comes in on the fourth day and he tells me that he isn't really a writer for *Rolling Stone*. Man, my face dropped. I was so damn mad I couldn't believe it. I've been entertaining this guy left and right, going to dinner and picking up the tab and everything. But with all of that, I still liked Boz. I liked him as a person. Boz is the kind of guy who could mess you over but you still liked him—that's kind of a rare quality in people.

After Boz told me he wasn't a writer for *Rolling Stone*, he knew that I was disappointed—all of my fantasies tossed out the window. So then he tells me he's a guitar player, and I'm sitting there thinking, *We've got Duane Allman, Johnny Jenkins, Dickey Betts, Pete Carr—all excellent guitar players right here in Macon already. We really don't need another guitar player.* What was he trying to pull? And then he told me he'd played with The Steve Miller Band and had three platinum records. He was with Miller on Atlantic and Capitol. We knew the same people, but it never occurred to me to question his stories. I had been in R&B for many years and I'd never had a platinum record. That kind of changed the whole tone of my attitude.

Boz and Steve were in school together at the University of Wisconsin in Madison, up near where Otis was killed. Boz was smart. He spoke with intelligence, and he was extremely well-read, in the music business and all subjects.

'Okay, what is the real reason you're in Macon?' I asked, figuring that eventually Boz would have to tell me the truth.

'I wanted to come in here and feel you out to see if you'd be interested in managing me.'

'Okay then. Now we have something to talk about.'

I brought Boz into an R&B session with Thomas Bailey after the guitar player scheduled couldn't show up. Boz had been playing R&B for years—here and in Europe. Anyway, Boz was Jann Wenner's friend—the editor of *Rolling Stone*. Jann used to spend about every other weekend in Macon. Maybe there was some hope for that cover after all.

Boz was very interested in Duane playing on 'Loan Me A Dime,' which Jann would wind up producing.

Duane waltzed into the office, guitar in hand.

'I'm going over to play with Boz Scaggs. I'm really looking forward to it. But I will show him he should never pick up a guitar around me.'

Duane walked into a Muscle Shoals Sound Studio bathroom with his Les Paul and closed the door. He played the entire session while someone kept passing him weed. He played his ass off, right there in the bathroom. The album, *Boz Scaggs*, came out on Atlantic.

I moved Boz into my log cabin—him and his very beautiful girlfriend, Carmella Storniola. She was a gorgeous woman—jet black hair, olive complexion, high cheeks, big lips—you could just sit and stare at her for days. The log cabin was at the end of a dirt road, and it wasn't exactly safe for an attractive gal. She'd leave the doors unlocked and was not at all security conscious. I went out there and found her in a bikini, walking down the dirt road.

'You don't do that in the woods in Georgia. Someone might come along and rape you and kill you in a heartbeat,' I explained.

But she wasn't scared. She was naïve about the whole thing and trusted everyone. No matter how many times I told her, she'd still leave the cabin door unlocked. I'd go out and have dinner with her just to make sure she was okay.

I didn't book Boz for shows. All he wanted to do was hang out in my cabin and play music.

Boz scored with 'Lowdown' in 1976: '*Dirty, dirty, dirty, dirty lowdown.*' He was a super entertainer. He could sing Jimmy Rodgers to Percy Sledge, and he always had a smooth, mellow voice. Boz was the first person I ever saw get a standing ovation at the *beginning* of their concert—that was when he played at the Freddie Brown Amphitheater in Peachtree City, Georgia.

TEMPORARILY INSANE DUE TO TOURING WITH A ROCK 'N' ROLL BAND
SCENE THREE

The Allman Brothers Band were playing in some pretty rough clubs at the beginning, during the tour for their first album. They starved and panhandled to get places and to get money enough to make it through the toll bridges in their Winnebago and buy food and beer—dues being paid for every mile traveled and every can of Bud opened. That's how broke they were, but they kept going and kept going. They had that old southern determination. You get a southerner that's determined and he's probably going to get where he's going. He might take a little longer, but if he's determined, he'll get there.

Up in North Buffalo, the Brothers were playing in a club popular with the mob called Aliotta's Lounge. The owner of the club, this big Italian guy named Angelo Aliotta, wanted to pay the band five hundred dollars instead of the thousand he owed them. Berry Oakley got Twiggs over at the hotel. Twiggs, pretty hopped up from eating speed—trying to stay awake to manage the details of the tour—grabbed a Dutch fishing knife he had bought as a present for Duane and headed for trouble over at the club.

'Man, I don't want to argue with you,' Twiggs told Aliotta. 'But you're going to pay us the money.'

So Twiggs called me, and I told him to leave Buffalo and we would deal with the problem from Macon. Some college kid who had booked the band at the club was there, trying to figure a way out of the mess, but the owner kept going after Twiggs and bullying him and getting in his face. I got on the line with the college kid and arranged that he would go somewhere out of the heat and give Twiggs five hundred dollars, which gave him the entire thousand.

Twiggs returned to the stage after we spoke to him, and then Aliotta was there again, chewing on the bit and giving more hell to Twiggs. The roadies pleaded with Twiggs that it was time to pack up and get the hell out of Dodge, but Twiggs's blood was up, and Aliotta wouldn't back down either.

'I'll kick your damned ass,' Alliota warned Twiggs.

'You ain't going to kick *my* ass. You owe us five hundred dollars, and you're going to pay it!'

'I think I just might kick your ass!' Alliota threatened, and charged Twiggs.

Twiggs pulled the knife as the club owner got on him. Twiggs stuck the man three times in the gut—stuck him real deep. The roadies jumped over the equipment and wanted to pull out fast. Aliotta was spurting blood from the three deep holes Twiggs put into him, and someone shouted to call an ambulance.

'It's a little late for that,' Aliotta moaned, and he dropped over dead, or as good as dead. He was dead in an hour. Twiggs just sat down on the stage and waited for the police.

'I stuck him,' he drawled. 'I don't care if I get the electric chair. I proved a point,' he added, as quoted in David Krajicek's account in the *Daily News*.

Twiggs was charged with first degree murder in Buffalo, New York, and The Allman Brothers Band headed for Cleveland without him.

Our lawyer was John Condon. John was known as a 'Perry Mason' type. He came to Macon and interviewed over four hundred people about Twiggs. He had two hearing aids, but he was the best criminal lawyer anyone could get.

In court, Condon proved that Twiggs was out of his mind and had been popping speed for three days to keep the band going during the grueling tour. Condon got Twiggs declared temporarily insane at the time of the stabbing—temporarily insane due to touring with a rock 'n' roll band. The judge reduced the sentence to six months in a mental hospital—he had been in jail for eighteen months before the trial began.

Phil and I called Twiggs at Christmas.

'Do y'all have Santa Claus up there?' Phil asked.

'We have nineteen Santa Clauses, twelve Easter Bunnies, and a good Tooth Fairy.' Twiggs replied.

Twiggs made the best of his time in prison. When he got to the psych ward, he organized an algebra class for the 'patients.'

After The Allman Brothers Band hit, everybody loved them. They could park their car on top of Macon City Hall if they wanted to. They even donated televisions to the jail—they put the televisions in the jail so they could watch television when they were arrested. But that wasn't likely to happen, because all of a sudden they owned the town. I think they just wanted to make someone's stay a little more comfortable. One day, they gave away sixty-four thousand dollars to charity, and they would play free dates on Sundays, inviting all the musicians from out of town to jam, and it was free to see some of the biggest names in the business. Those were some great days.

Then I got a call from my mother, and she told me that she just got a call saying that Duane Allman had crashed and was in a serious condition at Macon Medical Center. He collided with a large truck loaded down with a crane and slid along the road, sustaining massive bodily damage.

I headed for Phil's office—he was out traveling with Joe Galkin, somewhere down near Bimini. They were out on a boat and couldn't be reached for quite a long time. Carolyn finally got him on the phone, and the connection wasn't great.

'Is there anything I can do?' I asked Phil. 'I'll do whatever you tell me to do. I'm so sorry to hear that you lost another artist.'

'Duane Allman's death is a very personal loss,' Phil told Jon Landau, for his article in *Rolling Stone*, 'not only for the no-nonsense, straight-ahead music he created, but for the warm and sincere friendship we shared. To remember Duane is to recall his music, and that exactly is what the man was all about.'

Ordinarily, this would end the career of a band, but Phil had lived through the death of Otis Redding, and he knew how record sales were going to skyrocket. He immediately put them back to work and suggested they not be so sad and to get through it—to end the mourning and get back to work, like he said after Otis's funeral.

Phil wanted to push forward. That was the big thing for him. He put more energy into the band. Dickey Betts was trying to do all of the guitar work himself, but Phil added Chuck Leavell, which made it easier on Dickey.

The Allman Brothers Band made some fantastic history. These guys were the first band from the South to reach that very high level of success. They were authentic stars. At the Summer Jam in Watkins Glen, The Allman Brothers Band soared. *Brothers & Sisters* entered the charts at #1 with a bullet and went platinum—that was my brother's hard work. He understood promotion and how to run a record company. When they hit #1, I had to salute it—but, more importantly, I had to salute my brother.

The Allman Brothers Band did a lot of good in the early years but, after Duane's death, Gregg and Dickey started having problems. Dickey loved to drink, and he loved to fight when he got drunk. And he could fight. Big time. There was some dissension between them.

I used to love Gregg Allman. I thought the world of him. But he let me down. He burned our friendship and he ruined our friendship. He tore up people who helped him rise. He destroyed the bridges that were built for him to succeed. For him to say anything bad about my brother—who gave his wealth and his spirit to The Allman Brothers Band—was just so stupid, because nobody believed in Gregg more than Phil Walden. Phil had probably sunk four or five hundred thousand dollars into this band and pretty well stripped the company of all the other revenues. He drained the company for this band. Nobody believed in a band like Phil believed in this one.

Gregg accusing Phil of stealing money was petty and small. But Gregg always accused people of doing things. Phil put him in several institutions to dry him out—he was an alcoholic and a junkie. I think he was just paranoid because of the drugs.

I tried to get the two of them back together, but after about six days I knew that it was pointless. Gregg and Phil would never get back together because they kept adding more and more to the *he's got to* and *he's got to*. I was spending more time than I needed on healing a wound that wasn't going to heal. I did it out of friendship for Gregg and love for my brother. But Gregg let me down. He let a lot of people down—a lot of the people who helped him. It was a sad day for me when I had to write him off as a friend.

BROTHERS AGAINST BROTHERS
SCENE FOUR

Over time, Phil and I began to have more disagreements. With the success of the Allman Brothers, Phil started to act like a star himself. He was the celebrity of the whole thing. It all started going to his head.

Prior to my departure from Capricorn, I know I accounted for at least the same amount of income as Phil did. Some weeks, I'd book a hundred thousand dollars' worth of dates, and sometimes we had thirty percent commission—twenty percent for the management and ten for the agency. I was one of the true early pioneers of Capricorn Records, but I can't take credit for any of the success of Capricorn because I left just as The Allman Brothers Band put out their second record, *Idlewild South*. I don't take any credit for any of the success other than I put my money and my blood into it in the very early days, and I enjoyed recording there, and I used the facility after I separated from Phil. But while I was at Capricorn, I was the office manager, I was the accountant, I was the booking agent, I was a manager, I was a publisher, and I was a promoter.

I'd always let all the gold records and stories and everything be dominated by Phil, but I was the man behind the scene. I stayed in the background and just did my work. I didn't care about fame. I was money motivated. I loved music, but I also loved making money, and I didn't care about celebrity and the trappings that went with it.

We were in New York one night, and Phil was in another room and had gotten intoxicated. Very seldom did you see Phil drunk. He could drink a half bottle of scotch and get creative, like a genius at work—in fact, he probably was a genius, thinking about all the things he did accomplish. I call him the genius of the Walden family.

Phil was drunk and we started talking.

'All you ever think about is pussy,' he snarled.

'Excuse me, Phil. But what was that I just saw leave this room?'

And then he turned real ugly.

'You're just hanging onto my shirttail.'

I did the books for the company, so I knew how much I generated. When I did something good, Phil was complimentary. I pulled some deals that even surprised him—like when Percy Sledge gave us our first #1 record. I lived with that, but it never would go away. It hurt me. It was always on my mind.

Phil and I developed some hate for each other. I got tired of taking the shit. I was starting to make some real money myself. The next thing I knew, he needs to borrow money from me.

When Phil was doing a lot of coke, he was a real bastard. Maybe he and I were the problem, not the Allman Brothers.

Later on, if Skynyrd was going to play with the Allman Brothers, we'd have to bring our own piano. Chuck Leavell didn't want anyone playing *his* piano. I didn't know if it was Chuck or the road manager talking—just little things to aggravate every date that we did together, to the point I wanted us to just do our dates and let them do theirs.

One night, Billy Powell cut his finger and it was bleeding and getting on the keys of Chuck's grand. Billy was trying to wipe the blood off the keys and trying to be so careful. He was embarrassed. We knew how to respect a damn white grand piano. We wanted one for Billy Powell—and we got one.

I wanted to get as far away from Phil as possible. I couldn't shake it. My brother thought I was just hanging on. Maybe it was the coke starting to kick in. Drugs had a lot to do with it. Phil's personality changed. With the cocaine, he went on a big ego trip. He got to the point where he thought he was as much of a star as anyone else. He'd jump on everybody—a cab driver, a policeman—he didn't care. When he got hot, he was hot.

Phil and I physically fought a few times. I remember one particular fight with me, Phil, and Blue. Phil and I started fighting, and we had one of these big old open-faced fans without a grill and just the blades spinning. We were fighting and rolling and were going straight into that damn fan. Blue took those big hands of his and grabbed the fan blade and held it still—a miracle he didn't chop his fingers off, but he was that strong.

'Y'all go ahead and just work it out,' Blue told us.

I sold Phil all of my stock in every company except Redwal. I sold Phil my part of No Exit Music, which turned out to be a multi-million-dollar company. I sold my share of Capricorn Records and Walden Artists, all for nine thousand dollars cash. I kept my Eldorado, my adding machine, my phone book, and my IBM typewriter.

The stock alone was worth a half-million dollars. I let it all go for nine thousand, plus those few things, because I wanted to leave Phil in peace. I didn't want us to be arguing. I just wanted to do something on my own. Prove to myself that I could do it on my own. I didn't like the idea of riding on anybody's shirttail. So I left. And immediately went broke.

I was used to making about ninety thousand a year—kind of hard to do when it is cut completely off. Even when I had Lynyrd Skynyrd, I was still running out of money all the time. And Phil was over there getting filthy rich. He was smoking. He was starting to really sell records.

Did I make a mistake? I was over there making a lot of money, and now I'm over here broke and spending a lot of money I really don't have. Not only that but when I left Phil, a lot of doors slammed in my face. People who I thought liked us both didn't give a rat's ass about me because I was the one doing the audits.

A lot of people got mad when I went over their books and slammed the door on me. I didn't realize it, but a lot of people put up with me only because Phil was my brother. After I left, a lot of these people didn't return my phone calls.

A PRAYER IN A
COTTON FIELD
SCENE FIVE

In the beginning of trying to strike out on my own, I was going broke. The Allman Brothers Band were shooting up the charts, and I'm thinking, *God, if I was over there, I'd be making good money and here I am trying to pay the power bill.*

Alan, you really screwed up, I thought to myself.

I had to go to Muscle Shoals. I had to work in the studios for five or six months, doing what I could to promote and book acts. I was living off of canned salmon, onions, and vinegar. I made a few deals and made them some money, and I got some capital to roll with. There was a group called Smith, Perkins & Smith started by Wayne Perkins, a very successful and killer studio guitarist at Muscle Shoals. He worked with so many great talents—Eric Clapton, Steve Cropper, The Rolling Stones. And, man, the record company heard this band and they started talking like they had found the next Beatles right in Alabama. Wayne Perkins was something else.

I got the deal to a hundred thousand to sign them, and I could run the Muscle Shoals Sound Production company for at least a year. But a funny thing happened on the way to a deal. I kept seeing the deal dwindle and break down. The next thing I knew, the record company wanted the band to sign for thirty-nine thousand. I knew somebody was leaking information to weaken my position.

I went over to a meeting and told five different people individually, swearing them to confidence not to breathe a word, that I sold the band for a million dollars. About five o'clock that day, I heard five different lies, so every one of them leaked that I sold the band for a million dollars.

I was packing my bags when Barry Beckett from the Muscle Shoals Rhythm Section came in.

'What's going on?'

'No one here can keep their damn mouths shut, and I can't negotiate with all the leaking out information.'

The band had never been in front of a live audience. They went on a tour for a year but they couldn't hold, and it fell apart.

When I left Muscle Shoals, I had a hundred dollars in my pocket and a hundred-and-eighty-thousand-dollar debt, and my deal had just gone to shit. I got about forty miles out of town and my fuel pump went out in my Cadillac Eldorado. The tow truck arrived after five, so he charged me overtime.

I was heading down to the bottom. I had arrived at that old crossroads. I walked out in the middle of a cotton field and started to feel like Robert Johnson before he sold his soul to the devil, except I took a different tack—a direction with a much more positive backend. I started talking to God rather than the devil, right there in that cotton field.

'God, I'm not going to quit. I'm not going to give up. Help me, Lord, to keep going.'

A cool wind wafted in over the cotton, cooling me down and bringing me a bit of peace.

When I got back home, Gary Donehoo was discouraged with how things were working out. He had had enough of the music business. He married a young girl and she wanted him to settle down and sell insurance. And that was Gary Donehoo. He had been with me for a few years and was my most loyal employee. I trusted Gary with everything. I trusted him totally.

Gary drove me back and forth to Alabama probably a hundred and fifty times in that Cadillac. One night when he was driving, I woke up to the bumpety-bumping of the tires because he was driving the car down the railroad tracks. I panicked.

'What the hell are you doing? We're going to get hit by a train!' I screamed.

'It'll be okay! I can make a left at the next crossroads.' Gary told me back.

We were both exhausted.

I had shut down my office on Walnut Street and was living and working out in the log cabin and using the garage as my office. My secretary came out there when I needed her. I figured if I moved out into the country, I'd get some work done. I never missed a beat.

THE TOUGHEST KIDS
IN THE WORLD
SCENE SIX

I opened Hustler's Inc. on April Fools' Day, 1970. This was before Larry Flynt's magazine. I named it for my hard and strict work ethic. I set Hustler's Inc up as a publishing company first and then a management company. I wanted to find my band and very much expected to control the publishing. Publishing is everything. Songs. That's the secret of success. Songs. You want to own the songs.

I had made friends with Eddie Floyd. Eddie was Mr. 'Knock On Wood,' 'California Girl,' 'Bring It On Home To Me.' He was my original partner in Hustler's Inc., but I caught him at a bad time because he was having financial issues—bad investments and tax problems. I made Eddie a partner and took him in for a time, but he wasn't able to contribute anything to keep the doors open. We had to dissolve our relationship because of that. So I got Gary Donehoo to put in some money and take Eddie's stock.

Al Green was the best artist with Hustler's Inc. He was the first artist I sent a contract to. He had a country-music lawyer, and during the negotiations I told Al, 'If you go with your stupid, cornpone damn lawyer, he'll screw you. I ain't going to do it.'

I have lots of regrets. I regret being rough with Al Green. I said some very stupid things that I wish I had never said. Lots of regrets.

Al Green could out-sing anybody out there. When his first hit album came out, I picked 'Tired Of Being Alone' as the single, and I was right. It hit #11 on *Billboard*'s Top 100. Al cut so many beautiful love songs. When his girlfriend committed suicide at his house, he stopped singing secular music for a while and began singing gospel, and he even became a preacher in a church in Memphis. Al Green came close to capturing Otis's audience. He had a very soulful audience, and Al Green was soulfully pop.

My dream was to be like Brian Epstein with The Beatles and Colonel Tom Parker with Elvis Presley—Elvis stuck with Colonel Tom and The Beatles stuck with Epstein after success. I wanted to be like them. I wanted one band and to worry only about that one band—put my heart and soul into that one band. And so I went out and auditioned

a hundred and eighty-seven bands in one year. That's a lot of bands—
thirteen to seventeen bands in a day, sometimes. I covered Louisiana,
Alabama, Tennessee, North and South Carolina, Florida, Georgia, and
even went as far up as Toronto and Quebec City in Canada.

The audition and travel scene of trying to find my perfect act was
driving me even broker than I was, but I wanted to make sure I got the
right one. I had faith that that prayer in the cotton field was going to
come into play. I knew the band was out there somewhere. I traveled
the country looking for bands and had my share of burgers, cheap
steaks, and lonely hotel rooms. I was looking for magic. I didn't know
what it sounded like, but I knew when I heard it, I'd know it. It was
like hunting for a tiger: you may not know where it's hiding, but when
it jumps out of the bush, you know damn well you found it.

On my first trip out on auditions, I went to Jacksonville, Florida,
to an old warehouse. We had thirteen bands there, set up by a Mercer
student. The young man was a very straight type of guy, and he didn't
want anybody smoking grass or anything like that. He did a good job
of organizing the scene.

Skynyrd was band number thirteen—Ronnie Van Zant, Allen
Collins, Gary Rossington, Larry Junstrom, and Bob Burns. They came
out with both barrels loaded. Allen Collins was down on the floor,
doing splits, playing behind his neck, upside down—every gimmick
he could think of—he was always the one on the stage moving. They
did a fantastic audition, and that audition included 'Free Bird.' I made
a note about the group and the song—something to definitely think
about. After they finished, I told them that I was very impressed but
that I had other bands to hear. I explained that I was still going to
audition a lot of bands, but if they could stay with me and show me

that they could hold up on the road for a bit longer then I would be back. They understood.

'By any chance, do any of you boys have a joint?' I asked, and five or six joints came flying at me.

At the end, I did come back to band number thirteen—Lynyrd Skynyrd. I also wanted a band called Orgone Zable, with Mickey Thomas as lead singer—a great singer with definite star power. Mickey would go on to sing lead on Elvin Bishop's 'I Fooled Around And Fell In Love,' and then he'd join Jefferson Starship. Orgone Zable were a tight, southern band, and they had everything it took to get up the mountain. I signed the two bands with strange names and headed for Muscle Shoals to cut some demos.

I auditioned Grinderswitch on the same day I auditioned Lynyrd Skynyrd. Grinderswitch would later come out on Capricorn with their album *Honest To Goodness*. I wasn't hearing it that day, and I knew it wasn't quite what I was looking for. Guitarist Dru Lombar was the leader of the band. Larry Howard was on guitar. Joe Dan Petty, who had been working with The Allman Brothers Band as a guitar tech, was on bass, and Ricky Burnett was on drums.

Every time I saw Larry, he was messed up. He always had a cast on from breaking an arm or breaking a leg—he was always bandaged up for one reason or another. He stayed drunk and high most of the time. He was pretty much a basket case as far as I was concerned.

After many years, one day I opened my office door on Broadway, and there stood Larry Howard. I didn't even recognize him. He was clean cut, sober, and he was cast and bandage free. He was also drug and alcohol free. I would eventually do a gospel album with him.

Larry died not too long ago. I was asked to speak at his funeral.

When he was dying, a fund was set up for Larry, and he was asked who he wanted to accept the checks that came in. He insisted that I do it. The Georgia Music Hall of Fame paid tribute to him, and he asked me to come to the event.

Larry and his wife, Peggy, helped me through my second divorce. I was a mess and drinking like crazy, and I was one miserable human being. When Larry gave up booze, he became a minister and traveled the world, including deep into the Russian prison system, where no American had ever been. I was so messed up that I thought I was possessed. Larry grabbed me by the head and said, 'Lord, Jesus. Heal this man! Get him over his pain, Lord. I'm demanding it!' I had never demanded anything from Jesus.

I got through the pain, and I don't think I could have made it without Larry's help. I took him on for the big picture.

I started making demos for Lynyrd Skynyrd and Orgone Zable at David Johnson's Broadway Sound. The fellow who owned the studio with David Johnson was more interested in buying gold and playing golf, and he couldn't stand to be around any pressure. We didn't have a whole lot of time or money, and I had to keep things moving. Everything was going too slowly, so I moved both of the bands over to Jimmy Johnson at Muscle Shoals Sound. We had a week to record all of our demos. It was good to renew my relationship with Jimmy. He was so far ahead.

Skynyrd worked the graveyard and Orgone Zable in the day— Orgone Zable went home at night. Jimmy produced Skynyrd and Barry Beckett produced Orgone Zable. We kind of gave Orgone Zable the first-class treatment. They had an apartment with a television and a girl cooking for them, and they slept in beds—first class all the way.

Lynyrd Skynyrd slept in a second-rate truck-stop motel without even a television in the room. There was nothing to do but play basketball on a hoop nailed to a wall against the back of the motel. They walked to the market and bought a huge jar of peanut butter and bread, and for that week they returned from the all-night sessions, ate peanut butter sandwiches, shot hoops, drank, and slept.

Ronnie would go over to the studio in the day to learn as much as he could from being around the master, Jimmy Johnson. They didn't have any money. I didn't flaunt any money in front of them because I wanted to see how strong they really were. They were very strong, they were talented, and they had great attitudes. That is the combination that unlocks the mystery to success in the music business.

We got to the end of the week and I met with Barry Beckett and the band, and I listened to three very good songs from Orgone Zable.

'We got three good ones,' Barry told me. But the songs didn't have anything that showed the magic of being hits. They were tight, very good songs. But they weren't *great* songs.

Then I met with Jimmy Johnson.

'How many you get with Skynyrd?' I asked.

'We got fourteen songs,' Jimmy said. We listened and they were all as tight as a tick. Every song was slamming me in the head—every song a potential hit. That made up my mind to cut Orgone Zable loose and run with Skynyrd. I had found my band.

I moved to Muscle Shoals to make sure they got the album down, and we recorded about an album and half. Skynyrd really learned how to record at Muscle Shoals Sound. Roger Hawkins—Roger was with Muscle Shoals Rhythm and had been on dozens and dozens of hits, including 'When A Man Loves A Woman,' Wilson Pickett's 'Hey Jude' with Duane Allman on guitar, Aretha Franklin's 'Respect,' and so many others.

It took a couple of hours to tune Bob Burns's drums because they were so much out of tune. Bob had never heard about tuning drums. I didn't know you tuned drums, either. I never got into that technical stuff. I couldn't tell you if you were playing B-flat or what. I can't even tune a radio. But I've got a common ear, so I hear what the average public hears. I can pretty well spot a hit. I was good at picking hits.

LYNYRD SKYNYRD—
TURN IT UP!
SCENE SEVEN

Now Muscle Shoals has got the Swampers
And they've been known to pick a song or two (yes they do)
Lord, they get me off so much
They pick me up when I'm feeling blue, now how 'bout you?
—'Sweet Home Alabama,' Ronnie Van Zant,
Gary Rossington, Edward King

Lynyrd Skynyrd was a masculine band. Their music was tough and the band was tough. They let you know how tough they were in their music. They were *burning* in their performances. They weren't there just to play around. They were a serious band. They were the showstoppers. They could destroy any audience. When I walked onto the stage with these guys, the hair on the back of my neck stood up. I felt like a gladiator going into the arena. We were out to kill and be the hottest band at any concert.

I think about all of these record companies that turned down Skynyrd, believing they sounded too much like The Allman Brothers Band. I ask you to put on a Lynyrd Skynyrd record and then put on an Allman Brothers Band back-to-back. They both are playing southern music, but Lynyrd Skynyrd were *jukin'*. The Allman Brothers played mixtures of jazz and southern rock. Skynyrd were a honky-tonkin' rock 'n' roll band.

The Allman Brothers Band were not swampers. Skynyrd had a different sound. Later on, after I had stopped being their manager, they did cop a bit of an Allman Brothers feel on some of their songs. But earlier, there were no songs that sounded like The Allman Brothers Band. The only similarities were that they were southern boys, had lots of guitars, had long hair, had rough-sounding singers, and they all drank like fish—though nobody drank more than Skynyrd. Skynyrd came from the swamp, just like an alligator or a water moccasin, and they were just as deadly—musically and often physically. They were a swampy street gang with guitars.

Swamp music is music that comes out of the swamp. It has a special 'swamp' feeling to it—an earthy sound. Like heavy air on a humid night in the bayou. It came out of swamp blues—old swampers like Lonesome Sundown and Whispering Smith and Tony Joe White, with his 'Poke Salad Annie.' Skynyrd was dripping with swamp water. Ironically, Ronnie would die in the swamp.

Oh, Fetch me a cane pole mama
Goin' to catch a brim or maybe two

Part of the heartbreak of so much rejection early on was that record companies didn't tell us to send some more songs, they just passed—passed without comment. *We don't want you. End of the road, Jack. Ain't no sense in talking to us. We've made our minds up.* They passed, and they really meant it. Nine record companies had turned us down—including my own brother and Capricorn, as well as Atlantic, Columbia, Warners, A&M, RCA, Epic, Elektra, and Polydor.

Several times, it looked like there was no way in hell Lynyrd Skynyrd would get a deal, because there were too many people taking a pass—negativity spreads in the record business. But something in the back of my mind kept telling me that the record companies were wrong and I was right. That spirit kept me driving—kept me being a force. Maybe it had something to do with making the right decision standing out in that cotton field on my way home from Muscle Shoals.

When you believe in something hard enough, you can't be beat and you can't be torn up—can't be destroyed. There are too many great artists who never made it to the top of the mountain because of getting beat back so much. They gave up because they couldn't take it anymore, and I can't blame any of them. It had nothing to do with talent. Bear in mind, they turned down Skynyrd after hearing 'Gimme Three Steps,' 'Simple Man,' and 'Free Bird'! DON'T EVER GIVE UP!

Starting in 1971, during the southern music explosion, most of the time you wound up at Grant's Lounge. Our hospitality is famous. We rolled out the carpet to people we felt were going to be on the side of the southern movement. If a band wanted Phil and me to see them, they would book Grant's Lounge, and we'd check them out. When I put Lynyrd Skynyrd in there, they'd start singing a cappella on the stage and making harmonies—that would draw the crowd closer to them, closer to the stage. Then we kicked those amplifiers up full force and knocked them all the way to the back like a hurricane wind. The power was devastating.

We had people in from London and Paris and all over ending up at Grant's Lounge to hang out for a weekend. We did a lot of business in Grant's. People still come to Grant's to feel the vibe of those days. I guess you could say it was Macon's top club at the time—Boz Scaggs, The Marshall Tucker Band, The Allman Brothers Band, Lynyrd Skynyrd, The Outlaws, Wet Willie, Eddie Hinton, Tom Petty, Grinderswitch, Bonnie Bramlett. Everyone made the Grant's Lounge scene.

One night after a Skynyrd set at Grant's Lounge, Phil tried to convince me that Ronnie was too cocky, he couldn't sing, and his songs were weak, and to drop them because they weren't worth it—and of course they sounded too much like the Allman Brothers, in Phil's opinion. It was just denial, denial, denial.

Phil walked away from me and Ronnie walked up.

'What did your brother say?'

'Nothing.'

'What did he say, Alan? He must have said something.'

'Nothing important.'

'How's he feel about the band?'

'He wasn't talking about anything, Ronnie.'

I never had to tell him the truth because he knew the truth, and we didn't have to keep talking about it. Ronnie knew it was a turn-down. What was the point of hurting his feelings? He and I went out and had a drink. He never asked me another word about what Phil thought.

It was fantastic for an artist to be that way with his manager. I didn't want to sit there and go through all of that badmouth crap, though I could always be honest with Ronnie and give him my true opinions. I could tell him anything and suggest anything, and he would generally listen if he was sober—even on the creative side. I'm the one who came up with the song 'Saturday Night Special'—that was an idea of mine. I got it off the news. You were always hearing about some guy with a Saturday-night special heading straight toward the liquor store to hold it up:

> *Mr. Saturday night special*
> *Got a barrel that's blue and cold*
> *Ain't good for nothin'*
> *But put a man six feet in a hole . . .*

My brother and I had on days and off days. We had a couple of years we didn't even speak, except for Christmas and Thanksgiving—and that was for our mother's sake. Hearing his comments about Skynyrd hurt me, but something in my head said that the band was so damn good that Phil couldn't totally ignore them. I reckoned he'd come around, along with the rest of the world.

Tom Werman, the producer and A&R man at Epic Records, came down and loved Skynyrd and wanted to sign them. He got a vice president to fly to Nashville to see them. The problem was that the executive was so focused on getting laid by a southern gal that I don't think he even heard half the material—he was only hearing what was rolling in the background while trying to pick up a date. He came out with the same stupid statement—that they sounded like The Allman Brothers Band—and that killed any possibility with Tom.

Tom went on to produce Cheap Trick, Molly Hatchet, and more, but he could not convince the record company to sign Lynyrd Skynyrd. Tom was a good, solid, down-to-earth person. I liked him. Most of the record executives had their noses in the air and were a bit snobbish. Not Tom.

I'D LET HIM HEAR
THE WHISTLE OF A
TWO-BY-FOUR
SCENE EIGHT

Lots of times I had dreams about Lynyrd Skynyrd. I believed in a good many of those dreams because they were totally right. I felt like it was God letting me dream so I'd know what to do next.

Ronnie Van Zant grew up in Jacksonville, Florida, in a neighborhood where white folks stopped and Black folks started—right there on the line. Even though it wasn't technically a shantytown, Ronnie would refer to it as a shantytown. Everybody down there fought. I never liked going to Jacksonville because of all the damn fights and brawls. I'd get me a lady and head for the hotel and stay there until showtime.

Jacksonville had a lot of tough-asses who were out roaming the bars, just looking to fight. The navy is down there. These guys come off the ships, and all they want to do is fight and fuck. Ronnie grew up scrapping and fighting—that influenced his style and his music and his personality.

Ronnie did sing country songs in the cab of his father's truck. When his daddy, Lacy, was driving a truck long distances, Ronnie would go with him, and they'd listen to country songs all night. Old Lacy was as tough as nails. He would fight with eighteen-year-olds and whip them. I never messed with him. Lacy was one of those old ball-peen-hammer men, and he'd tear up your ass bad.

Sister, Ronnie's mother—her real name was Marion—could get as rough as a man, though she was as sweet as a peach to me. She'd be at the concerts, and every time any of the band members were arrested— usually for fighting—she'd bail them out.

When Skynyrd hit the stage, they took it and they kept it. We could always count on fights after 'Free Bird.' The song would move people to fight. It kind of uplifted people's spirits—sort of satisfied the inner need to get back at someone for doing something. That's what 'Free Bird' did to people—it made them feel tough. Sometimes there were six or seven fights in the crowd, and Skynyrd got sued for inciting people to fight.

Fights were a regular thing around Skynyrd. If they weren't fighting someone out on the street, they were fighting each other. They loved to fight. Ronnie would beat up Bob Burns for missing his beat. Ronnie enjoyed hitting people. I also think he enjoyed being hit.

Sister stood up for Lynyrd Skynyrd and she stood up for those who dug their music because they were her kind of people. Everyone knew Sister, and no one gave her any shit. She was tough like Etta James.

Ronnie loved his parents. He loved them deeply. I think he could feel their struggle. I think he respected their struggle. Their struggle formed who he was.

Lynyrd Skynyrd were real rednecks, but they were the hardest-working rednecks I ever met. They rehearsed six days a week, from nine to five, like clockwork. That's what made them so tight. They were as tight as any band in the world. They even rehearsed their guitar solos—nothing was unplanned or improvised. They played it the same way they played it every time, note for note. A word to the new bands coming up who think they're too hot to rehearse: Skynyrd was the most rehearsed band that ever walked into a studio.

At the 'fruit and nut' bar Funochio's in Atlanta—a club for drug addicts, heads, ass-kickers, and some damn nice-looking women—Skynyrd would do five or six sets a night, killing it until dawn. We would pack the place, shoulder to shoulder. I reckoned if they could entertain those damn fucked-up junkies who had joneses and monkeys clawing into their backs, they could entertain the world. I was totally right. They got an education there—like The Beatles got in Hamburg. They would be extremely tired, but they played and played and got better and better. Damn, they could play. They might go home with two to five dollars in their pockets for their effort, because they usually drank up most of their pay, but those boys always went home laughing and talking about what a great time they'd had while they were performing. They loved every moment of what they were doing.

One night, I decided I was going to have a drinking contest with Skynyrd—teach these kids a thing or two about drinking with the big boys. Johnnie Taylor and I had been drinking a lot of scotch when I was with him, so I figured I would show these young kids how to put the booze away. These scrappy rednecks consumed three-fifths of liquor in less than thirty minutes. I had to go to bed to pass out, but they stayed up and ordered two more bottles.

There was no way I could ever out-drink Lynyrd Skynyrd. They had been drinking since they were young teens and had been working in joints since they were fifteen. They drank from jugs in those days, and they could really put a lot of booze away. I never saw anything like it. But they never missed a beat, and they never missed a gig—Skynyrd never underestimated the power of showing up.

They also understood the importance of promotion, like playing a free date in Macon just to get a story in the *Macon Telegraph*. They drove from Jacksonville and back without any expense money—that's about two hundred and seventy miles. The lady at the *Macon Telegraph* wrote a real nice story about them.

Lynyrd Skynyrd could play better drunk than they could sober. Skynyrd drank so much for so many years, by the time we hit success, they were all alcoholics—and that includes me, I'm not ashamed to admit it. We had to have a drink just to get right. I remember standing on the stage one night at Funochio's, trying not to have a drink. I made it all the way to 'Free Bird.' When they kicked into 'Free Bird,' I gave myself an excuse to salute the song and have a drink. That's what alcoholics do—they make up excuses to drink.

The band sometimes would go through countless cases of beer and bottles of Chivas Regal for the shows—of course, that includes the crew. Skynyrd were an alcohol band until they got into cocaine. Once they got into cocaine, they didn't slow down on the alcohol, they just added cocaine to it for another high. This band was the roughest, toughest band I ever saw in my life. They lived like tomorrow didn't exist.

One night, Ronnie ran into a monster at Richard's Rock Club in Atlanta. Skynyrd had played a great show with The Who, so I bought Ronnie a bottle of Chivas. The monster worked behind the bar at Richard's, and he figured that Ronnie had stolen the bottle of Chivas. He grabbed the bottle out of Ronnie's hands and leaned against the bar. Ronnie walked over to me with a smirk on his face, which meant that someone was going to get hurt. I felt it was my job, in this case, to convince him to back down—something Ronnie didn't know how to do very well.

'He's too damn big, Ronnie.'

I had seen Ronnie take down some big guys because he wasn't afraid to hit first. But this one was as big as I ever saw. I had a .25 automatic sticking in my belt, but that wouldn't do anything but make him mad. So Ronnie walks up to him, and this guy must have been a good two feet taller than Ronnie. Ronnie said something to him, and the big guy was in shock and didn't know what to do. Ronnie grabbed the bottle of Chivas and walked back to me.

'What did you tell him?' I asked.

'I told him that I was going to rip his dick off and shove it down his throat.'

'What would you have done if he started something?'

Ronnie paused, thought about what he would do, and smiled.

'I'd let him hear the whistle of a two-by-four.'

I feared no man when I was with Otis. And I feared no man when I was with Ronnie Van Zant. He wasn't a big man, but he was ferocious, like a caged lion. When he got mad and someone swung a fist, he'd jump up and beat them unmercifully.

One night in Atlanta, I thought Ronnie was going to beat a guy to death over a girl. Ronnie beat him real bad. The band jumped in and started stomping on the man and hitting him in the middle of a circle—they kept hitting him. When they finished with him, his face didn't look human. All over a girl.

'I told you,' Ronnie said to the beat-up man. 'She's with me.'

Then someone hit someone else, and the place erupted into a bar fight. Everyone wanted to get into it. A guy grabbed me and told me he was going to whip my ass and I knocked him into yesterday. Ronnie and I and the girl got into my new Lincoln, and the girl puked all over the inside of the car.

We drove around for a bit with the windows open and then went back to the club so I could check on the guy who was beat up. I found him nursing his wounds over a boilermaker.

'Do you want to go to the hospital?'

'I'm going to sue all of you motherfuckers,' he said.

'Listen, man. I came in here to help you. You've already had the shit stomped out of you. I came in here to help you, and now you can go fuck yourself.'

That man, who turned out to be a bail bondsman, tried to put out a contract to murder Ronnie. He approached one of Ronnie's friends and spilled the plan. When Ronnie found out about the contract, he called me and asked me what I thought he should do.

'I think that you all need to pile into the car and come to Macon. We'll park your car here and we'll take the Lincoln and head up to Atlanta to pay that guy a visit.'

I spent the whole afternoon shaving bullets for my .38 special so that when it hits you, it may not kill you, but it sure will knock you down. Of course, close up, it sure as hell would kill you.

We got to Atlanta and went to three different clubs, just missing the man at the first two clubs. When we got to Funochio's, the manager told us he'd never heard of the man.

'You're a damn liar,' I told him. 'He's your bail bondsman.'

'Okay,' the manager said. 'I don't want anything to do with it. I just want it all to go away.'

'Just let him know that we're here if he wants to get down to business—knives, guns, or whatever the hell he wants.'

The message was delivered. We never saw him in Atlanta ever again.

I can remember seeing the fear in people's eyes when we walked into a place. You could see it: *Get away from these killer musicians.*

My wife made me a skull-and-crossbones ring. She made it the way I wanted it. I got the idea from the *Phantom* comic strip in the newspaper. It had the jagged edges stuck out on the cross so that when I hit someone, the ring would cut them, and my idea was to leave the mark of the skull on them. That was a redneck thing.

THESE BOYS ARE NIGHT CRAWLERS
SCENE NINE

I talked Ronnie Van Zant to bed almost every night when I wasn't on the road with him. He would get drunk and call me at four in the morning. He'd wake me up and want to tell me about the day and what he was feeling. He needed to be talked to sleep. I'd listen to what happened to his day and talk to him about it, and I kept talking until he drifted off to sleep.

'Why don't you tell him we need our sleep, and to call in the day?' my wife asked.

'Honey, you don't understand. Ronnie doesn't know what daylight is unless he's fishing. These boys are night crawlers. They stay up all night partying and then they try to go to sleep, but they can't sleep.' Allen Collins could not go to sleep until he saw the sunlight coming through his window.

Sometimes, Skynyrd would have cases of whiskey on the stage— cases of everything. They would have a ton of cigarettes. This was a seven-man operation—I was the eighth man. Two roadies made ten. We were uncapping the bottles and setting them out on the stage, and we'd let anybody in the audience who wanted a drink come up and take a big slug. They'd get the front rows drunk, and then the people behind them, and you could see the crowd open up like an accordion.

During our first album-cover photo session, the photographer was a bit intimidated and wanted me to go along to the session as a sort of escort. He was a little nervous because of the band's reputation. But he went out there and started drinking beer with them and began to party. He took a bunch of photos, and afterward he was greatly relieved, walking across a beautiful field.

'When I got here, I was nervous. I thought you were so tough and mean. You have been perfect gentlemen,' he told Ronnie. 'I thought you guys fought a lot. How about a shot of you getting angry and mean?' the photographer asked.

'You got your camera ready?' Ronnie asked. And he turned to Bob Burns, punched him in the face, and flattened him right in the field. 'That tough enough for you?'

The photographer went back to being scared again.

Every man in Skynyrd knew how to fight except for Ed King. Ed came from L.A. and Strawberry Alarm Clock—they had a #1 hit with

'Incense And Peppermints'—and Ed was sort of a flower child. He wasn't into all the southern raise-hell kick-ass life. When there was a fight, Ed would head for the hotel or out back, which was very smart of him. He just wasn't into the fighting like the rest of them.

Skinny Allen Collins could fight like hell. Gary Rossington could fight like hell. Bob Burns was a wild man at fighting. Leon wasn't a real big fighter, but he would be in there with them. Allen, Gary, and Ronnie were the three that were deadly fighters. They'd be fighting at Funochio's and fighting out in the parking lot during intermission. Some guy would give them trouble, and they'd take him out in the alley and kick the shit out of him. Billy Powell could fight, being a former roadie for the band. He wasn't as anxious to run into a fight, but he could fight.

One time, Ronnie backed up in the corner and told them all, 'I'm going to whip everyone of you. One at a time or all at once.' And then he did it.

I am the man who suggested the three-guitar sound for Skynyrd—a great contribution I did make for this band.

We were in Atlanta, at Doodle's Showcase. Ed King was playing bass, with Allen and Gary on guitars. Leon Wilkeson was in the club, and I went and talked to him. Leon had been the band's bass player before Ed, but then some guys down in Jacksonville convinced him he was going to be a star in another band, so he left. Ronnie Van Zant did not believe in giving anyone a second chance. If you messed him up once, you were gone.

I found Leon listening to the music over by the bar.

'Would you like to play on "Free Bird"?'

'Yeah, I'd love to. But I don't think Ronnie would let me.'

'You let me go talk to him,' I told Leon.

I went down and first suggested Ronnie let Leon play.

'No,' he said. I'm not ever going to give him a chance.'

But I was able to convince Ronnie to let Leon come up and play just on 'Free Bird.' Leon came up and he played, and he burned. Everybody in that club realized that *this* was 'Free Bird.'

When Ed King came offstage, he went over to Ronnie.

'I will never be able to play "Free Bird" like he just did. I will never be able to play it that good.'

'Let's move Ed over to third guitar,' I suggested to Ronnie.

'No. They'll be stepping all over each other. It won't work,' Ronnie said.

'Hey, at least give it a try. It's an idea. Then we'll know if it does or doesn't work for sure.'

Well, it did work, and it made the band twice as strong. Adding one more different style player. Ed King was technically perfect, and he could come up with some hot licks.

Billy Powell and Leon Wilkeson were the last two who signed on before we started tearing off onto the road. Leon was a tremendous asset to the band, and Billy's audition was really something. He played Mozart and classical music—just beautiful piano.

'Billy, that sounds wonderful, and I love it, but I got to ask you . . . can you give me that Little Richard honky-tonk jammin'?'

And, man, he sure did. He ran up and down those keys.

Ronnie flipped at Billy's playing, so we added Billy as the seventh man. Billy was so talented. The three-guitar sound worked, and it worked extremely well.

A BEAUTIFUL DAY IN THE SWAMP WITH GATORS, TADPOLES, AND 'SWEET HOME ALABAMA'
SCENE TEN

I went to Jacksonville, Florida, to meet Ronnie and took my oldest daughter, Jessica, and her mother with me, and a fellow who I was considering as a road manager. I thought we were going to the rehearsal house. It was called *Hidden Hills*—it was just a little shack right in a cow pasture at the edge of a river. Psilocybin mushrooms were all over the place.

We got there and started heading into the house when Ronnie came out of the shack.

'No, no, no. Come around here.'

He took us around the house to the creek. Ronnie called it a creek. To me, it was a river with black, black water. Ronnie had rigged out a little fishing boat with rods, trolling motor, gasoline outboard, tackle, and even a cooler full of beer and sandwiches. Ronnie had set up a nice lounge chair for my wife so she could enjoy the adventure.

'I want you to go up the creek here about two or so miles,' Ronnie explained to me. 'We'll be playing here, and you'll be able to hear us. We wrote a song, and we want you to hear it over the water and the woods.'

So we headed upriver. We got up there about two or three miles, shut the engine off, and started drifting down. I put a line into the water. I was conscious of alligators swimming around us, going after millions of tadpoles that had been recently born into this world— born into that death-black water. I couldn't imagine what kind of mysterious creatures were crawling around in that dark water.

In the distance we could hear some great guitars through the woods and up the river. There was a real beauty to hearing music like that— the sound moving up the river like a warm mist.

I got a couple of nibbles and then hooked into a damn bass that felt like a monster. It jumped up on the line, and it was the biggest bass I had ever seen. And I've got lightweight tackle. I brought him in and let him run and get tired and then brought him in a second time, and I'm telling my man to get the net but he can't find it. My friend pulled the fish in close to the boat, leaned over to pick the fish up, and the line snapped. I was plenty pissed because that future road manager who was with me couldn't find the net. It happened to be under his foot the whole time.

And then we heard it. A melody flowing through the air as we drifted closer to the rehearsal shack. 'Sweet Home Alabama.' We were drifting through the swamp listening to that song, and it was a mighty spiritual experience.

When we got to the shack, I ran up to Ronnie.

'Man, you've got something special here,' I told Ronnie.

We were the first civilians to hear 'Sweet Home Alabama.' Ronnie wanted us to hear it the right way. And we sure did.

Al Kooper and Skynyrd got together one night at Funochio's. Al happened to waltz in wearing a white mink coat, past people who were lucky to be wearing shoes. Al requested to jam with the band. Why not? Al Kooper was a legend. Skynyrd let him come up and jam—this black-haired Jewish guy from Brooklyn. Al had paid his dues to jam on any stage with any group in the world, and that was fine with me.

After the session we sat down, and Al explained that he was starting a label, called Sounds of the South and that he was definitely interested in producing Skynyrd's album. The problems started, and I could see that the company was going to tie the band down every way they could.

Al Kooper made a deal with MCA for Skynyrd. I met the band over at the Macon Coliseum parking lot and had all of the contracts spread out on the hood of my '73 Ford pickup with a gun rack in the back and a cooler of beer tucked into the bed. The deal Al made for them was terrible.

Ronnie asked me, 'What do you think of our record deal?'

'It's the worst piece of shit I've ever seen,' I told him.

'What else do we have?' Ronnie said.

'Nothing,' I told Ronnie. 'But with this contract you've got less.'

'Give me that damn pen,' Ronnie responded. And then he signed the contract.

Later, Ronnie and Ed King wrote a song called 'Workin' For MCA,' because that's what they ended up doing.

EVERYONE KNEW THEY HAD JUST WRANGLED A MONSTER
SCENE ELEVEN

A lot of people used to ask me what it was like going from working with a liberal Black man to a redneck, wild, street-gang fighting band. It was easy. All I had to do was get a pickup, stock a cooler full of beer, and work my ass off.

Ronnie loved my Lincoln Town Car. One morning, a bit after dawn, we were riding back to Macon from Atlanta, and Ronnie was sitting in the backseat. Allen and Gary were asleep, and I knew Ronnie was wiped out too, but he was wide awake.

'Why aren't you taking a nap?'

'And miss this ride?' Ronnie said. 'When I get famous, I want to buy my momma a car like this,' he told me. When he said that with sincerity, it kind of stuck with me.

After Ronnie died, I gave the Lincoln that I loved so dearly to Ronnie's mother, Sister, at his funeral.

'Sister, I didn't bring you roses, but I am bringing you something that Ronnie wanted you to have.'

Even when Ronnie and I went our separate ways, Sister and I would have dinner. She'd cook me a southern meal, and she appreciated what I had done for Ronnie. Both she and Lacy had a lot of class. It broke my heart when I saw Lacy a year and a half later.

'How's the Lincoln, Lacy?'

'You know, those kids jumped into that car. It had to be parked on the side of their bedroom, and they just tore it up like rats.'

'We're not going to call Al Kooper and ask him to record "Sweet Home Alabama,"' I told Ronnie. 'We're going to do exactly what we want to do. We're going to *tell* Al Kooper that we're coming to Atlanta to record this song while it's hot. Before you polish it too much and the feeling goes away. I want you to go in there hot, right now, fresh.'

Al wasn't used to anyone putting demands on him. He was very strict. It was going to be the Al Kooper way or no way, but he agreed to be there.

209

I was not at Studio One in Doraville, Georgia, when they recorded *Pronounced 'Lĕh-'nérd 'Skin-'nérd*, I arrived in the afternoon. I kept everybody I could out of the studio—total lockdown, so they could concentrate on what they were doing. They had buddies who were let in, and their friends were always tough-ass guys, but they did look after me great.

I was friendly with everybody. That's one thing I could say. I was friendly with the roadies and drivers. They were all part of the organization, and sooner or later you're going to depend on them for something. Why not go ahead and have a good relationship with them, instead of trying to treat them like employees? I think I successfully managed the band that way—trying to keep them on the uplift as much as possible.

Al Kooper had almost complete control with Skynyrd until they came in and wanted to record 'Simple Man' over in Doraville.

'No way,' Al said. 'I don't like the song. We don't even need to put it down.'

'Hell, man, that's one of our best songs,' Ronnie told Al. 'What's going on here?'

Ronnie was pissed. He thought about it and followed Al to his car.

Al got into the car and rolled down the window.

'We'll call you when we're finished,' Ronnie told Al.

Ronnie went in and handled it himself. Thank God, because 'Simple Man' is a great song and one of my favorites. I think one of the most powerful songs they had.

By the time I got to the studio, about three o' clock in the afternoon, they had already finished 'Sweet Home Alabama,' and Al Kooper had 'kidnapped' Ronnie Van Zant, put him on a plane, and got him to L.A. to meet all the people at MCA. They were going to hand-deliver what would be 'Sweet Home Alabama.' When they got there, the record company let them know they were going to start pressing *Pronounced* and wanted to hold 'Sweet Home Alabama' for the second record— they loved it to death but wanted to save it for the next single. So that's what we did.

Everyone knew that they just had wrangled a monster, and they knew that when it was set loose it would devour the world. Al Kooper produced *Pronounced* in Georgia and *Second Helping* at the Record Plant in Los Angeles, but they were also my records, and I can tell you now, with all honesty and humbleness, that I built the foundation for Lynyrd Skynyrd that they're still living off today.

Skynyrd didn't like the environment at the Record Plant at all. They wanted to go back to Muscle Shoals, but instead they went to Doraville, where Al had his connections. Al got to choose the studio, but Tom Dowd came in and helped. We did the fourth album, *Gimme Back My Bullets*, at Capricorn, and it came across, but Capricorn specialized in the dead sound. That was different from what Skynyrd liked.

I didn't work in the control room with Al that much. We had sort of a clash. Being the band's manager, I felt like I had to stand up for the band all the time. Al felt like he was the chief and in control. At one point, he wanted me to work for him, to run a booking agency, but I didn't build Lynyrd Skynyrd to work for Al Kooper.

We kind of made a mutual understanding without saying it: when I was in the studio, he wasn't there; when he was in the studio, I wasn't there. We weren't in the studio together. I'm not really a technical expert by any means. Musicians would show me their guitars, but those things were not important to me. It was the sound that concerned me. What can those instruments do, and how much control did the musician have over his instrument?

I was going to rule the world with Lynyrd Skynyrd. I had more determination in my mind than I ever had.

Finishing is everything. I don't quit. If I am committed to a band, I'll stay right there with them, and I was committed to Lynyrd Skynyrd. I ate, slept, and everything with Lynyrd Skynyrd. Ronnie was the best man at my wedding, and the band were my only guests. I'd wake up in the morning and think about what I could do for them. I'd get to my office and plan out a whole tour.

One thing about MCA: they would always give me the sales figures and show what areas were good and what were weak, so I would take those undeveloped areas and put them on the development list—calling radio stations and getting more play. We might be playing for ten thousand a night in some places, but the next show we might play for fifteen hundred, because we were weak in that market. Then we'd work it up to ten thousand by creating more demand.

I once told Al Kooper that he sweetened the sound of Lynyrd Skynyrd. He did influence how they sounded during that period. He tried to get them out of the swamp. But the swamp beckons a group like that. The swamp is where their music lives.

EVERYONE IN THE ROOM
WAS VERY INTERESTING AND
I WAS VERY INTERESTING
AND EVERYTHING WAS
VERY VERY INTERESTING
SCENE TWELVE

I had a big meeting with Mike Maitland and MCA in California. Phil called me that morning—he was in town for other business—and told me to go in there and give them hell. Take it up the mountain and keep the high ground—tell them what you want and take it. Joe Galkin called and told me the same. I always appreciated Phil's support, and I was humbled by Joe's. Between Phil and Joe, I was primed.

I think I was staying at the Regency, and Phil was there as well. He told me to get over to his room because we hadn't seen each other in a while. I get over there and Phil and his buddies are tooting cocaine, so they offered me some.

'I don't do cocaine, Phil.'

'Ah, come on, man. You know I wouldn't turn you onto something bad. Take a bump of this.'

I am wondering today how many people heard that line.

'Pot gets me high enough. Maybe a codeine pill on occasion,' I said, starting to go into a sort of anxiety attack. The brain of the family is now trying to shove cocaine up my nose.

I left his room, ran to my room, hit the toilet, and vomited for two hours. I collapsed in the bed and the phone started ringing again.

'Alan. Come on back up here, man. We haven't been together for a long time. Come up here, brother, and have a party.'

To make Phil happy, I walked back, and the next thing I know he's shoving that stuff right under my nose again. Okay. So I tried it. And, man, in a few moments I'm feeling great. I'm feeling like I could lick the world. I could talk my way into or out of any deal. I was feeling alive. I did not remember ever feeling so good.

'What did I tell you?' Phil asked.

I was warm all over. My body was in great shape. And with the next few snorts, everyone in the room was very interesting and I was very interesting, and I had very interesting things to say. What the other people were saying was fascinating—just not as fascinating as what I had to say. Where have you been hiding all my life?

I have sinus problems, which is why I am still alive, because otherwise I would have been on that plane with Otis. Sinus problems saved my life.

My nose wasn't dripping, it was flowing like an open faucet attached to my forehead—and it didn't stop. I had to be at Mike Maitland's that day, so I stuffed some Kleenex up my nose and headed for MCA.

Mike and I got along great, and in about fifteen minutes he wanted to call in Rick Frio, the head of marketing, so he could hear some of my ideas. I kept going with my marketing ideas for Skynyrd and the touring, and then Mike called in Vince Cosgrove, in charge of promotion, to get him into the picture. The Kleenex was holding, though I could feel the pressure building. After a few more minutes, Mike called in Lou Cook, head of finance. Lou entered for a bit longer, and then we decided to take a little break, since we had been at it for a couple of hours. We would meet back up in a bigger room after lunch.

I knew one of the publicists in the office, a beautiful Italian American named Michelle. She was a knockout, and her office was down the hall. I sat with her for a little bit and I could feel the pressure in my head was getting critical.

'Michelle, I want you to turn your head. I'm going to do something that isn't going to look good.'

'What are you talking about?'

I started pulling out the Kleenex and throwing it into the trash.

'You got some more Kleenex, Michelle?'

'What you need is another bump,' she said. 'That will dry it up.'

Michelle opened her drawer and handed me a little brown bottle. We both had a couple of hits, and my dripping went away.

I walked back into the meeting and my energy was burning. I went back to work full speed—all pistons firing and rockets red glare. I even convinced them to put Lynyrd Skynyrd in every adult magazine out there—full-page ads in all of the magazines aimed at the adult male. We were the first rock 'n' roll band to ever market to that crowd. That was strictly my idea. We had *Rolling Stone* and *Cashbox*, and the record company agreed to support us if we needed help. I insisted that they had a representative of MCA on the band's upcoming tour with The Who. When they got off the plane, there was always a man in a suit picking up this raggedy hippie band, Lynyrd Skynyrd.

Bill Graham was a great guy, and probably the best show promoter in the world. He once asked Otis what he wanted to drink, thinking he wanted some kind of alcohol. Otis wanted a Coke. Since Bill didn't have a Coke, he walked two blocks to get one. It was Bill who put on The Who and Skynyrd at the Cow Palace in San Francisco, in November 1973. Later on in the tour, Roger Daltrey got down on his knees in front of Ronnie Van Zant and told him he was the greatest singer in rock 'n' roll.

Bill insisted that a group needed to get a ten-second applause to give an encore. We got the encores.

For some reason, there was a bit of confusion about our transportation from the hotel to the Cow Palace. The limo didn't show up, and a Mexican fellow suggested that he drive us over in his big sedan. We all crowded into this raggedy car, and when we pulled into the Cow Palace, everyone knew that Lynyrd Skynyrd had arrived.

A couple of nights later, we played the L.A. Forum, and we were staying at the Holiday Inn. The clerk saw us coming into the lobby and wasn't very impressed. I told him who we were, and he informed me that we did not have a reservation. I gave him the confirmation and opened my wallet—my roll of twenty-six credit cards went to the floor. (Twiggs and I had a little competition going on how many credit cards we could acquire.)

'How long is this going to take?' Bob Burns asked.

'Almost done, Bob.'

Bob took the ashtray—one of those old lobby ashtrays filled with sand—turned it upside down, emptying out the sand on the floor, and sat on it.

'I'll just wait here until you're ready.'

Skynyrd decided that it would be a good idea to see if they could throw a television into the swimming pool from their window. Impressed that they could, they got some long extensions from the roadies and threw another television into the pool while plugged in. The result was quite spectacular—the television blew out when it hit the water. Fortunately, nobody was in the pool, because they would have been electrocuted to death, and I didn't have enough credit cards to deal with Skynyrd being arrested for electrocuting people in a hotel swimming pool.

I'm not sure what was happening with the limos. One showed up to take us to the Forum, but it was in the form of a Ford Econoline van—one that had driven its share of rock 'n' roll bands around Los Angeles. We pulled into the backstage alley behind the limos for The Who, and then, after the show, we couldn't get the van started to move out of the way. We all went out and pushed the van up a ramp and away so The Who could leave the Forum. Finally, the car started, and Skynyrd headed back to the hotel.

THE TRUTH OF
THE MATTER IS . . .
SCENE THIRTEEN

In 'Sweet Home Alabama,' Ronnie sings that '*in Birmingham we loved the governor,*' but then he put in '*boo, boo boo, but we all did what we could do.*' He played the middle line so he wouldn't be misunderstood and be called a total racist.

This song was definitely aimed toward white audiences, for sure. I love the song—I think it's a masterpiece—but many people have tried to read a lot of things into it.

The truth of the matter is, Ronnie had a pretty Italian girl over there that made his life interesting while he was in Alabama. I have a picture of her—there is a picture with all of us in the back of a truck.

There are two girls in the photograph. The one wearing the bathing suit and kneeling down in front of Ronnie is the girl who probably inspired the song.

African Americans objected to the song more than anybody. They saw the Confederate flag as racist. It didn't matter if it was us just saying we're from the South and identifying with the South—it said racism to them, and that's all there was to it.

I think the Confederate flag represents the South. I don't see the flag as racist. There are a lot of racist sons of bitches—truthfully, I can't think of anyone who flew the Stars and Bars who wasn't prejudiced, or a bit so—but some of us are just proud of the South, and that flag was part of our history. People want to erase it out of everyone's memory now—take down the statues and all of that. I don't believe in destroying art that has any sort of history to it. I don't believe in destroying art or history for any reason.

I have a flag as a collector's item, but mine was actually the Georgia state flag, which had the Stars and Bars from 1956 to 2001, and then a tiny Stars and Bars on a banner up until 2003. The flag was a gift from Jimmy Carter. I have friends of all different races and of all different religions, rich and poor. I don't judge a man by the color of his skin or the thickness of his wallet. I don't care what race he is or what religion he is—is he an honest man or not an honest man?

Looking back, we were originally in the building called the Professional Building and then, later, the Robert E. Lee Building. Otis Redding Enterprises' mailing address was Robert E. Lee Building, 310 Mulberry Street, Macon, Georgia. It was on his letterheads and all of the promotion—kind of amusing now, with all of this Confederate flag business. Times change.

Ronnie Van Zant was a southern man. He was a redneck and so was I—though I was a sort of an educated redneck. I knew how to play like southern boys play—fast cars, drinking whiskey, guns, chasing women, fishing.

Ronnie hung a Confederate flag as a backdrop on stage. It wasn't catering strictly to the white audience, but that's how it turned out. The fact is that the white redneck crowd went to his shows and waved the Confederate flag, like at NASCAR and a lot of other events in the South. That's the reality of it, and there's no denying it.

Was 'Sweet Home Alabama' a white anthem? No. Was it taken by some as that? Maybe. They were really just talking about Alabama being good to them. There's a lot of good things in that song, though Ronnie was a George Wallace man all the way. Yes, he was. Tried and true. I got him to get behind Jimmy Carter. Later on, I think Ronnie felt that I talked him into supporting Carter—he was still a Wallace man. Skynyrd did do a benefit for Carter, and the Allman Brothers raised a half million dollars too.

I don't think 'Sweet Home Alabama' was aimed at slamming the African American people at all. But it was taken that way. I don't think it was written with that intent. There's nothing in the song that makes reference to African Americans. The controversy came from the spirit around the song, and the audience for the song.

Until the press started picking up on it, Ronnie didn't give a damn if it was or wasn't perceived that way. After people wrote about it, Ronnie kept saying he didn't mean this or that. He kind of backed away from it and got a little less convicted. Usually, he really didn't care what people thought.

I loved the song. I didn't foresee the accusations of being racist because of that song. It was just a good song about Alabama, though it was one of the more racist states to be in at the time. When I heard it, I never thought that we might be controversial on this or that verse. It was Ronnie talking his philosophy, and I wanted it to be the way he thought, and that's what 'Sweet Home' is. Good or bad, it was Ronnie's truth—not everyone's truth but his truth. He wasn't the kind of guy who would throw bricks at Black people in cars and things like that. He did have some experiences in his life that made him more prejudiced than most. He was a product of his time and place.

It wasn't until after I stopped managing Skynyrd that the controversy started heating up. 'Sweet Home Alabama' was originally just accepted as a great song. Somebody started picking it apart and it grew and grew, and all of a sudden it was a big issue and Ronnie Van Zant was a racist. I didn't defend it or deny it. Nobody ever asked me. I never really had to face the issue.

Some people turned Ronnie Van Zant into a little god. They believed everything he said and would take up his philosophy on a lot of different issues. Flying the rebel flag just represented that the band was from the South. It wasn't aimed at Black people. Ronnie treated Black entertainers equally. We had a lot of Black musicians get up and jam with them, and he always made a point of getting them a bigger amp or anything else they needed. Ronnie supported music and musicians, Black or white.

Phil was a liberal southern boy. He didn't like the way white people treated Black people. For as long as I can remember, Phil's heart was into, and supportive of, the Black experience.

Phil had bought Debbie Reynolds's white Rolls-Royce. He was

riding down Cotton Avenue and stopped at a red light where there were three African American teenagers who had just finished playing basketball and were wet with sweat.

'Hey, man,' one of them said. 'That is one cool car.'

'Hop in,' Phil said.

The kids hopped into the back seat of the Rolls. They didn't know Debbie Reynolds from *Debbie Does Dallas*, and they didn't know Phil from anyone. But Phil drove them around the streets of Macon for a couple of hours, riding on a dream come true.

TAKING IT OVER
THE MOUNTAIN
SCENE FOURTEEN

We looked up to The Allman Brothers Band in the beginning. They were the ones who paved the way. But as Lynyrd Skynyrd gained strength, I kind of had the Allman Brothers shoved down my throat too damn much. Every time I'd come around, Phil would tell me all about how successful his band was. He never asked what was going on with me or my band. Even when we were setting up the show at the Atlanta Braves Stadium with The Marshall Tucker Band and the Allman Brothers in 1974, Phil thought we shouldn't be paid as much as either of them. I acknowledged that the Allman Brothers were the #1 southern band, but I resented having them thrown at me so much, and I felt like I wanted to put a foot up their ass.

We picked the date of June 1. Lynyrd Skynyrd appeared on the stage in front of over sixty-one thousand people. Grinderswitch opened the show, followed by The Marshall Tucker Band. Skynyrd went on third, and then The Allman Brothers Band closed the show.

Lynyrd Skynyrd had one of their best days ever. They played perfectly. Even the encore was outstanding. We burned the Brothers' asses up. We hit that stage and we didn't give the audience a chance to applaud between songs—the set just *rolled*. 'Sweet Home Alabama' lifted people off the ground. They ended the set with 'Free Bird,' and nobody looked back. We came to an Allman Brothers show and beat them bad. We put a boot right where it belonged.

The Marshall Tucker Band were good, but the rain started coming down and the bottom fell out of their set. People started leaving. When the Allman Brothers started up, it didn't take long for Gregg to pass out on the organ. Lamar Williams, the bass player, was so dosed up that Joe Dan Petty, one of the guitar techs, had to take over. Thousands of people walked out. They weren't going to get drenched to watch a train wreck. The Allman Brothers had one of their worst days ever and we had one of our best. By the time the Allman Brothers came out, half the people had gone home. They saw what they needed to see—Lynyrd Skynyrd.

Phil did acknowledge, somewhat reluctantly but sincerely, that we were the highlight of the show. He and the Allman Brothers didn't really respect us until after Atlanta Stadium.

A month later, we were playing at the Orange Bowl, in Miami Florida, with the Eagles, Leon Russell, and The Band. Man, I wanted Skynyrd to kick the Eagles' asses so bad because Irving Azoff and I had become enemies. He managed the Eagles and I managed Skynyrd. I wanted to stomp them bad.

I didn't like Irving at all. He and Phil were enemies, so naturally he was my enemy too. Later on, he was the one who created most of our problems with Skynyrd. He's the kind of guy who saw a band and, if he couldn't get them, he'd figure out a way to mess up their career and convince them that they needed new management in order to survive.

It was a big, big crowd. Skynyrd went out there full tilt, jukin'. I mean they were jukin' and jukin' and gave it one of their best shots ever. Well, the Eagles came out in their cutoff shorts, charged those mics, fired up those harmonies, and soared all the way over the mountain. They shoved it right back down our throats. We didn't burn any Eagles that day.

We had just played with the Eagles, and before that with The Allman Brothers Band. We had eight or nine major acts we were playing with. We were happening. We had gone from middle-class band to top-rated band—from fruit-and-nut bars to stadiums. Cincinnati Gardens with the J. Geils Band; Memorial Stadium in Charlotte; and Municipal Stadium in Cleveland with The Beach Boys, REO Speedwagon, and Joe Walsh.

In Memphis, Tennessee, Skynyrd played with Eric Clapton, and we shook him good. Skynyrd kicked Clapton's ass.

Ronnie had gone to see Eric Clapton before the show.

'Man, you ought to get down on your knees and kiss the ground Duane Allman walked on,' Ronnie told him. 'Duane Allman was the greatest guitar player in the world. I know you're good, but Duane Allman is the king.'

Even though Ronnie was drunk, I really do think that shook Eric up.

Sounds magazine wrote of that show, 'English guys who surround people like Eric Clapton don't seem to be interested in the music. Their pleasure comes from throwing people bodily off the stage for no apparent reason as often as possible. Lynyrd Skynyrd know who their friends are. They have a crew who would and have worked for free when the band was starving. As Ronnie Van Zant says, We're the real brothers of the South.'

I caught up with Eric down in Miami sometime later. I was recording Mama's Pride at the Criteria, over on Ocean Boulevard, where Clapton had cut one of his albums. Eric treated me like a friend. He knew who I was. Such a gentleman. He played me a couple of his songs to get my opinion, and I felt quite honored by that. He was and is a great artist. I had been a fan of his since Cream, and it was a real thrill.

CRY FOR THE BAD MAN
SCENE FIFTEEN

Lynyrd Skynyrd had me talking to hotel managers and the police and all these people that took up my time—time I should have been working radio stations and getting more dates in the weak areas. I didn't want to be a damn road manager. Someone else ought to have been taking care of that job.

I would get calls from the road, and Ronnie would ask me to pay off a hotel because of them busting up the place—ripping doors off and breaking windows. They were turning into crazy, violent, spoiled kids. Their response to the hotel who wanted to get paid was, 'Go buy yourself another door.' They'd tear the doors off the room, and each door was about a thousand dollars to replace and install. Skynyrd had no concept of money and they didn't care about other people's property, except for Ed King—Ed was different. But I was getting very sick of this behavior.

One night in St. Louis, after they had been thrown out of a hotel for busting all the emergency exit lights in the hallways, they called and cried to me that they wanted me to find them new digs.

'Listen, Ronnie. It's two o'clock in the morning. And I'm going to tell you something. There is a convention in St. Louis, and these were the last rooms available. You just got kicked out of the only place we could get. You're going to have to sleep on the bus.'

Ronnie started yelling at me, and I laid into him.

'You want to see my balls? I'll show them to you. Cut this shit out! I'm sick of it.'

Show Ronnie my balls? That's probably the stupidest statement I ever made to Ronnie Van Zant. But Phil got away with speaking to his bands like that on a few occasions, so I figured I'd try it on for size.

I have to admit that lots of times I copied Phil. I had a 'Phil Walden' act, and it was nothing but me doing Phil Walden. I copied his mannerisms with my hands and the way he lowered his voice. Sometimes I just said what I thought Phil would say, or what I had heard him say.

I did share my issues about Skynyrd being wild with Phil, and he had one very smart response.

'Don't take any shit from the band,' he said.

All of these bad-boy behavior issues created the resentment—from Ronnie to me, and from me to Ronnie.

It just so happened that Irving Azoff was there in the city that night, and he ended up talking to Skynyrd about what he would do if he managed the band. Perfect timing on his part—like a buzzard landing on a dead squirrel.

Skynyrd told me that they had been talking to other managers— one of them being Irving—and a couple of others, and they didn't want to tell me who. I had told the band in the beginning that if they ever wanted to change management, I would help pick their next manager, because I didn't want to see my work go down the drain. I wanted to still find a way to make some money out of this project. I felt terrible, but I was kind of ready for it.

'Well, I'm going to tell you,' I told Ronnie and the band. 'We can go into a lawsuit if you want to and attach your equipment and all of this, but what will that accomplish? It will only get the lawyers a bigger piece for them bullshitting us back and forth.'

Ronnie listened.

'If you're that dissatisfied, I guess the whole camaraderie thing is out the window.'

'We're a machine now, Alan. We work like a machine.'

I found out that Ronnie had taken meetings with my own brother and Peter Rudge, as well as with Azoff. Finding out that Phil had met with Skynyrd without me knowing broke my heart.

Ronnie called and asked what I thought of possibly working with Phil.

'That's pretty shitty for my brother to do that,' I told Ronnie. 'And it's pretty shitty for *you* to do that. What do you think he'll do to you if he is willing to fuck his own brother? You'd be sucking up to the Allman Brothers for the rest of your life. If I were you, I'd look at Peter

Rudge. Peter has the Stones and The Who. He's got a nice stable of artists.'

Ronnie liked Peter. Peter used all of these big words and he'd put on that English accent, and Ronnie ate that up. Sometimes, when Americans hear an English accent, they get impressed—they like to relate it with intelligence and sophistication.

The band took a vote and voted me out seven to one. I don't know who voted for me.

'Do you want to know who they were?' Ronnie asked.

'No, I don't need to know that. I don't want to be bitter at anybody. We'll leave it at that. If we're going to do this, I want to do it and know together that we're all going to still make some money.'

So I did the deal with Peter, and I hung onto the publishing for everything that I released under my time—'Free Bird,' 'Sweet Home Alabama,' 'Simple Man,' and 'Gimme Three Steps'—all of the first two albums, and they were the best records they made. Personally, I was hurt, because I thought I was doing a fantastic job. I don't think I could have done a better job than I was doing. I just should have never got into talking to the hotels and the police and all of that other junk. I should have let the road manager work that stuff out for himself.

Peter even told them he could get them into the movies. Why does everyone want to be in the movies? I don't know. Maybe they would have made some pretty good redneck street fighters.

Lynyrd Skynyrd audited me when we were in the middle of trying to settle our differences and get to mutual ground. They did an audit on me, and my books were off by thirty-nine cents. I mailed Ronnie Van Zant a check for thirty-nine cents. That's when I got the nickname 'money miser.' And that's when Ronnie wrote a song about me.

The thing about that song, Ronnie always knew that I wanted a song written about me, but I kind of thought it would be a song about how I helped musicians—a good song. A complimentary song. Then he got mad during these negotiations—my lawyer wasn't giving in—and he wrote the song 'Cry For The Bad Man.'

Lynyrd Skynyrd ended up with a bunch of lowlife hangers-on, carrying suitcases full of cocaine and giving them coke every time they turned around. That's the end for a band, if they don't get rid of that lifestyle. I tell young people trying to get into the business to always watch out for drug dealers and drug use. Dealers will find a way to get to that artist, and they will tell that artist everything they know an artist likes to hear, and only long enough to get them addicted to drugs. Dangerous people are always surrounding the artists. I did a good job at keeping them away because I could recognize danger. A lot of these young artists couldn't.

I went into Percy Sledge's bus one time and fired twenty-six people in one day. There were twenty-six people on that bus who didn't have a function except to tell Percy how good he was and how talented he was. And Percy was paying the hotel bills and all of that. I bought them all a bus ticket home.

That night, I had my first migraine headache. I went back to the hotel and told my daddy about my headache and went to bed. When I got home, I found out that the bus waited until I drove off and circled back and picked them all up again, and they kept the bus money. That one really got to me. I was always trying to save Percy money.

A BULL BY
THE HORNS
SCENE SIXTEEN

We had a Capricorn picnic in 1976, and everyone was there—lots of bands and lots of record people and beautiful women. Capricorn picnics were something else. At this particular picnic, Andy Warhol was there, Don King was there, Jimmy Carter, Bette Midler, The Allman Brothers Band, Lynyrd Skynyrd, The Marshall Tucker Band—people from all walks of life were there for the party.

Ronnie and I wound up in a hotel room to have a chat—just the two of us. I guess we were both looking for something, but to this day I still don't know what.

We started talking about things, and something was said that made my temper flare—I can't even remember what he said. I jumped up and grabbed Ronnie by his hair and slammed him against the wall, knowing that he could easily hit me with one punch and end it. With his fighter knuckles, Ronnie's punch packed a hard wallop.

'Man, you and I were supposed to be back-to-back, covering each other, and you let them stab me in the back.'

'I guess you're going to take that pistol out and use it on me,' Ronnie said.

'I don't need a pistol to do you tonight. I'm that damn mad.'

I took my pistol out and threw it to the farthest corner of the room.

I was willing to fight if he was. But I got him up against the wall and I looked into his eyes, and he's got tears coming down his face. Then I started crying. And I turned around and I walked out, knowing that our relationship was completely over.

I ran into Ronnie again the next day.

'I guess you know you had a damn bull by the horns,' he told me.

'Yep. And I wrestled him too, didn't I?'

In some ways, Ronnie admired that I would fight if I was mad enough. Up until that year, our relationship had been perfect. He did everything I asked for. My decisions generally stood.

Before I left Skynyrd, I was talking to Ronnie about doing more dates with Pep Brown. Pep Brown had a very unique voice, like Percy Sledge. He could write real deep, meaningful songs. I loved him. I could sit around and listen to Pep sing eight hours straight and not be bored, he entertained me that much. He was a self-taught guitar player. He may jump a key, but we'd just go back and overdub that.

I met Pep in the sixties when Otis was still alive. He came into the office and sang a cappella for me right there at the desk. Man, he sounded just like Otis, but he had tempered it with his own unique style. We eventually cut an Al Green song called 'Are You Leaving Me' with Jimmy Johnson at Muscle Shoals. He wrote some very unique songs.

Pep Brown and Bill Coday both played with Skynyrd when they played Grant's Lounge. We also did it at the Coliseum one night. We did the show just for the story, to get some publicity started in Macon.

Ronnie did not mind working with Pep Brown or Bill Coday. Bill had a great record. The first time I heard his record, 'Get Your Lie Straight Baby,' I just about died:

If I ask you this same question ten years from now

The answer better be the same
Get your lie straight...

That's something I would say. Maybe that's why I liked the song so much.

I was heartbroken after Lynyrd Skynyrd. I had been working them hard for four years. Every day I did something for that band. I wasn't satisfied unless I could accomplish something every day. Some days I'd get ten or twelve things done. I learned that when I'm on, I'm on. I don't make a lot of mistakes, and I get very creative under pressure. When I'm tired and worn out, and when I really don't have my heart into it, I can be bad.

I was heartbroken but I didn't cry. It was almost like a big concrete block sliding off of my shoulders, with the amount of pressure that I had been under with Skynyrd. I was a one-man army handling their careers. It was a lot of work, and I was doing it all.

I didn't even want to hire a lawyer—I just wanted to do it and make our own contracts. Peter Rudge drew up the contracts and then cut off all communication with me. Sometime later, I called him about something I knew about that I thought he wouldn't know about, and he wouldn't return my phone call. He finally did call me when he received the gold and platinum records that were mailed to his office— they were my records, so I had to go by there and pick them up, and then got the hell out of there.

I spoke with Ronnie a few times after that, when The Outlaws played with Skynyrd. We did thirty or so dates together, and things were cordial but distant. We loved each other, but there was nothing more to be said.

THEY GOT THEMSELVES A BIRD SONG!
SCENE SEVENTEEN

As I was going out of my relationship with Skynyrd, I signed The Outlaws.

I first heard of The Outlaws from Ronnie Van Zant. He had been on the bill with them in Nashville, at the famous Muther's Music Emporium, which was owned by Joe Sullivan, the legendary manager and show promoter.

Ronnie gave me a call and told me about this hot group who were playing there that night.

'There's a band up here in Nashville called The Outlaws, and they're trying to kick our ass.'

'*Are* they kicking your ass, Ronnie?'

'They're giving us a run.'

'Well, are you putting it back to them?' I asked.

'You bet. We're shoving it right back up *their* ass.'

'That's what you do.'

'But I got to tell you, Alan, they got themselves a bird song!'

'A bird song?'

'They got themselves a "Free Bird."'

I made a call to Joe Sullivan, who managed Charlie Daniels. Joe was a legend in his own right, and aside from producing and promoting great shows, he managed many artists, like Dobie Gray, Wet Willie, and Wolfman Jack.

I had first met Charlie Daniels in Nashville when Skynyrd played there. We had already begun our hot roll—we had one of the albums up, and we were smoking. Charlie Daniels came by to say hello to Ronnie, and they talked for about an hour, and then Ronnie took Charlie over to meet me. We spoke for a good deal of time, and then Charlie left. Charlie really liked Ronnie's spirit.

'You sure can tell he's a hick,' Ronnie said.

'How, Ronnie?'

'He still has yesterday's food in his beard.'

Charlie Daniels and I became good friends, and we remained good friends right up to the end. He was a wonderful man. Never had cross words with him. It was always good.

I called Joe to ask him his opinion, and he told me that if he weren't so damn busy with Charlie, he'd sign The Outlaws himself. Joe thought they were a great band, so that was a huge endorsement.

'You need to get right on them,' Joe advised me adamantly. So I did. I went to the Paragon Agency to see Terry Rhodes and told him what I had found out and what I had heard, and he dove in with me. He helped me find Charlie Brusco in Florida. Charlie was the show promoter for The Outlaws down there, and he booked the band into clubs.

Finding Charlie was like discovering another hot new super-band. He and I had a nice long conversation that went well, and then I went to see the band first down here in Macon, at Grant's Lounge, and 'Green Grass And High Tides' just knocked me on my tail. Lord have mercy, that was a good one. When I heard 'Green Grass And High Tides,' I realized that Ronnie was one hundred percent right.

The Outlaws came in from Tarpon Springs and around Tampa. They were a three-guitar band, and they were referred to as the Florida

Guitar Army: Hughie Thomasson, who wrote the song and played guitar and sang; Henry Paul on guitar and vocals; Billy Jones on guitar and vocals. Monte Yoho played drums and Frank O'Keefe held the bottom on bass. And they were ready to record.

Hughie got married after I signed the band, and he was always the guy who stayed away from the women on the road. He loved his wife and really tried to be a good husband. Hughie also tried to be a good guy—he had a very friendly personality. It took a lot to rile him up, and he was the undisputed leader of The Outlaws, the same way Ronnie was with Skynyrd.

Big Henry Paul was a founding member of the group, and he was always my support. He was born in New York but was raised and started playing music around Tampa. I could depend on Henry Paul as a musician and a friend—he was steady and true. A great man. Billy Jones was a real gentleman, and he wrote a lot of the love songs on the albums.

The Outlaws had a fellow named Hawaii Five-O. He was a real Hawaiian, and he could handle almost any situation that came up, though not a killer like Huck. When we were done playing and having a party at the hotel, we always put Hawaii Five-O at the front door, and he could approve who came in—mostly, he kept people out. He was the main road man, the bus driver, and he actually sang on occasion with Charlie Daniels.

The Outlaws just blew me away. I didn't want to push Charlie out of the management—I wasn't out to do that—so I ended up making Charlie a partner in a new management company called Walden & Brusco. He and I also became partners in the production company, Outlaw Productions. Charlie and I became very close friends.

We had a well-rehearsed routine. We made four record deals out of four tries. We were a fabulous team. Before we went into a record company, we rehearsed what we were going to say. Then, when we set up the key words, the other would take over control of the conversation like a tag team. I came in as soon as he finished, before they could say anything. We took control of the conversations and usually got what we wanted. We started to knock off major acts left and right.

When I came across The Outlaws, I felt that God had delivered a replacement for Skynyrd. I figured I'd come back to beat Skynyrd at their own damn game—to sic a band on their ass that is going to rip them up. And I did. But more important than a replacement, I found a great, great band.

These guys had paid some dues. They were starving on the road on many occasions, and they had to pool their money and put enough together to eat. Henry told me about having to go into a store and buy a ham, which they brought back to the alley behind the club and cooked slices of ham over an open fire. That's all they had: ham and ham and ham.

And I had to start paying my dues again.

A lot of people don't remember The Outlaws, but more and more people are beginning to appreciate them. They are now becoming legends in their own right. We had one big single and three great albums, but we sure were one hell of a touring band—just not known like Skynyrd and The Marshall Tucker Band. Possibly because The Outlaws were a great southern band that actually broke first in the North before the South. Usually, southern bands broke in the South.

After Macon, Charlie and I flew to Tampa to see what The Outlaws were doing in their hometown. They were playing at the Depot. The place was packed, and it had people waiting outside, listening through the windows. They only sold beer, but there was a disco bar up the street where people could get whiskey.

'After we finish, we could go to that disco, and I'll buy you all some drinks,' I told the band.

'They don't allow us in the place,' Hughie said.

'What do you mean, they don't allow you in the place?'

'We played there one night. They threw beer caps at us and harassed the hell out of us the whole time, so we stopped playing. They hate our music and they hate us. Now they won't let us in. This crazy woman and her old man run the place.'

'That's against your civil rights. Civil rights applies to kick-ass rock 'n' roll bands as much as anyone else. They can't do that. I'll tell you what: when we get off tonight, we're going to drink in that bar. Get all of your friends in here—and the other band, Dogwood—and tell them to join us as we march toward this club to exercise our civil rights!'

Man, the word got out that we were going to do this and force ourselves in with a little rock 'n' roll civil disobedience. We were going up the street with about thirty people and looked like the Texas Rangers in that old television show—looking for some downhome street justice. But some cops dressed in riot attire had positioned themselves on the steps of the Performing Arts disco.

I didn't have enough money to get all of us out of jail, and I didn't have any cop pals in Tampa, so I suggested we head back and have some beers. Everyone agreed with me and were anxious to turn back. They turned back, and I grabbed Charlie.

'We're the managers. We have got to go on in.'

Just as we reached the doorway, Henry Paul roared up behind me. He whispered to me.

'I have a lead pipe in my boot. I have your back covered.'

We went in and there was the crazy woman that had been acting real mean. The bar at the Performing Arts was her roost, and she was the one who *really* hated The Outlaws. The place was dead except a few people at the bar, and it looked like it hadn't seen any great business in a while. Disco was dying, but she wasn't getting the message.

I decided to come down hard on her.

'Hey, lady. You can't be throwing my boys out of here.'

'I don't like their style of music.'

I found the husband standing in there and gave him some more of the same. When I had run out of steam, Charlie took over. When Charlie ran out of steam, we were thirsty and wanted a cold beer.

'How about a beer?' I asked the husband.

We went back to the bar, and they opened up the beer section and popped a couple of Blue Ribbons.

'I don't drink that shit. Give us a couple of Buds.'

We stood at the bar and contemplated the room. At this point, Charlie and I were controlling the table.

'I'm going to tell you something. Things are kind of slow in here. You should be booking The Outlaws, not throwing them out. Your customers are old and dead. They're packing the club down the street beyond capacity, and the joint is jumping. You could be playing them over here and making a lot of damn money yourselves. We should get together and join forces to make something big here, rather than fighting and arguing and all of that.'

The owners agreed, and I took a swig of Bud.

'Now my point has been made,' I said.

The husband booked The Outlaws into that club, and we broke every attendance record for almost a year. This was in the early days, when we played Tampa a lot. We became the stars of that club. The Performing Arts became our place.

WE GOT YOUR ASS, CLIVE
SCENE EIGHTEEN

The Outlaws originally recorded at Capricorn, but the real time for recording came when I took them to Muscle Shoals to lay down some demos with David Johnson at his Broadway Sound. David and I had developed a friendship, and to this day we are very close. He produced the original Skynyrd demos and the original Outlaw demos, and he knew exactly what sound I wanted. I didn't have to stay around. I could leave the band with David, come back later, and they pretty well had what I wanted.

Clive Davis flew out to Columbus, Georgia, himself. He'd never changed planes in Atlanta in his life until he came to see The Outlaws. I put him up on the soundboard next to the engineer and watched his reaction. I saw that foot going with the band and knew we had him. I remember thinking, *We got your ass, Clive.*

I went back and sat on a trash can by the stage door and waited for Clive to come back. Just as he came back, Ronnie Van Zant stumbled in from the alley, drunk. I can't imagine how much he drank to get in that shape or to fire up the courage to pop in on us, but he did, and I'm grateful.

Ronnie got right into Clive's face.

'If you don't sign this band, you're going to be the biggest fool in the record industry,' Ronnie told Clive.

That coming from Ronnie was a big boost to the record deal. Was he trying, in his way, to thank me? Was he trying to make sure I would be okay?

We didn't ask for a big bundle of money. I'd learned that you take a large percentage rather than a big amount up front. If your band is a success, you get rich fast. If you get all of that front money and a lower percentage, you're going to spend that front money, and then you'll be stuck with the lower percentage.

From those Muscle Shoals tapes, we got signed by Clive's Arista Records. We were one of the first rock 'n' roll bands to sign with the label.

When we signed with Clive, the band headed for Los Angeles and started working at the Record Plant with Paul Rothchild. Clive put Paul on the job. One good thing about Clive: he always wanted to be involved in choosing the producer, and he liked being involved and hearing the songs before they were cut.

Clive was an excellent record man. He followed through with almost everything. He has brought a lot of careers back to life. He was a smooth gentleman, and I had nothing but respect for him. He knew his business.

The Outlaws scored with Paul Rothchild, too. Paul was a legend. He had produced The Doors, Janis Joplin, Eric Clapton, Bonnie Raitt, and so many more, going all the way back to his Boston days in the early sixties. He was a slave driver, though. By the time I got to the West Coast, the band was so beaten down, I was worried about them falling apart before they ever left L.A.

Clive had stuck them in the Hacienda Motel, out in El Segundo—the same place where Sam Cooke had been murdered back in '64. There is a lot of controversy about the night Sam was shot by the hotel manager after spending some time with a woman of questionable character. A lot of people think it was a setup. Sam always carried a lot of cash. At the time of Sam's death, the Hacienda was where you could get a room for three dollars an hour. It had improved a bit since then, but it was still pretty funky, and all The Outlaws caught scabies. There were a lot of mites crawling over people during the seventies. I think it had something to do with the wild sex scene. I went out and got them scabies soap and shampoo.

I was worried about the band getting run down and not being able to do their work. I needed to rescue them from Paul. He talked very rough to them and had to control every little thing. He made great records, but the guys needed a short break to get some fresh air.

I went out and rented two limos and told Rothchild that we were taking the day off and spending it away from him. He was pissed, but he had no choice.

I put The Outlaws in the two limos, and we rode all over town—through Beverly Hills and past the *Beverly Hillbillies* mansion, and they thought that was pretty cool. We drove out to the beach and just had a very relaxing time. The Outlaws went back into the studio the next day and were full of fire and totally relaxed and ready to make some great music.

We were on Arista for nine months before our record ever came out—
that was a long time. We chose 'There Goes Another Love Song' for the
single, and out it came, hitting #34 on *Billboard*'s Hot 100. And the
album, *Outlaws*, came out beautifully. It got to #13 on *Billboard*'s top
LP list. The Outlaws were solid.

The next album, *Lady In Waiting*, reached #32. We ended up doing
one track in Atlanta with Paul Rothchild, but after that we cut ourselves
loose from him. The third album, *Hurry Sundown*, was done by Bill
Szymczyk and Ed Marshal. Bill was a great producer. He'd worked with
B.B. King, the Eagles, Elvin Bishop, the J. Geils Band, and Johnny
Winters, among many. *Hurry Sundown* turned out to be one of their
biggest sellers. It was a decent album. It was put together much faster
than the first albums, and it had a few loose ends here and there, but it
was very successful.

Henry Paul left The Outlaws after *Hurry Sundown* to strike out on
his own. They got a new singer, Freddie Salem, who was a fabulous
guitarist but not so great a singer. They chose Freddie so they would
sound more rock than cowboy.

The Rolling Stones heard The Outlaws on one of their tours and
they flipped over them. They asked them to do some shows on their
1978 tour, and they also asked Henry Paul to open for them with his
new, Henry Paul Band. I made it to two of the shows. One was in
Buffalo, New York, and the other was in Anaheim, California. I had
never seen that many people in my life. We busted our ass and did the
best we could, but those shows belonged to The Rolling Stones. The
applause at the Stones' entrance was phenomenal. It was louder than
our encore applause. We did our show and split.

Charlie Brusco and I started expanding with other bands—Buckacre, Mama's Pride, Albatross, Thermos Greenwood. We had five or six groups and got record deals for all of them, except for Thermos Greenwood & The Colored People. This was the one time I was talked into taking on a novelty band. They were actually colored—one was pink and another was blue—all different colors. They did a sort of comedy routine rock 'n' roll show, and they were very clever and funny, with a lot of potential for stage and television.

I talked Mike Maitland into coming to Tampa to see them. It was a big thing for Mike to come from L.A. to Florida to hear what he thought was going to be the next great novelty act. It was a disaster. Everything went wrong. They were running into each other, smashing each other in the face with guitars, tripping over their own feet and falling down. Not one of their routines worked. They had a song called 'Trouser Of Worms.' The guy unzips his pants and this big old green slinky is supposed to come tumbling out of his pants, but he forgot to put the slinky in his pants, so he just opened his fly in front of the audience and that was it. It was so bad. I apologized to Mike, and he understood.

When I went back to the hotel, I told Charlie that I didn't want to talk to anybody. It was the worst case of stage fright I had ever seen. I immediately backed down on trying to do anything with the band. It was a short-lived management arrangement, and they eventually came out with an album called *Pin Head Teddy* and a single called 'Who Gave The Monkey A Gun?' Live and learn. Maybe they were ahead of their time.

We put Albatross on CBS. They were my band of blonds. These guys were good-looking, and they played hard rock—they were a real rock 'n' roll band all the way, with a lot of fans in Atlanta, but they never graduated past the club stage. They got into a fight with the producer in the studio and CBS dropped them. They ran up a twelve-thousand-dollar hotel bill—and they were only in the place for a week. More trouble than they were worth.

Buckacre were a band from up north in Illinois that Charlie and I signed right as The Outlaws were getting very, very hot. They used to open a lot of the shows for The Outlaws down around Tampa and Clearwater. They were a harmony band and sounded a bit like the Eagles, and they were very good.

I had convinced MCA that Buckacre were a hundred-thousand-dollar band, easy, and I had gotten a fellow named Bob Davis to help me to see what they were like on the road—to see if they could do it every night. Then Mike Maitland came down himself and approved them personally. Naturally, we signed with MCA.

Boz Scaggs's favorite producer was Glyn Johns. Glyn had produced everyone from the Stones to The Beatles to Led Zeppelin to Bob Dylan to Boz Scaggs. He was a master and a star. Boz thought so highly of him that when I made a deal with MCA for Buckacre, he insisted that Glyn produce their records.

Glyn liked Buckacre so much that he recorded them at his home in England, instead of going into the studio. They felt very comfortable recording in Glyn's home—they were damn nice kids. They had a guitar player named Al Thacker who could *wail*, and a country singer, Les Lockridge, who could turn rockabilly out.

Buckacre were a good band, and Glyn really enjoyed working with them. They had a song called 'Morning Comes' from the first album of the same name that was as pretty as some of the Eagles'. They had one great album and one good album, but neither one was a hit. I put them on the road but Les, who was really the key man in the band, had bad health, and he had to come off the road a couple of times because he couldn't hold up to the pace.

We had a lawyer who went crooked as shit, and the next thing I knew, he and I ended up in Atlanta in front of a couple of bottles of scotch. He set it up to get me drunk, and I did. He took the band away from me, and that was it for Buckacre.

Mama's Pride came out of Missouri. I went to audition them in Augusta, Georgia. They had a song called 'In The Morning.' The singers were two brothers—Danny and Pat Liston—and both of them sounded like Gregg Allman. They were a kick-ass band. By the third song that I heard at their audition, I was ready to sign them.

I got Mama's Pride a huge advance from Atlantic and bought them all the equipment and arranged their transportation. They were one of the bands that made it to the charts. I did all I could until Atlantic dropped them. After a record company drops you, you have very little chance of ever getting a record deal.

Chris Hicks should have been right up there with Clapton and Duane and all of the rest. This cat plays fantastic guitar—not good guitar, *great* guitar. He's since pretty well taken over The Marshall Tucker Band. Chris Hicks is a powerful singer, too, and he has genius guitar knowledge. I would put Chris Hicks up against anybody in the world. Pay attention to him.

Mama's Pride had another song called 'Where Would You Be' that I recorded later with Chris Hicks and dedicated to Ronnie Van Zant: *'Where would you be, girl, if I hadn't shown you the light?'*

THEY PUSHED IT
TOO HARD AND
CRASHED IN A SWAMP
SCENE NINETEEN

Peter Rudge put Skynyrd in an old, raggedy-ass, thirty-year-old Convair 240 flown by negligent pilots. Peter should have been more watchful over his band. They should not have been in that plane. If I had been managing them, they would not have been. The Skynyrd people knew that the engines were spewing out flames on occasion. The plane was a dangerous piece of junk, and Rudge should have known it.

They were headed toward Baton Rouge, where they had a gig at Louisiana State University. Their new album, *Street Survivors*, had just been released, and things were looking up.

The plane ran out of gas. The pilots were stupid and incompetent. When they went to switch to the reserve tank, one of the pilots panicked and turned the lever the wrong way and emptied all of the fuel, so they went down. The pilots were killed. Everyone on the plane was in bad shape or dead. Ronnie, Steve Gaines and his sister Cassie, and Dean Kilpatrick, the band's road manager, were all dead. It was a nightmare come true for several of them, because they didn't want to get into that plane. It was just too dangerous.

When I heard about it on the news, I called Lacy Van Zant. He hadn't heard about his son being killed. I was the one who had to tell him that the plane went down, and man, that was a hard phone call. Two of the hardest calls made in my life—telling Lacy that Ronnie had crashed and telling my daddy that Otis had crashed.

A lot has been written about the crash. I can't add anything. It was just a lousy deal.

'How do you feel about your boys now?' Phil asked.

'They always pushed it too hard,' I told him. 'They took too many chances.'

THE END OF MY FRIEND TWIGGS
SCENE TWENTY

By 1979, Phil had stopped managing The Allman Brothers Band—there were disputes and lawsuits and things—and Twiggs felt like he was in line for management. Twiggs was real sure that he was going to get the job, but they didn't give it to him.

Rightly, Twiggs should have gotten that gig. Duane was killed when Twiggs was in the mental ward. When he got out, he went back to work with the band on the road, but he felt that he should take over Phil's old seat. He came to see Phil beforehand and asked if it would be all right.

'Twiggs, I'd be glad for you to have the job,' Phil told him. 'You're more than welcome to it, and you deserve it.'

'I'll be working with them, but you know I'll be talking to you. You know everything that is going on in that band.'

But they didn't choose Twiggs, and that broke his heart. He started working with The Dixie Dregs instead. Twiggs and The Allman Brothers Band really loved The Dixie Dregs. But the damage was done.

Twiggs always told me that if he got killed jumping out of an airplane, not to worry about him. He was an experienced skydiver. He told me that if he ever was killed doing that, it wouldn't be an accident. And that's what he did.

Twiggs geared up and headed over Duanesburg, New York. He jumped out of a plane over Duanesburg, and his chute didn't open. I believe he killed himself.

Rest in peace, Twiggs.

THE MUSIC OF MOTORCYCLES— THE HELLS ANGELS MEET THE OUTLAWS
SCENE TWENTY-ONE

It's always fun to run into the Hells Angels, and I ran into them in New York City, when The Outlaws were performing at the Beacon Theater over on the Upper West Side. There were about thirteen of them, and the smallest man was probably two-fifteen. Real rough giants. They were hanging around all over the theater and blocking the door to the dressing room. They were angry because The Outlaws had a song called 'Angels Hide,' and since the Outlaws Motorcycle Club was one of the Hells Angels' rival gangs, they didn't want *our* Outlaws to sing it, because they interpreted the song to mean that they ran from the Outlaw gang.

A couple of them paid me a visit. One of them had blood dripping down the side of his face and looked like he had been in a bad fight not long before. He was jumping up and down needing to hurt someone, probably loaded with speed.

I got myself out of the room and went over to the dressing room and sat down with Freddie Salem.

'Hey, I don't know about you, but I don't want to be around these guys,' I told Freddie.

All of a sudden, *thump thump thump*—it sounded like they were beating somebody. We charged out of the dressing room and one of the Angels had Hughie under his arm. Hughie looked like all of the blood had been drained from his body, and they were talking plenty rough to him. A bunch of them went down and blocked our way to the stage. We agreed not to sing that song.

I knew a lawyer in Manhattan (not to mention Joe Glazer) who told me he could get two torpedoes over there and waste all of them.

'No. We're not going to do that. We're going to drop the song, and the damn song ain't that strong to begin with.'

We actually had to walk through the line of Hells Angels to get to the stage. But we also thought of the idea, and they agreed, to come to the show on the following night as our guests and listen to 'Angels Hide,' so they could understand that the song was about dark spirit stagecoaches and freight trains and angels, not about motorcycle gangs. You'd have to be on drugs to make that connection, but that may have been part of the problem.

The next night I was in the wings with Jessica, who was a baby, and her mother. The show begins, and we're thinking we've got things worked out, and we looked to our left and there's the damn Hells Angels beside me, getting too close for comfort.

One of them just stood there and listened to the band—really starting to check them out. His hair was like George Hamilton's— big and beautiful and healthy. His boots were shined, and his silver polished and his colors were crisp and sharp—a well-dressed Hells Angel. Turned out he was one of the leaders.

The band kicked into 'Angels Hide,' and we all held our breath. I was looking around for a place to pray. After the song, the Angels started clapping.

'Sorry my guys gave you a hard time,' the leader said. And all was at peace.

I didn't realize it, but the Outlaws Motorcycle Club were, in fact, fans of the Outlaws band. They had been following the band for quite some time. The first time I heard about them, they were throwing beer caps at the band onstage.

'Hey, man,' I said, 'we're just a band trying to make a living. Why are you screwing with us? If anything, you should get the band to play a concert for you. They probably would if you asked.'

The Outlaws were always steady as a rock. One of the greatest thrills I had with them was watching Hughie Thomasson take a dead audience, do a solo, and bring twelve thousand people to their feet with a guitar and a whole lotta soul.

In 1976, we were playing at Cobo Hall, a historic convention center in Detroit. It was the location of Martin Luther King Jr.'s first 'I Have A Dream' speech—he did it there before Washington. The Outlaws were supporting Aerosmith, and they were not a good match as far as a show went. The Aerosmith crowd was definitely not our crowd. They were a northern band out of Boston. The Outlaws sang songs that attracted the southern sensibilities. At the time, Aerosmith were dark, druggy, and heavy.

The Outlaws were there, but it was the house of Aerosmith that night. The Outlaws would play a song and maybe a few people clapped, but it was primarily, for us, a dead house. Then the Outlaws Motorcycle Club showed up, and they put everyone in a very agitated state—they were actually rougher than the Hells Angels. If there was ever an anxious, weird show, that was it, especially since the motorcycle gang had been 'suggesting' people move out of their seats so they could have them. But then Hughie, who was one of the most talented guitar players in the world, went into his guitar solo on 'Green Grass And High Tides,' and the whole place fell apart. Hughie took that song and that gang right up over the mountain. Echoes of King's 'I Have A Dream' rippled through that old building that night.

The Outlaws Motorcycle Club became sort of like our bodyguards. They actually paid for Hughie Thomasson's solo album to be recorded at Capricorn Records, and they paid cash. They came and put down seventy-five thousand in cash. The studio had never seen anyone walk in with that kind of money.

The gang kept wanting to get a bigger percentage of the solo album, and I finally laid into them, while Hughie was standing there with the president of the gang.

'I'm going to tell you,' I said. 'You might as well just take it all, because you keep coming in every day and asking for a little more and a little more—taking bigger bites every day. Just take it all and get it over with. I'll keep the damn publishing and you all make the record deals, and you can have all the money from that.'

Of course, I knew they couldn't make a record deal. Nobody in the gang was that smart. I didn't want anything to do with going into business with a motorcycle gang. Those old-school motorcycle gangs were notorious and dangerous. I didn't want to wind up at the bottom of a ditch.

In 1979, The Outlaws made it to Madison Square Garden, with Molly Hatchet as their opening act. Everyone had earplugs that night. I don't know why, but I didn't think about them. I was already hard of hearing in my left ear from the Skynyrd shows and getting too close to the amps. Peavey had set us up with a wall of monster amps, and that night my right ear got smashed to pieces.

I eventually stepped back and let Charlie Brusco take over the whole management and kept up with the production and the publishing. I didn't have to do anything but be around backstage and talk to Hughie about his publishing. I left Charlie to manage the band. After all, they were his band when I signed them at the beginning. We worked for our hits. Having Charlie on my side was like having another good band.

I loved The Outlaws. I still love them today. We had a lot of fun. I had a lot of successful years with The Outlaws—twenty-nine years is a pretty long run, and I still have relations with them. There is a real brotherhood between me and Monty and Henry Paul and Charlie, because we were the originals.

BEING A GOOD MANAGER, BOOKING AGENT, PROMOTER, FRIEND
SCENE TWENTY-TWO

I will always advise a young person getting into the business not to let your band manage *you*. A lot of bands want to tell their manager this and that, thinking they know more or being told that they know more by someone else who may have a stake in that opinion. Sometimes they do know more than a manager, but then again, sometimes they don't.

That's what happened with Skynyrd. They wanted to manage me instead of me managing them. I didn't fit. I could have held those guys for another three years with bullshit and made almost my full commission, but I know when to leave the show with my dignity intact. I wish them well and thank them for every dollar that I made from them. I'm not an ungrateful person.

Many years later, after I had gotten out of the business, I became aware of one of the best groups I had ever heard. They were called Blackbird, out of Tifton, Georgia. The soundboard man at Riverfront Blues, one of the local nightclubs, called me up.

'Man, I've got a band you really do need to hear.'

'I'll try to come see them, but I'm not making any promises.'

'Alan. The club will be closed, and you'll have them all to yourself.'

My wife Tosha and I went over to the club to hear this group. Blackbird played so good that they had me bawling. I'm not talking about crying. I'm talking about bawling! I had tears just flowing everywhere.

Tosha asked me if I was all right, and there was a simple answer.

This band had every damn thing that I look for in a band. They got everything—regional songs, hot guitar players, killer drums and bass, and kick-ass talent. I listened to each song—one taking me to the end of the world and the next taking me higher and the next even higher still. They were all in their teens—cute guys. One particular guy had a lot of sex appeal.

They were an incredible band. I took them out of the nightclub and booked the Capitol Theater and sold the place out. I just stepped into the next Lynyrd Skynyrd, or maybe something much greater. Well, they talked me—or, more truthfully, I talked myself—out of retirement to manage this band for a time, to see how things played out. That's how much I liked them.

I built these boys up to the point where they were already getting reactions from record companies—right off the bat. Every musician in this band was red hot—the drummer, the bass, the guitars, the lead singer—it was all fantastic. And then I got a call and they wanted to get rid of one of the guitar players.

'You got a great sound,' I said. 'I personally don't think you should change right now.'

'He won't make rehearsals and all he cares about is smoking dope and chasing women and he doesn't want to rehearse and he's a real problem.'

In my guts, I knew that this guitar player was the magic. But the lead singer's father had been taking care of them before I met them, and he was pushing for this. I don't know. Maybe he thought this guitar player was taking too much of his son's juice. Against my wishes, they fired the guitar player. I went to see the new band, and technically they were solid, but something was missing. Maybe that smoking guitar. I couldn't convince them to hire him back. They wanted to do it their way or no way.

That kid had been reaching for those notes way on out there and making mistakes and covering them up and making it sound like it was supposed to be. He smoked and the girls loved him. I had gotten the brilliant Rodney Mills out of Atlanta to produce four sides. Rodney had engineered the Atlanta Rhythm Section, Lynyrd Skynyrd, Gregg Allman, The Outlaws, James Brown, and so many more. He was a master engineer. I talked Rodney out of retirement. I respected him that much. He's the only one who turned the knobs on 'Sweet Home Alabama' and 'Free Bird.'

'You know, Alan, I'm retired, but if you do the project, I'll go in,' he told me.

We went into Atlanta and cut four sides, but their spirit had been cooled when they got rid of that little guitar player. I had a four-year option and I didn't pick it up. They rejected almost everything I suggested. They wanted to do things their way, without paying any of the dues necessary to make such decisions. And so they got what they wanted.

TRUST
SCENE TWENTY-THREE

I wanted all of my artists to trust me. I remember writing a letter to each artist telling them how proud I was to be their agent, and how much it meant to me and my life for them to be involved with me, and that built up a family spirit tighter than ever. They loved that letter.

Just imagine what my Friday afternoons were like. I had to get over fifty acts to their dates on time, all over the country. I knew which ones were going to ask for extra travel money. I knew each personality so well. If one wanted travel money, it would be waiting for them at Western Union, because that is what I anticipated. I always tried to stay ahead of the acts. Some had a reputation for being slow and late, so I encouraged them to speed it up to get to the gig—so they sped up. I took pride in representing my artists. I was very proud of most of them. I was proud of the company.

In my life and career, one main thing I have learned is that initially, I don't trust anyone in the music business. The entertainment business is full of people who will take advantage of you. Unfortunately for me, that was the first hard lesson I learned. You think someone is your friend, and the next thing he's ripping your ass out. It got so bad that I woke up every morning wondering not *if* someone was going to rip my ass out but how *much* they were going to rip out.

Companies would hide money and they would steal money. I did an audit and found about a half million dollars for Sam & Dave. I hired CPAs that did the examinations on many major record companies. I knew where to tell them to look, and they usually found it.

When I got into gospel music, I realized real quick that the gospel scene was loaded with thieves and some of the most poisonous snakes in the swamp. These guys were worse than gangsters. There was just too much stealing and cheating going on. I got out of the gospel business because hardly anyone could be trusted.

Sometimes you've got to out con the cons. That was just the name of the game. Could you be slicker than the record companies, managers, promotion guys, and, sometimes, artists? There was always someone trying to mess with you.

Don't trust anybody. You'll find that even your close friends in the music business will find a way to hide royalties. Most companies do that. My company never did. You will find that you will be better off keeping people at a distance while you are working with them until they show you in some way that they can undoubtedly be trusted to a point, and you know that they are sincere about it. Then you take those people and treat them as your special friends.

It is a tough business. If you let people run all over you, they will. In New York, they'll tell you that they'll fuck you and then fuck you. In L.A., they'll tell you what they can do for you and then fuck you.

Everybody thinks the music business is all fun and games. It's a lot of hard work. You better have some stamina if you're going to get into this business. I used to be the last man standing in the studio. I made sure I was the last man awake—I was the one who called the session. I'd work all night. We called them suicide sessions—just kept going two or three days straight. We put a big old pot of vegetable soup on the hotplate and that's what we ate during the session, and we drank a lot of Budweiser beer.

Some people liked to play games. They don't want you to have success. They want you to stay below them all the time. Friendship is something we all need, but it was not really a good thing in the music business to become too close to the artists. Sometimes, when you became too close, they wanted to start calling the shots more and more. Bands love to fire their managers after other managers promise them the world and put the buzz on them. You can expect that when you sign someone to a contract, someday they will try to fire you. They resent you because they will believe you have more power than they do, and sooner or later they want to tell off the manager.

It's the same old story. You help an artist achieve a hit and he tells you that nothing will change. And then, after the legitimate hit, he decides to make a change. He may change for the worse or he may change for the better. Sometimes the band will fire members that shouldn't be fired, and then the band loses the magic.

We tried to save our management relationship with Sam & Dave, but they had already been convinced that another management team was going to get them in the movies and all of that—things they said we couldn't do. They weren't popular enough to be in the movies. What would they have done in the movies?

Ninety percent of my stable was dependable. There were always some goof-offs, and I didn't tolerate any messing up their dates. I had to think ahead. You had to think ahead all the time and think about all the problems that exist and solve them. That's why we were such good managers. When we managed somebody, it was like marrying them—like taking another wife. You had to live out their problems and help them out with family life and everything else—totally committed to supporting them any way you could.

I would explain to the artists about the accounting and the breakdowns—a statement showing every date they played and what the commission was and any advances we gave them.

We were looking for acts that would go on into history and change the whole scene. It's always a great honor for all of us from the South to achieve recognition all over the world with respect and honor. Not just the South and not just America, but all over the world.

Go in there being malicious or dirty and you're going to get caught and you will pay with your reputation. We did our best on every level.

Phil and I were some of the best managers of all time. Not as big as Colonel Tom or Brian Epstein, but we were up there somewhere. All of us took pride in our work. My daddy, my brothers, my mother—she worked the Otis homecoming shows in the box office.

James Brown came to Macon from Augusta, Georgia, because he couldn't get a break in Augusta, and he'd heard about a young man named Clint Brantley who was a local promoter and booker. Clint wasn't that good, but he was good enough and smart enough to introduce James Brown to Ben Bart, who became James's lifetime manager.

After Ben Bart died, Jack Bart, his son, took over the agency, but he had no idea how to manage James. His father had a knack for it.

I was with James several times. I booked him in Auburn University in Alabama, and I think I got him five thousand dollars for that night.

'You should have charged them twenty,' he told me.

'I had a hard time getting you five, James.'

Many years later, James came to play in front of City Hall in Macon. A large outdoor stage was set up. Jack Ellis, our first Black mayor, called me to see if I could go down and entertain James in his dressing room. I went down there, and James and I spent the afternoon together before he performed his show.

James was impressed about how much I knew about his life and the musicians that had played in his bands. I knew where James had bought all of his cars, and I knew most of his best friends. We had wonderful conversations. His wife strolled in with his new baby. Then Tosha brought in my son, Christian, who was about five at the time.

'Well, I guess it shows that us old soldiers still shoot real bullets,' James said.

He laughed at that for quite some time.

I remember stories Otis told me about James. Otis would let James kid him for this or that. Otis looked up to James and respected him. James had so much success.

One time, James flew his Lear jet into Macon and pulled up to Otis's old single-engine plane.

'When you going to get those white boys to buy you a real plane?'

I guess those white boys were Phil and me. But Otis just laughed it off.

When it was time for James to take the stage, I decided to leave. When we were saying our goodbyes, James turned to Jack Ellis.

'You need to keep Alan around. He knows his shit.'

That was a pretty high compliment coming from the Godfather of Soul.

At my peak, I had thirteen albums on the charts from my publishing company, and I owned about eighty percent of the publishing on all of those albums. I was very fortunate to deliver a lot of hits. That's what kept me on top. If we were told we couldn't do something, that was an invitation to do it. We delivered the message.

The Outlaws and Lynyrd Skynyrd made me wealthy. I am committed to them for the rest of my life, and even though we may have had our differences and some may still carry grudges, I do wish them well and thank them for every dollar that I made from them. I'm not an ungrateful person, and I would love to stay friends, but that is not always meant to happen.

I'm still friends with The Outlaws. Henry Paul calls me often just to say hello. He's been doing that for over thirty-five years.

In this business, that's pretty damn good and meaningful.

THE WHITE GIRLS WERE GETTING TOO EXCITED
SCENE TWENTY-FOUR

I tried to find work for as many local acts as possible. I believed in supporting them. Some were great and some not so great, but most of them were sincere and decent people. And you never know who might break and head right up that mountain.

Shaka-Plenty was actually a guy in drag, and he would occasionally strip down to his underwear. He put on one heck of a show, and the crowd loved the way he teased them. It was a wild show. There was this guy I went to high school with—he was always the guy who was number one in everything and a real conceited type. Before the show, he 'fell in love' with Shaka-Plenty. He had a fantasy to get real close to a beautiful Black woman, and the next thing I know he's got his tongue all the way down Shaka's throat, with me sitting there with a grin on my face because this guy didn't think too much of me, and he just started to kiss away, slopping all over Shaka-Plenty. I started to tell him, but I decided I'd just sit there and watch it and enjoy the show. After Shaka got up on the stage, and this guy saw that Shaka-Plenty was a man doing his thing, he disappeared. I never saw him again. If I had told him he was a guy, he probably would have beat Shaka to death on the spot. Shaka's real name was Carmen—a very nice person. I booked a lot of dates for Shaka, and he made every date.

Hugh Boynton was out of Jeffersonville, Georgia. He had a good voice, but he was one of those performers who thought if he recorded one song it would be a natural hit and shouldn't miss at all, so he was really disappointed when his record didn't hit. He ended up becoming a preacher. He used to hustle people out of their paychecks by convincing them they could hit in the numbers racket if they paid him money. Nobody ever really won the bug racket.

Herman Moore was a good singer from Macon. Phil took him to Stax and he cut one side. He had a great song called 'Got To Get Away From Here.' The problem with Herman was that he liked to drink a whole lot, and when he did drink, he spent his nights on the streets, so he didn't have a real promising career, since you would see him intoxicated and crawling around on the sidewalk.

Sheila Waters was a preacher's daughter—the Reverend Jimmy Waters was a very well-known preacher in Macon. She married a state senator, Richard Green. He and I really got along great. I used him as my lawyer a number of times. I set Sheila up with a session at David

Johnson's studio at Muscle Shoals, and she recorded a whole album. We remain friends.

Thomas Bailey was a local singer from Macon. Boz Scaggs actually played on Thomas's audition recording—his first demo. Another promoter got hold of him and made him a bunch of promises, so he went with him, and I haven't seen him since. He wasn't a bad guy. I enjoyed being his friend. He really put on a good show. He went with the other team and suffered the consequences of never getting a hit.

Alice Rozier was a local singer out of Parrott, Georgia, but she was living in Macon when I met her. She did some dates with Johnny Jenkins when she was handled by Clint Brantley, and she came out with a very cool song called 'I'm Gonna Hold On To You' with Little Joe Clower, who was known as Little Joe—Joe was occasionally a guitarist for Sam & Dave.

Maddie Vaughn was a singer from Macon, and Otis took her out on the road after she performed at one of his parties. She probably stayed about a year. She was not a very attractive lady, but boy could she sing. She had a range that was just unbelievable.

Willie Morris was probably the best singer to ever come out of Macon. I had signed his band, The Black Exotics. Willie was the lead singer. This was a killer band—they sounded like Earth, Wind & Fire, and they put on one great show. At one of the sorority parties, the chaperone asked me to tone 'those boys down.' The white girls were getting too excited, and they had a line all around the band.

'I can't do that,' I told the chaperone. 'This is what it's all about. Let them have some fun.'

Gloria Walker came out of Milledgeville, Georgia. Gloria probably had one of the worst bands I ever heard in my life, but the girl could sing very strong and could still entertain the crowd even with a raggedy-old band. She had a hit and a couple of other releases—'Please Don't Desert My Baby' came out on Flaming Arrow.

Nancy Butts came out of Sparta, and the same thing was true with her. Eugene Davis produced her and Gloria Walker, and Nancy had a couple of good records, including 'Go On To Her' on Flaming Arrow. Eugene delivered the two girls to us, but they couldn't hold up.

The Cotton Brothers were a Macon gospel group who were really good. On the same night Otis and I wrote 'Chained And Bound' and 'Your Man,' Otis had been working with them on their material before we got started. I met them all and liked them. They never had huge success, but they still have a group known as The Cotton Brothers, with different people—the name still plays around Macon.

In the R&B years, what I loved about my job was that I never knew who I was going to meet the next day. It was always somebody new coming to Macon. One morning, I heard a knock on my door. I opened the door and there was Joe Frazier, the boxer, standing in front of me.

'Man, you're Joe Frazier.'

'Yes, I am.'

'What are you doing down here, Joe?'

'Can I come in?'

'Of course you can come in. What can we do for you? Whatever you need, Joe. You've got a big fight coming up. What brings you here?'

'I want to know if I can meditate in Otis's office for a while.'

'You want to meditate in Otis's office?'

'Would that be all right? Just for a little while.'

'Of course,' I assured him. And so I led Joe Frazier straight into

Otis's old office, and he stayed there for about two hours. I didn't hear a thing. He didn't make a single sound.

Two weeks later, Joe beat Muhammad Ali at Madison Square Garden. I guess Otis was in Joe's corner.

NASHVILLE CAT
SCENE TWENTY-FIVE

Phil went to Nashville in 1980 because he owed everyone money. He probably owed twenty million dollars.

Phil had left Warners and made a deal with Polydor. Polydor were Germans, and they had tons of money. Phil found out that they would advance him money when he called, because he was a genius to them. So he and his pals would be sitting around snorting, and it was, 'Let's call Polydor and get a million.' And they would send it. He owed them eleven million before they wanted to talk about it. They wanted to see something for their investment, and then they closed him down.

All the people in Macon fed on Phil like sharks. In one month, he went from being the most popular man in Macon to the scourge of the earth. His friends turned to enemies. He owed everyone in the world.

Phil did so much for Macon, Georgia. He preserved the history of Macon. The Old Town section, the Douglass Theater—it was going to be torn down. He put imagination back in Macon. But when you owe everybody, things change, and none of that matters. So he had to leave and go to Nashville.

At this time, Phil was very much addicted to cocaine. He didn't buy a little bit of cocaine. He bought a lot of cocaine, and he could snort a lot. He went to Nashville and continued to do that until he was down to a one-room apartment and his dog, Twinkles. His wife had divorced him. He met a priest and the priest got him on the path to recovery and converted him to being a Christian. He never went to a treatment center.

When Phil got in trouble, he borrowed a lot of money from me. He had to wire into my electricity box because his had been cut off so many times. I had some cash and he needed it real bad, so I loaned him about a hundred and twenty-five thousand dollars, and that took all of my savings. He paid me back, borrowed it again, and then couldn't pay me back. So he paid me back in real estate, antiques, a Mercedes, and different things of value, but I was stripped of cash. All of a sudden, I didn't have anything for my overhead, and that put me into a bad spot.

NEVER GIVE UP
SCENE TWENTY-SIX

A lot of years, a lot of fun, a lot of headaches, a lot of sadness. I thought the tragedies would never stop. People used to wonder if Phil and I were jinxed—so many of our artists were dead. I don't know. Maybe it was just the law of averages. We had a lot of artists. And I have thought about it a good deal and wondered about it, but I came to the conclusion that God brought them to us so they could achieve what they wanted in life—I believe that. After you see so many young people die in the music business, it gets to be hard to make some guy famous, knowing that he'll probably end up killing himself trying to live out some wild fantasy.

In the early nineties, my brother came up with a band called 311 and they went #1, and then the money flowed in like a river, looking like it was never going to stop. And then he had a band called Widespread Panic. They weren't a big record seller, but were a huge success on the road, like the Grateful Dead. The audience showed up from everywhere, breaking attendance records at all of their shows. They were a different band. They let everybody download their songs. They were encouraging it. They wanted to be the people's band. And they became the people's band with a huge following.

Phil had a new deal with Warner Bros, and Mo Ostin gave him a top deal. Phil was back. He hired his son, Phil Jr., to come and work for him, and he hired my nephew, G. Scott Walden. He also wanted me to come back.

'Big brother, I'd love to work with you again, but I've been my own boss too long. I'm making a comfortable living and I'm happy with what I'm doing, and I don't want to leave Macon. I want to stay in Macon.'

After he sold his record company in early 2000, Phil found out he had a lump on his lung. They did a biopsy and it came back negative.

'I don't care if it was cancerous or not. I want you to get that lump out of my body. I've read up a lot on this and I don't want to take any chances. I don't want a possibility of cancer.'

They went in and did surgery and found that he did have cancer, and they took out half of one of his lungs. They assured him that they got it all and that he didn't need chemo.

'I want chemo,' Phil told them. 'I want to make sure my body is rid of this disease.'

The doctors tried to insist that Phil was fine, but then the cancer showed up in his brain.

Okay. Phil was told that he was fine, then the cancer showed up in his brain, and they went in and cut it out there, and again they thought they got it all. Then it showed up in his spine. And that was the end, and he deteriorated super-fast.

My brother and I had an unusual relationship. We had a love/hate relationship. When we loved each other, we loved each other. But when we hated each other, we hated each other. But God, I loved my brother. He got me into the music business. I loved my brother.

COME CLOSE TO ME AND GET WARM
POSTLUDE
BY S.E. FEINBERG

Alan and I were sitting down on the shore of the lake. The catfish would come up to the edge of the shore and stick their heads out of the water, waiting for Alan to feed them bits of dog food. It was peaceful on that shore—especially in the late afternoon. The fish were jumping at the bugs flying low over the still water. I gazed over the woods and thought about the history of this place. I will often think about the Civil War when I am in Georgia. The tragedy of the war bleeds out of the woods and echoes through the warm air like the gentle whistle of a mockingbird before dawn. You think about things—not what was right or wrong about anything, just the human story—the struggle and the tragedy. Not opinions so much as empathy.

After the war, Robert E. Lee wrote, 'What a cruel thing is war: to separate and destroy families and friends, and mar the purest joys and happiness God has granted us in this world; to fill our hearts with hatred instead of love for our neighbors, and to devastate the fair face of this beautiful world.'

The edge of the lake was a good place to talk and a good place to think. It brought a peace and a serenity to the mind.

I asked Alan what he would say to his brother, Phil, if he could. He paused for a time, fed some bits of food to a catfish, thought about my question, and then found the words.

'*All those years you thought I hated you. I never did. Deep down inside, I loved you, and I always will. You were the biggest influence on my life. Thank you for all the things you taught me. So many things. You were a very educated man and I lacked the education. You were, without a doubt, the leader of the Walden family. You were the king of the Walden family. You changed history. Thank you. And thank you for getting me into the music business. Thank you for all of your advice—even when you were mad at me, you gave me good advice. You took a ragtag bunch of southern boys and turned them into an army. I love you, Brother. I always will.*'

Alan turned to me. He put his Dr. Pepper down and felt the cool air of this Macon night—taking in all that was Macon.

'*We all defended each other. Even though there might be a big competition between the bands, we kept it friendly. There was a lot of camaraderie about us southerners sticking together and to keep this thing going full force. We all bonded together because we were southern bands. We were a family. We will always be a family.*

'*When Phil and I were little boys and waiting on the school bus, I would be freezing cold. We'd be standing out there on the road for thirty or forty minutes so we wouldn't miss the bus. One morning it was especially cold and my teeth were chattering away and I was shaking. Phil opened up his coat and pulled me into it and held me close to him to keep me warm.*

'*When Phil was in trouble and he had to move to Nashville to get away from creditors and had gotten strung out on cocaine and booze and had lost almost everything, I went to see him. I opened my coat. I'm here for you, Phil, I said to him, and pulled him close to me. Come close to me and get warm.*'

END CREDITS
ACKNOWLEDGMENTS

Alan Walden wants to thank all of y'all, and I am dedicating this book to Tosha Walden, Jessica Walden, Georgeanna Walden, Christian Walden, Walden and Jamie Weatherford, David Johnson, Jimmy Johnson, Gary Donehoo, Charlie Brusco, Rumer, and Jerry Womack.

—A.W.

To my darling wife, Alice. I love you.

Thanks to Tom Seabook for his patience and wisdom during the development of *Southern Man*. To Nigel Osborne, for allowing us the opportunity to fulfill this dream.

To Rumer, who had an inspiration and, with perseverance and faith, forged it into reality.

—S.F.

All photographs used in this book are from the author's private collection.